THE

STEAL

THE

STEAL

MARK BOWDEN &
MATTHEW TEAGUE

Atlantic Monthly Press

New York

FIRST EDITION

Published simultaneously in Canada
Printed in the United States of America

First Grove Atlantic hardcover edition: January 2022

Library of Congress Cataloging-in-Publication data is available for this title.

ISBN 978-0-8021-5995-3
eISBN 978-0-8021-5996-0

Atlantic Monthly Press
an imprint of Grove Atlantic
154 West 14th Street
New York, NY 10011

Distributed by Publishers Group West

groveatlantic.com

22 23 24 25   10 9 8 7 6 5 4 3 2 1

To the real patriots

Contents

THE
STEAL

1

Election Day

Donald Trump really did believe he would win. His staff had assured him of it, and he could feel it in his bones.

But . . . what if he lost? A man who grounds his very identity on winning has strategies for handling loss. For years, Trump had been laying out his. If the votes did not add up to victory, there was a reason. An obvious one. Everybody could see it. He had spelled it out again and again, warning even before his shocking victory in 2016 that the system was "totally rigged."

Rigged by whom? Trump's promise to "Drain the Swamp" was a sure applause line at his rallies. The expression long predated him, of course, referring to the nefarious ties between lawmakers and lobbyists, but Trump's usage implied something more and kept enlarging. In time it became simply "The Swamp," a thing he never clearly defined but that eventually seemed to encompass every entrenched institution in America. There was the "Deep State," the career employees who made up the enduring machinery of government; the Democrat Party, stem and branch; unprincipled "career" politicians; the "lying" mainstream press; the technocrats who created and controlled the very internet platforms he and his supporters used; the Republicans who dared to criticize him; liberal academia . . . on and on the meaning expanded. Left-leaning and corrupt, The Swamp was an unyielding suck on Trump's native genius, determined to drag him down, and with him the American dream.

Campaigning against Hillary Clinton, he had predicted "large-scale voter fraud" and had decried the American electoral process as fundamentally unfair. He forecast a sweeping crime capable of changing the nation's course but was always vague about how it would actually work. Indeed, despite his claim that everybody knew it, there was no evidence of it in modern times. The Heritage Foundation, a conservative think tank that tabulated voting fraud cases nationwide going back more than thirty years, listed only widely scattered instances committed by members of both political parties, capable of influencing—and even then only in rare instances—local election results. But the charge resonated with those who feared big government, the growing number and power of minorities, the whole modern drift of American society. Drawing on antiquated stereotypes from the era of Tammany Hall, Trump especially stressed corruption in big cities, where Democrats ruled and the population was heavy with African Americans.

"They even want to try and rig the election at the polling booths, where so many cities are corrupt. And you see that," he said, campaigning in Colorado in 2016. "And voter fraud is all too common. And then they criticize us for saying that.... Take a look at Philadelphia ... take a look at Chicago, take a look at Saint Louis. Take a look at some of these cities where you see things happening that are horrendous." In his final debate with Clinton, he had refused to say whether, in the event he lost, he would even acknowledge the results. In that event, the numbers would be crooked.

Even victory did not allay this gripe. He continued to throw shade on the contest, questioning the validity of Clinton's winning margin in the popular vote, eventually setting up a commission to investigate voter fraud. Asked whether Clinton's certified numbers were accurate, the commission chief, Kris Kobach, said, "We may never know the answer to that." Even after the probe found nothing and disbanded, Trump continued grooming his supporters to expect fraud.

Throughout his White House tenure, he used his elevated platform to spread this message. In November 2018, prior to midterms, Trump and his attorney general, Jeff Sessions, warned of wide-scale voter fraud. They offered no evidence. Trump said, "Just take a look. All you have to do is go around, take a look at what's happened over the years, and you'll see. There are a lot of people—a lot of people—my opinion and based on proof—that try and get in illegally and actually vote illegally. So we just want to let them know that there will be prosecutions at the highest level." As ballots were still being counted in Florida's races for governor and US Senate, Trump claimed on Twitter, "Many ballots are missing or forged, ballots massively infected." No evidence of this surfaced, no one was prosecuted, and both Republican candidates ultimately won.

Still he continued impugning the voting process. The move to allow more mail voting during the pandemic gave him a new target. "Mail ballots are a very dangerous thing for this country, because they're [Democrats] cheaters," he said at a coronavirus press briefing on April 7, 2020. "They go and collect them. They're fraudulent in many cases. . . . You get thousands and thousands of people sitting in somebody's living room, signing ballots all over the place." Pressed the next day about the "thousands and thousands" claim, Trump promised to provide evidence, and did not. There wasn't any. He wasn't making a case; he was sowing suspicion.

So Trump did have a strategy in case of defeat. He used fear of fraud to raise millions of dollars for his 2020 campaign, soliciting contributions on his campaign website with the words "FRAUD like you've never seen," asking for donations "to ensure we have the resources to protect the results and keep fighting even after Election Day."

On October 26, one week before votes would be cast, campaigning in Allentown, Pennsylvania, he said, "The only way we can lose, in my opinion, is massive fraud."

GEORGIA

In the darkness of election morning, the first drop of water fell from the lip of a urinal in an Atlanta bathroom, splashing onto a black concrete floor. Every flood arrives with a first drop.

For months, within the walls of the State Farm Arena, water had risen in a pipe that led to the bathroom in the Chick-fil-A Fan Zone on the upper level. The arena's maintenance staff had shut off the water on that level during the coronavirus pandemic, since crowds couldn't come watch the ice skating shows or listen to Harry Styles sing. But thanks to a valve not quite shut or an O-ring worn by time, water in the pipe inched upward. Sometime in early November, it topped a curved trap and began filling the basin of the urinal, a Toto Commercial model in Cotton porcelain.

Now it spilled into the world, pouring onto the floor, seeking the lowest point in concrete worn smooth by ten thousand pairs of sneakers. It seeped into crevices, into the arena's structure and interstitial spaces, down through the wires and ductwork, and finally collected and poured through the ceiling of the room below.

About five thirty in the morning, a few blocks away at the county's election headquarters, Rick Barron's phone rang and chirped with the bad news. He was director of Fulton County's elections, and stood surrounded by banks of phones and televisions. Workers back at the arena should have started sorting early ballots, but now calls and text messages said they hadn't. When the first workers arrived, in the dark and quiet, they'd heard the impossible sound of what seemed like indoor rain. Someone flipped on the lights and the workers found themselves standing on the edge of a storm.

Now Barron watched a video of the indoor flood. The image showed a vast room, with an array of ballot-processing machinery, tables where the workers normally sat, and big plastic bins full of ballots. Two of the workers always made an impression, even in grainy arena security footage. Ruby Freeman stood out with an Afro that matched her big personality. In normal times she ran a kiosk at the mall selling handbags, socks, and other ladies' accessories, which she called Lady Ruby's Unique Treasures. But during election season she helped out with temporary work. Her daughter, thirty-six-year-old Shaye Moss, wore her hair in recognizable long blond braids, and had worked for years for the Fulton County elections office. Doing election work meant early mornings and long hours but it gave the mother and daughter a close-up view of democracy in action, right in the room where ballots were gathered, sorted, and counted. But now this—water pouring from above—had brought the machinery of freedom to a stop.

Behind his pandemic mask, Barron sighed. He would hear about this from higher-ups at the state level, which was the last thing he needed. He already didn't fit in here; he was the only white member of his election staff, to start. And the Atlanta political class found him odd. He was from Oregon, for one thing. At that moment, he wore a lanyard emblazoned with the logo for the Portland *soccer* team, of all things. He might as well drink Pepsi.

Now a rain cloud had burst, somehow, in his counting room.

Bonkers, he thought. He showed the video to Johnny Kauffman, an Atlanta radio reporter who had covered local elections for years and had embedded with the Fulton County staff. It seemed funny, in a bleak way. "Oh my God," Kauffman told him. "It looks like it's raining from the ceiling."

"It could only happen to us," one of the election staffers said. What could Barron do but laugh?

He didn't know he stood on a historic precipice; soon he would realize that in this election, any detail, no matter how small, could be manipulated. And any event, however mundane, could be contorted into conspiracy.

The downpour in the Atlanta arena turned out to be a brief squall. The arena's maintenance crew found the source, fixed the urinal, and sopped up the mess. No ballots got wet; no equipment damaged. Shortly after eight, when the polls opened, the counting resumed.

Barron thought, *No big deal.*

PENNSYLVANIA

Proud, hopeful, and vigilant, Leah Hoopes arrived at her local polling place in Bethel Township before the doors opened. There was already a line. She had come not just to cast her vote for Donald Trump and the rest of the Republican slate but also to serve as a watchdog. She had formed a group by that name: the PA State Watchdogs. This was a fateful day for herself, her family, and her country.

The year before, Hoopes had been elected a Republican committeewoman in Bethel, in Delaware County, or Delco, as natives prefer, a sprawling suburb that stretches west and south of Philadelphia. Soon to be given a measure of fame by the fictional HBO series *Mare of Easttown*, it was home to more than half a million people, of whom only 9,500 lived in Bethel. The county contains disparate worlds, stretching from the city's swanky, storied Main Line suburbs to the densely packed rows of blue-collar townhouses of Upper Darby. Bethel lay twenty-six miles southwest of Philadelphia at the Delaware border. The county was one of those traditionally red suburbs that in recent years began turning blue. In 2020, Delco had sworn in a Democratic majority on its governing council for the first time in a century and a half. But along the leafy curved lanes of Hoopes's precinct, the vote still leaned Republican.

Hoopes is a slight and very energetic woman of early middle age, big-eyed, occasionally blond, cheerfully social—she loved a stiff drink—and fiercely opinionated. Trump had won only 37.4 percent of the vote in Delco four years earlier, but he had narrowly edged Hillary Clinton in Bethel. Two hundred and ninety-one votes had made the difference. Ever since, as best she could, Hoopes had rallied the Trump troops, mostly through pungent and frequent Facebook postings. She maintained two accounts, one featuring her face superimposed on an old tourist ad of a woman in a polka-dot spring dress with a red carnation in her hair, inside the slogan "Everyone Is Welcome on the Trump Train," and the other with her in a Rosie the Riveter pose, with her hair tied in a red polka-dot kerchief, flexing her bicep over a "Trump-Pence" banner. Each had a following in the hundreds. She posted multiple times on most days, about, among other things, gun rights, the glory of God and America, Democratic perfidy, the necessity of cracking down hard on the leftist antifascist group called Antifa, and lately, vehemently, against all public health efforts to curb the COVID-19 pandemic, which she regarded as less threatening than the seasonal flu. For Hoopes, masks, vaccinations, and shutdowns were needless, and to the extent they were mandated or encouraged by government, liberal tyranny. When the statistics she posted to support her arguments were labeled false by Facebook, it just underscored her point. Mark Zuckerberg and the other social media titans, along with the mainstream liberal media and Democratic leaders, were out to push a liberal agenda, to stop Trump, and strangle freedom. Hoopes fought back with outrage and sarcasm. She was a cheerful and outspoken warrior, telling it like it was to anyone who would listen.

The term she self-applied was "patriot," by which she meant something much more than showing the flag on Independence Day. And it wasn't just a matter of degree. Her use of the word signified allegiance to a particular idea of America, one in tune with God, with the nation's commonsense core—as these patriots saw it—where men were men and women were women, where justice meant protecting hearth and home and cherished values, where the heroic stories of American greatness learned in elementary school remained true, where folks lived and earned and thrived free of meddling government or so-called experts, where the old usually trumped the new, where gut feelings counted for more than science, where good people were free to carry guns to protect themselves from bad people, where America was respected worldwide and its power feared. As used more widely, the definition was loose by design and wasn't always coherent. There were "patriots" who deplored racism and those who were white supremacists. There were those who both embraced America's immigrant traditions but also wanted to build a wall to keep foreigners out. Some wanted to remove the United States from foreign entanglements but also wanted it to flex its muscles more aggressively overseas. The tent was wide. It included Christian fundamentalists and conspiracy theorists and ordinary God-fearing, gun-toting wives and mothers like Leah Hoopes. But all shared a conviction that the America they revered lay under siege. The "patriot" stood armed and ready at a conceptual Bunker Hill, holding the line against the erosion of faith and decency, against big government, multiculturalization, affirmative action, or any other force that threatened their traditional ideal, or to abolish freedoms in the name of some cockeyed communal purpose. This especially included repressive, expensive, harebrained programs and policies to reengineer America, like those to redress "institutional" racism and sexism, to confuse the concept of gender, to enforce safety and health regulations in the name of public safety. "Patriots" recognized each other. It was less an ideology than a *feeling*.

And Donald Trump got it. Hoopes had been sold on him since the moment he descended the escalator in his Manhattan tower on June 16, 2015, to declare his candidacy for president. Here she saw a powerful, savvy messenger for those like her, who felt America lazily slipping away from greatness. The eight years of Democratic governance under President Barack Obama had been one tortuous disaster, with elitist nanny-state policies supplanting sensible tradition and good old-fashioned patriotism replaced by self-hatred. Trump understood it all. He waged war against apologetic Americans who held a jaundiced view of their own country, who saw it as flawed, racist, and in need of improvement, who had rendered it impotent, unwilling to carry a big stick abroad and incapable of policing its cities and borders. Trump had the guts to call out immigrants as drug dealers and rapists—not all of them, of course, but those who were tearing at the fabric of the country. His words infuriated the lefties, which is what she liked about him particularly. He never apologized, and he didn't mince words.

Not that she was starry-eyed. A lot about him made her cringe. He had a huge ego. He was often crass. But he saw America as she did: as the hope of the world. It was still the place millions envied and yearned to live in, which was fine, so long as they arrived legally. Some of Hoopes's dearest friends were immigrants. But through three years and more in the White House, Trump had withstood relentless liberal persecution and mainstream media assaults as he fought for her and other patriots to restore the unabashed, righteous, proud image of America they held dear.

So the consequences on this Election Day were, as President Trump would say, *huge*. He simply could not lose to Biden, whom she called a "stuttering prick." The cost would be catastrophic. As her Facebook writing made clear, Hoopes regarded Democrats less as fellow citizens with whom she disagreed than as a threat to the very idea of America, out to destroy her way of life. Weeks earlier, after a discussion with her husband, Zach, she posted a plea for her fellow patriots to rise up as if it were 1776. She spelled out the consequences of a Democratic win: "Our business will cease to exist . . . the luxuries we have will no longer exist, our freedoms diminished, our opportunities gone, our schools have crumbled, the middle class will no longer exist." Rioting and looting in the cities would spread to their own quiet neighborhoods; in fact, she wrote, "It is the goal of the left to destroy suburbia." Only thirty-five people liked her post, which illustrated the challenge. But Hoopes would reach a much bigger audience soon enough.

The truth is that ardent Trumpists like her were outsiders, even with the local Republican Party. Delco's GOP organization viewed them the way mainstream churches viewed evangelicals. They shared the same religion but not the same zeal. Trump rallies filled Hoopes with exhilarating passion. At them, she felt engulfed in fellowship, immersed in a rising, egalitarian, class- and color-blind tide of those who believed America was pretty near perfect exactly as it was and had been. Trump had beaten the staid old Republican guard, who had failed to grasp the urgency of the moment. This passion was a big reason she had gotten herself elected as committeewoman and had scored her pass as an official poll watcher. As Election Day approached, Hoopes believed that Trump and the patriot tide was unstoppable . . . unless something happened. Unless the Democrats cheated.

Trump had asked them to prepare. He wanted them to monitor their polling places closely. The PA Watchdogs existed, in her words, to "expose and bring to light election fraud." They linked themselves with the Thomas More Society, an activist Chicago-based law firm that figured prominently in Trump's effort to challenge voting procedures. Hoopes had joined an October lawsuit by the organization attempting, without success, to bar districts from accepting grants from the Center for Tech and Civic Life, a philanthropic organization partly supported by donations from Zuckerberg. Delco had used one such grant to purchase new vote-counting machines for the anticipated flood of mail ballots—the pandemic would prompt millions to cast their ballots in advance from home. When she met Greg Stenstrom, a navy veteran who presented himself as a "data forensic scientist," she recruited him, telling him, "I could use some help if somebody knows fraud." Neither he nor Hoopes had ever worked on or observed an election, but they planned to pay close attention and make a public record of what they expected to find. In one of her posts, she had called the Democrats on the county council and election board, her county neighbors, "lying hacks."

Here was the animating principle behind Hoopes's concern. The Democrats who had won Delco in 2019, those at the state capitol at Harrisburg, those walking the federal halls of Washington, DC, and those embedded throughout all levels of government bureaucracy, the Deep State—along with their allies in the party's mainstream, in academia, and the press—were not simply fellow citizens with competing views. They were subversives. *Anti*-Americans. They could not be trusted to run a fair election.

Plenty of fervent Democrats had a similar way of looking at Republicans. They were racist, ignorant, xenophobic, and determined to impede the popular vote. This Election Day felt more like combat than friendly competition. A day of pent-up emotion.

So Hoopes arrived early and keen-eyed at Bethel's Precinct 5 polling place, the Belmont Community Club House, a low, tan building in a tony village for the elderly wrapped around a shallow pond. It was about as placid a location as you could imagine. But the atmosphere felt charged. Feelings were running high. Hoopes knew many of the poll workers and voters. Quite a few were seniors. They were afraid of catching the COVID virus and afraid they might encounter violence. Trump's son Donald Jr. had called for an "army" of Trump supporters to show up at polling places around the country.

"The radical left are laying the groundwork to steal this election from my father," he said. "We need every able-bodied man, woman, to join [the] army for Trump's election security operation . . . we need you to help us watch them, not just on Election Day, but also during early voting and at the counting boards."

So the mood, even in quiet Bethel, felt tense. The lines Hoopes saw on arrival persisted throughout the day. They fed into a large well-lit conference hall, with long tables to one side manned by poll workers. Voters were checked against the registration books and directed to curtained pods to cast their votes. Hoopes tried to keep things calm, and the Democratic poll watchers seemed composed and professional. She directed people and looked for ways to be helpful.

Problems started right away, though. The voting machines Delco had purchased to record ballots were new. Voters marked paper ballots, which the machines then scanned. The process created an electronic image of the ballot, stored in the machine's memory and backed up by the paper copy. The machines, provided by Hart InterCivic, had been the subject of a misinformation campaign two years earlier, in Texas, that suggested they might be used to switch votes. Texas secretary of state Rolando Pablos had felt the need to issue a statement defending them. They were originally designed for votes to be cast on an electronic slate, but out of continued worry about vote-switching, they had been redesigned to accommodate a paper ballot, so there would be a physical record. Because of the pandemic, most Delco poll workers had not received in-person training on the new machines. Either because of human error or some issue with the batch they had been given, the paper ballots kept jamming, which meant each had to be discarded and the voter asked to fill out another. This slowed the flow and kept the lines long.

One of the county's roving repair vans arrived that morning to take a look and diagnosed a paper problem, not a machine problem. A fresh batch of paper ballots was delivered, but Hoopes saw little improvement. It seemed fishy to her. It looked more like incompetence than outright fraud, but what if the clumsiness was deliberate? Considering the narrow margin Bethel had given Trump over Hillary Clinton, she wondered if the Democrats now in charge had intentionally provided clunky machines and hapless operators to her precinct to gum up the works. The idea grew. She would later liken it to a "Nazi operation," with "little monkeys" following orders after being set up by their superiors to fail.

Across Pennsylvania, millions voted that day without incident, but some, as always, encountered problems. Voting is a complicated and highly decentralized process with many people, machines, and procedures, all of them working quickly. There were new machines in many counties, and the pandemic had created a host of new rules, often irregularly enforced. So there were screw-ups, delays, and, in many places, confusion. Urged on by their candidate, Trump voters and observers stayed attentive.

Gary Phelman, a rare Republican voter in Philadelphia, had a gold slip of paper that he believed authorized him to watch the voting on behalf of Trump at any polling place in the city. When he heard a rumor that observers like him were being turned away at a polling place in South Philly, he drove there. It was a funeral parlor. He entered and was asked to leave. He showed his gold certificate.

"That's not good here," a poll worker told him.

"It is!" he insisted and asked her to read it.

They stepped outside, and Phelman's friend videoed the exchange.

"I'm the eyes and ears of the president of the United States," Phelman said. He was gently turned away.

Barbara Sulitka, an elderly Trump voter in Fairview Township in rural central Pennsylvania, voted for the president, but when she received a printout, it confused her. She did not see his name on the slip of paper. She complained to a poll worker who assured her that her vote had been recorded, but she remained concerned that the names for the presidential slate didn't appear on the printout. She was told that this was to protect the secrecy of her ballot, but she stayed worried. Had they counted her votes?

Another Trump voter from Drums, a township in central Pennsylvania, was confused by how to use the new machines and wasn't sure his ballot had been scanned. He found the poll workers unhelpful. Olivia

Jane Winters of Philadelphia found confusion at her polling place over voters who showed up with mail ballots they had not filled out. She felt the workers there had been rude to her when she complained that some of those people might be voting twice. There was no evidence that any had.

There were plenty of incidents like these. In an ordinary election, they might result in an angry letter to a precinct captain. But this year, they, like the leaky urinal in Atlanta, were all going to become a *big deal*.

Hoopes stayed all day at her polling place in Bethel, happy to participate and only mildly concerned by what she had seen. She left shortly before the polls closed at eight that evening in order to witness the sealing of the township's ballot drop box. By law, the box had to be secured when the polls closed. She watched that happen and then drove to the nearby McKenzie Brew House to celebrate with her fellow Watchdogs.

They were thrilled by the early returns strongly in favor of Trump and other Republican candidates. In her precinct alone, Trump had received 67 percent of the in-person votes tallied so far. Her own candidate for the state legislature, Craig Williams, was also winning handily. The first sign of trouble came in a call she took from her fellow poll watcher Greg Stenstrom.

He said there were big problems at the counting center.

MICHIGAN

Antrim County, Michigan, seemed an unlikely setting for the attempted overthrow of an American election.

In the mitten shape of the state's lower peninsula, Antrim makes up a fingertip in the far north. It sits on the eastern side of Grand Traverse Bay, which took its name from French voyagers who in the eighteenth century paddled canoes across its lonesome width: *la grand traverse*, they called it.

About twenty-three thousand people live in Antrim. Many work in fruit production, including the cherry farms that make the region the "cherry capital of the world." They grow sweet cherries and sour:

Montmorency cherries, Balaton tart cherries. Cavaliers, Sams, Emperor Francises, Golds, and a particular local favorite, Ulsters.

In spring, those cherry trees cover the landscape with pink and white blossoms. And the county features what people here call the chain of lakes, a series of fourteen terraced lakes and rivers starting with Beals Lake at the top and finally flowing into the Grand Traverse. The largest and deepest body in the chain is Torch Lake, where long ago Native Americans fished by torchlight. Today Antrim's residents sail their boats up and down its length on turquoise waters.

So Antrim County sits on a peninsular outcrop, its people are few and scattered, and its landscape is sublime. All of which makes it seem outlandish as the stage for what followed: private jets arriving in the night, intrigue, threats of violence, and an effort to subvert the will of the American people.

Election Day started with coffee for Sheryl Guy. She poured it from the old Bunn coffeepot into her teal-colored mug. Then she placed a lid on the mug, because you never know what might go wrong.

Life had carried the Antrim county clerk toward this moment since her first breath in a sense. In a concrete-block room, here in the Antrim County Building, her own birth certificate sits in a chunky black binder: Baby Sheryl Ann, born May 1961, eight pounds and ten ounces.

She graduated from the local high school on a Friday, and the next Monday she started work in the county building as a receptionist. She worked her way up and sat in every chair in the building along the way: clerk 1 and 2, deputy 1 and 2, chief deputy, administrator. For thirty-one years she worked under the previous county clerk, whom she viewed as a mother figure and who granted Sheryl—maiden name Kirts then—a license to marry her high school sweetheart, Alan.

Now Guy was almost sixty and county clerk herself. The people of Antrim had elected her for the job eight years earlier, and she loved it. It's a small county, so on Election Day she and her staff of four handled election duties along with the everyday responsibilities: collecting court fees, paying the county's bills, certifying births and marriages. "Busy," she said.

The vote itself went smoothly. Michigan counties are divided into grid-like townships, which are home to what they call villages: Elk Rapids village, Central Lake village, and so forth. People across the county voted on issues specific to their villages—on school boards, on a proposed marijuana shop—and bigger questions like the US presidency. There was a last-minute change, adding a candidate for village trustee to the ballot, but people voted without confusion or incident. Guy voted to reelect both Trump and herself.

Poll workers in precincts around Antrim fed people's ballots into scanners, which printed out tally tapes that looked like thirty-foot strips of receipt paper. The scanners also recorded the votes on memory cards.

At about 6:00 p.m., Guy walked from the county building to buy dinner for the staff—"the girls"—at Short's, a pub that sells sandwiches with names like "Sketches of Winkle" (salami) and "Old Man Thunder" (braised beef). They worked while they ate, and after the polls closed the results started to come in. Poll supervisors from around the county brought their memory cards to Guy at the county office, and she plugged those results into her central computer. It placed the votes into what amounted to a spreadsheet, sorting about sixteen thousand votes into columns and rows.

It took hours. Guy is quick to admit she's not technologically adept. "I'm not a techie person," she said. "I type, and I use my computer when I have to."

They finished just before 5:00 a.m., in total exhaustion. Guy had spent hour after hour peering at the columns and rows and, by the end, was too tired to step back, figuratively, and consider a broader view of the election. She knew she, a Republican, had won reelection as county clerk because she ran unopposed. But she felt too weary to even note how many votes she got. She registered, vaguely, that Joe Biden had won the presidential vote.

She locked the office about 5:00 a.m. and headed home briefly to shower. No time for sleep. She said a brief good morning to Alan, a machinist, then gave him a goodbye peck and drove back toward her office. Along the way she stopped at McDonald's to buy breakfast for the girls, who wanted sausage and egg McMuffins. Between placing her order and arriving at the pickup window, she received an email from an early-rising citizen who had seen reports of the presidential vote in Antrim. The short message was ominous: "Things don't look right."

The results she had posted, unofficially, showed Joe Biden beating Donald Trump by about 3,200 votes, which would be nearly impossible in a county as reliably Republican as Antrim. That kind of sudden shift in long-standing voting patterns signaled a problem, and the realization awoke Guy like a shock of cold water. "Oh *CROW*," she cried. She wanted to race to the office but could only sit trapped in the drive-through. Finally, after picking up the McMuffins, she gunned her car toward the county building.

She quickly put out a statement on Antrim's official Facebook page. "By this afternoon, we expect to have a clear answer and a clear plan of action addressing any issue," she said. "Until then, we are asking all interested parties to bear with us while we get to the bottom of this."

That sounded confident enough, but inwardly she felt baffled. What could've happened? She suspected a culprit: *computers*. They probably weren't talking to each other right. So all day, she and her staff totaled up votes directly from the official tape printed at each precinct and entered that by hand into the central computer. Then they republished the results, which now showed Trump as victor.

But a new problem arose. Now the totals showed more than eighteen thousand votes, which was two thousand too many. And the world was starting to notice tiny Antrim County.

CROW.

ARIZONA

Lynie Stone didn't like to vote. She didn't trust it.

Four years earlier, she had instead prayed and meditated, and set an intention that Donald Trump would win, which had worked! But this year, she had changed her mind, not about Trump—she liked him—but about her role.

"I'm voting in this election," she told her husband. This admirable, civic-minded decision would lead her down a trail of disillusion, to a public stand on a national stage.

A mail ballot wouldn't do. A voice inside her told her that she needed to vote in person and early, and Stone listened to her inner voice. So a week before Election Day, she drove from the ranch she and her husband owned outside Tucson to the modernist Pima County Recorder's Office, a big white-and-black box with five stone pillars in front that appears to have been designed to look like a giant computer component. She brought her passport and driver's license. Arizona law required only one photo ID, but Stone was on a mission.

An animal chiropractor, she looked like someone who just stepped off a ranch, with sun-bleached long brownish-blond hair and a pink complexion that looked mildly baked. Her sunny mood clashed immediately with the hushed gloom of the office.

"I'm here to vote," she told the clerk, an older man, seated behind the front desk.

He just smiled.

She told him that she had brought her IDs, and he thanked her but didn't seem to care. The look on his face and his tone implied they weren't necessary, which she found odd.

She was given a ballot and made a mistake filling it out. She offered to take it home and shred it.

"Oh, no, no, no," he said. "You can't do that."

The clerk drew lines with a black marker through her votes and wrote "SPOILED" on both sides.

"This ballot has to be accounted for," he explained. She watched as it was placed in a box with others marked the same. Then they gave her a new one, which she filled in correctly, voting for Trump and others. She signed it and sealed it in an envelope. It was placed in a locked box with other ballots. Then she received a slip of paper with a website printed on it—Pima.gov/VoteSafe—where she could, in three days, track the processing of her vote online.

On her way out, she noticed that there was a drive-up ballot collection window, which struck her as inappropriate. You could vote the way you picked up a burger and fries? She didn't see photo IDs being checked nor the ballots themselves. What if these drive-up voters made a mistake, too? Was there a "spoiled" box for them? She left the center with an uneasy feeling.

Stone waited three days and then accessed the website to check on the status of her ballot. She downloaded a three-page Excel spreadsheet. This would lead her down a complex path that others might find hard to follow.

The recorder's office had assigned her ballot to a batch labeled "Q2." At that point, the numbers for this batch listed thirty-nine *duplicated* ballots but no *rejected* ballots. This worried her. In fact, hers had been counted as "duplicated" because she had been handed a duplicate after she'd made the mistake. "Rejected" ballots were ones with mistakes where the voter was unavailable to fill out a new one. She didn't understand the difference and so was confused enough to wonder why her "spoiled" ballot hadn't been counted as "rejected." If that spoiled ballot had not been counted, had her corrected one?

She called the recorder's office and failed to get a satisfactory answer. The person she spoke to didn't seem to grasp the nub of her confusion. "What are you saying?" he kept asking and left her with the classic bureaucratic brush-off "We'll have to study that."

This sent Stone back to the spreadsheets, which only grew more worrisome. Out of 454,633 total ballots—she was now looking beyond her batch—only 20 were listed as "rejected." This seemed way too few. Given her understanding, she wondered how it was that more people, like her, hadn't made mistakes on their first try. The spoiled ballots of those who had were, like hers, noted in the category "duplicated," but she hadn't made that connection. If she had, she would have discovered that she was right about the number of voters who made errors. And each day, as more votes were cast, they grew more numerous. There were now more than forty "duplicated" ballots in her Q2 batch alone.

When the votes were all in, something caught her eye about that "duplicated" column that chilled her. The total of "duplicated" ballots countywide was 6,660. The number 666 is, in the Book of Revelation, the "sign of the beast," the mark of the Antichrist. Stone followed QAnon, the conspiracy theory that posited an international group of Satanic pedo-philic sex traffickers as the secret power behind forces fighting Trump. And here was Satan's signature, right there in the county's spreadsheets! The Pima County vote was not just fraudulent, but *evil*.

On election night, she was watching TV with her dogs when Fox News called her state for Biden. This was just minutes after the polls closed.

It made Stone's blood boil. She knew what was happening!

Was she the only one seeing this?

COOPED

Across the country, a handful of Americans had arrived first at a new and precarious place: a historic ridge dividing the way elections worked before and the way they would work after.

To survey America's electoral record is to look back on a landscape of these ridges, for better and worse. The millions of followers who applauded Trump's declarations of fraud seemed unaware how long and hard the country had struggled to refine the vote. Some failures and victories loom so large they barely need naming; women gained suffrage only in 1920, for instance, and many African Americans won real access to polls only after the civil rights acts of the 1960s. But the history of voter fraud, in particular, describes two general styles.

In the first, broadly, perpetrators tried to sneak phony votes *into* the ballot box. During the "political machine" era of the 1800s, for instance, parties printed their own ballots and stuffed collection boxes. Even less subtly, political bosses sent thugs into polling places to beat up any voter not holding the right-colored ballot. In New York City, the Society of St. Tammany—Tammany Hall—instructed its followers to grow full beards before voting on Election Day. Later in the morning they shaved their beards into mutton chops and voted a second time, then shaved down to moustaches and voted again.

Tammany Hall and similar outfits in other cities "cooped" voters by throwing enormous parties with free booze in their locked basements a day before elections or by kidnapping victims outright. Then on Election Day they hauled their half-conscious captives to the polls, often forcing them to change clothes and vote multiple times, between which the victims either took more alcohol or beatings. Some scholars theorize the author Edgar Allan Poe died a victim of cooping; Baltimore reeked of voter fraud in 1849, and on Election Day a man discovered Poe semiconscious at a tavern that also served as a polling place where coopers often brought their victims. Instead of his own clothes, Poe wore an ill-fitting farmer's outfit, including a straw hat. Poe gave the concerned man the name of a magazine editor who also was a doctor, so the man quickly dispatched a handwritten note—

Baltimore City, Oct. 3, 1849

Dear Sir,

There is a gentleman, rather the worse for wear, at Ryan's 4th ward polls, who goes under the cognomen of Edgar A. Poe, and who appears in great distress, & he says he is acquainted with you, he is in need of immediate assistance.

Yours, in haste,

JOS. W. WALKER

To Dr. J. E. Snodgrass.

—but too late to save Poe.

So there was a colorful history of this style of fraud, but the nation had prevailed against it, mostly with simple innovations. Colored ballots, for instance, gave way to secret ballots around the turn of the twentieth century, state by state; once voters stepped behind a curtain, political bosses' bribes and threats became useless. Nobody knew how they'd voted. States set boundaries at polling places to restrict electioneering that could intimidate voters. And in recent years, more sophisticated technologies have allowed election officials to sift mountains of data to search for patterns of illegal votes across entire populations. These safeguards so thoroughly snuffed out illicit voting that in the weeks after the 2016 election, when the *Washington Post* combed legal records searching for confirmed cases of fraudulent presidential votes, the paper found exactly three: a woman in Iowa voted twice for Donald Trump, a man in Texas voted twice for Trump, and a woman in Illinois tried to vote for Trump on behalf of her dead husband. A fourth case involved a local mayoral race. None of those votes were counted. Others almost certainly went undetected, and authorities may have discovered straggling cases later, but the report made Trump's claims—ballot boxes stuffed with millions of illegal votes—a farce.

In the second style of voter fraud, culprits tried to keep legitimate votes *out* of the ballot box. For instance, southern authorities suppressed votes with ham-fisted rules like land ownership requirements, poll taxes, and literacy tests. A more insidious technique raised the specter of the first style of voter fraud—ballot stuffing, dead voters, and so forth— even when there was none. In this case, politicians often played on their constituents' fear of outsiders who threatened to snatch away control of the country. In the 1840s, for instance, a political cartoon showed an Irish immigrant dressed in a whiskey barrel and a German immigrant wearing a beer keg, stealing an American ballot box. Such propaganda stirred nativist sentiment and gave politicians a pretext for restrictive voter laws. More recently, as technology extinguished the first style of election fraud, the technology itself became seen as a vulnerability. Could foreign hackers meddle with the count?

The human suspicion that *there's something funny going on here* is universal. The US Constitution delegates the responsibility for handling elections to the states, where a patchwork of party loyalties defines America's political map, and modern politicians, both left and right, have alleged voter fraud with varying degrees of credibility.

In 1960, Republicans claimed that corrupt political bosses in Cook County, Illinois—Chicago—handed a narrow victory in the state to John F. Kennedy over Richard Nixon. Historians have since analyzed the vote and concluded that yes, corrupt counting favored Kennedy, but no, it didn't decide the race in Illinois. At the time, Nixon didn't know that, of course. Even so he, one of the shrewdest and most grasping of all American politicians, declined to object to the outcome. He conceded to Kennedy and told a friend, "Our country cannot afford the agony of a constitutional crisis."

After the presidential election of 2004, some Democrats expressed suspicion that voting machines in Ohio may have tilted the vote there toward George W. Bush over John Kerry. The *New York Times* said otherwise, in an editorial: "There is no evidence of vote theft or errors on a large scale." The *Washington Post* dismissed the claims as "conspiracy theories."

Even so, Democratic US representative John Conyers, then ranking minority member of the House Judiciary Committee, led an investigation into irregularities in Ohio and issued a report called *Preserving Democracy: What Went Wrong in Ohio*. The report accused then-secretary of state Kenneth Blackwell of using his position to purge voter rolls of minority citizens who hadn't voted recently, and detailed various computer irregularities, but didn't offer evidence of mass fraud.

The left-leaning magazine *Mother Jones*, in a closer investigation of its own, found that, yes, Ohio politicians had used their authority to influence the election, but no, it didn't add up to fraud. Even so, the next year Robert F. Kennedy Jr. took up the cause, writing in *Rolling Stone* of a "media blackout" and that "indications continued to emerge that something deeply troubling had taken place in 2004"—language that would later become recognizable from the other side of the political aisle. But in *Salon*, Farhad Manjoo dissected Kennedy's case, saying "the evidence he cites isn't new and his argument is filled with distortions and blatant omissions." Further: "If you do read Kennedy's article, be prepared to machete your way through numerous errors of interpretation and his deliberate omission of key bits of data."

None of the squabbling on the left mattered, though. After the election, a spokesman for the Democratic Party had said, "The simple fact of the matter is that Republicans received more votes than Democrats, and we're not contesting this election." And Kerry, to the point, had conceded to Bush.

In May 2017, Trump created a commission headed by Vice President Mike Pence and Kansas secretary of state Kris Kobach, who would hunt down evidence of the fraud Trump had claimed. The clear message was, *Now that I'm president, we can finally get to the bottom of this.* The probe ended a little more than a year later, without documenting a single instance. One of the commission's own members, Maine secretary of state Matt Dunlap, attacked it, saying it had "a pre-ordained outcome," which it could not deliver. A draft of its unissued report listed categories of election deceit, but the spaces for documentation were, according to Dunlap, "glaringly empty."

"It was a dishonest effort from the very beginning," said Dunlap in an interview with journalist David Daley. "It was never really meant to uncover anything. It was meant to backfill an unprovable thesis that there's voter fraud—then to issue a fake report justifying laws or executive orders that change the fundamental nature of how we run elections. I think that might have been the real danger that we averted."

In 2018 in Georgia, Stacey Abrams lost a race for governor to Brian Kemp, then secretary of state there. Abrams, who is black, alleged Kemp had suppressed minority voters by using his position to purge them from registration rolls. Afterward, she refused to concede and weighed a legal challenge to the result, but decided against it.

Never in America's history, though—however many sideburns Bowery barbers shaved or immigrants came ashore—had a losing presidential candidate argued that the whole nation had been swindled. When Abraham Lincoln won the presidency in 1860, his victory so outraged his opposition that an entire region of the country broke away. But in loss Stephen A. Douglas never claimed the election was "rigged."

Now, though, a few scattered Americans—and through them, the entire country—stood on the brink of something new.

Pennsylvania

Greg Stenstrom didn't need to see Arizona go for Biden to think fraud. He had anticipated it and was ready.

Stenstrom is a big and broad-shouldered fellow, whose square face in middle age was softening around the jaws, chin, and neck. His hair was short and graying. He retained his youthful vigor, and his size and military bearing were imposing, which he knew and used to his advantage. He had identified himself to Hoopes as a fraud expert, and she had leaped. He was exactly the kind of person she needed to catch the Democrats in the act.

He fully embraced the role. On Election Day, he regarded himself as having been "deployed" by the PA Watchdogs. With her help, he had gotten certified as a poll watcher in Chester, the only city in Delco, and had visited twenty-two polling places that day, calling out some mishandling of provisional ballots—which was politely corrected—before deciding that he was wasting his time. This was petty stuff. The real action was at The Wharf, Delco's new counting center, where the number of ballots was far greater and where The Steal was no doubt in full swing.

He arrived there at about six in the evening of Election Day with four of his buddies, whom he would describe as "ex-military." Stenstrom planned to inspect things with his own eyes and already believed what he would find. When Hoopes had first approached him, he had predicted exactly what was going to happen: "I've been telling the Trump administration for four years," he said (he said he had friends in the president's inner circle). "Whatever ballots you have, whatever votes you have [election] night, the next morning, you'll be losing by one hundred thousand."

How? By a sneaky infusion of bogus Biden ballots. He was sure of it and sure that inside the counting center it was happening *at that moment*. But when he entered The Wharf and attempted to mount stairs to the second-floor counting room, officials stopped him. His credentials, good for Chester polling places, did not authorize him to observe at the counting center.

Delco had faced daunting challenges, holding this vote. In the best of times, a national election was a biannual miracle. Holding them was an ongoing chore for every jurisdiction in the country and one of its core responsibilities. Even at the level of a single county, the logistics were dizzying. There were 250 polling places in Delco alone, each staffed by a minimum of six. Thousands of part-time workers and volunteers were needed to check registers, scan and record ballots, and then transport them, every step governed by rules to ensure integrity. And this year, Delco faced two new complications: the introduction of new voting machines and the pandemic.

Making matters worse, newly elected Democrats found that departing Republicans had, in a gesture the newcomers saw as pure partisan gamesmanship, neglected to budget money for no-excuse mail voting. Since so many people were afraid of contracting the virus among crowds indoors, Pennsylvania, like most states, had loosened rules for voting by mail. In the past, voters had to show they were out of town or disabled in order to send in their ballots. This year, the privilege had been extended to all. Republicans, who in general resisted making voting easier, opposed the changes. In Delco, there had been several legal battles over the summer, with courts nearly always siding with the county. The pandemic did, after all, present a major unforeseen challenge that was no one's fault, and the option of effectively disenfranchising hesitant voters was a hard sell. So even though mail ballots ordinarily had been just a tiny fraction of those cast, this year there would likely be as many or more of them than those cast in person. Having failed in their efforts to stop it, the departing Republican council had simply not budgeted for it.

Incoming councilwoman Christine Reuther, a Delco native who had gone to Harvard and then to Berkeley for her law degree and then worked at a major Philadelphia law firm, and who had served previously as a clerk and then judge for the county board of elections, foresaw trouble immediately. In addition to the budget snub, the county lacked a full-time election director, and then its IT department announced it could no longer provide support. The new Hart voting machines, which replaced the lever-operated hulks that had served for decades, were unfamiliar to the county's poll workers. Given pandemic fears and restrictions, in-person training would be minimal. Then there was the likely flood of mail ballots. How were these to be processed? The old method of opening them by hand at individual precincts was out. What all this meant, Reuther saw, was a certain mess. She spoke up and, in time-honored fashion, was assigned to fix it. This being the first election handled by Delco Democrats since the nineteenth century, any confusion would be blamed on the party, Reuther knew, and on her.

At times, the crash effort to prepare seemed snakebit. Finding workers during a pandemic shutdown was hard. Ultimately, this election would require not only part-time hires and volunteers but an all-hands summons of county employees, everyone from Delco's executive director to council members to support staff to park workers and police. Much of this manpower would go to handling the mail ballots, which would turn out to number roughly 130,000, nearly 40 percent of those cast. To make it easier and to ease the burden on the post office, the county installed forty-one solar-powered ballot drop boxes, like the one Hoopes observed being locked on election night. Each had to be continually monitored by security cameras to ensure against tampering. They were distributed throughout the county according to need, with densely populated areas receiving more. This was interpreted as favoritism since there were more Democrats in urban neighborhoods than in the country.

To cope with the mail ballots, the county purchased—with the aid of grant money from Zuckerberg's philanthropic Center for Tech and Civic Life—BlueCrest sorting machines, which automated the process. Each mail ballot came in two envelopes, an outer and inner one. The outer one was marked with a barcode, affirming that it had been sent to a registered voter who had applied for it. It also contained the voter's signature and a date. Inside was an unmarked envelope that held the ballot. This was to ensure its secrecy, a feature of American elections designed to shield voters from intimidation and to check bribery—who would pay off a voter without knowing how he or she had voted?

The BlueCrest machine was a marvel. L-shaped, it stood about eight feet high and six feet wide, with its longer leg extending about thirty feet. It scanned the outer envelope, reading the barcode, then sped it down the long leg toward baskets for the appropriate precincts. The machine worked so fast that envelopes being processed were not even visible. The machine recorded an image of every envelope and notified the state's central voter data bank that it had been received. This process had begun weeks before Election Day. Voters received an email confirmation.

Cutting into the inner envelopes had to wait until the polls opened on Election Day. This employed a second group of machines that sliced open the outer envelope and removed the inner one. The outer envelopes were collected and stored, providing a paper trail for the images in the machine's memory. The actual ballots, still enclosed in the blank inner envelope, were then delivered to a third machine, which opened them, removed the ballot, and batched it with others for delivery to the scanners. If the ballot had been torn or damaged in handling, volunteers would replicate the choices by hand on a clean ballot so it could be fed into the scanner and counted.

To manage all this required shifts of between seventy-five to one hundred workers and would need much more space than the old counting rooms at the government center in Media, the county seat. Howard Lazarus, the newly hired county executive director, settled on The Wharf, a monumental century-old brown-brick power plant on the Delaware

River waterfront that had been retooled as an office center. Set on a pier in Chester, it stood more than seven stories high with battlement-like towers at each end of its river-facing front. Its enormous Beaux Arts facade featured rows of imposing stone pillars from just above the first story to the roofline. The counting would take place on the spacious second floor. Only after the lease was signed did Lazarus learn that the building's elevators were too small to accommodate the new BlueCrest machines. A portion of the building's outer wall had to be removed to hoist them up and in, only to discover that there were not enough electrical outlets for them.

By Election Day, all of these problems had been sorted, and Lazarus felt good. At the same time voters would start stepping into polling places, the first of the mail ballots would be sliced open at The Wharf. The procedures were comparable. At polling places, voters were first checked against lists of those registered in their precinct, and a note would be made that they had been given a ballot. They were then directed to a curtained booth to make their choices. At the counting center, these steps were automated. At both places, marked ballots were then scanned and recorded in the machines' memories for retrieval when the polls closed. In both places, the paper ballots were saved so they could be checked against the machine tally in the event of a malfunction or discrepancy. When the polls closed, votes cast in person were reported immediately. At The Wharf, the process was expected to last for several days. This introduced a dynamic that fed suspicion.

President Trump had discouraged his supporters from voting by mail and may have cost himself reelection because of it. He had warned, falsely, that mail ballots were particularly vulnerable to fraud. But voting by mail was easier and involved no risk of COVID exposure. In the end, far fewer Republicans mailed in their votes than Democrats. In Delco, more than eight of ten mail ballots were for Biden.

Because of this, a "blue shift," a leap in Biden's favor following Election Day, had been widely foreseen. To Trumpists, this would look exactly like what their candidate had predicted, a win snatched away by the vote-counting process—*The Steal*.

Greg Stenstrom's credentials did not entitle him to enter the counting center at The Wharf. To avoid a mob scene there, permits for the nearly one thousand authorized poll watchers in Delco, both Democratic and Republican, had specified particular locales. Most, like his, were for polling places. Other passes had been issued for observers at The Wharf and they had been watching there in shifts. Stenstrom's name was not on that list.

He raised enough of a fuss for Bill Martin, the county solicitor, to be summoned.

"Hey, I'm a poll watcher," said Stenstrom, with his entourage. "I have a certificate. I want to get in."

With long experience in Philadelphia government before taking the county position, Martin had dealt with his share of pushy citizens, and he was having none of it. Like Stenstrom, he did not shy from confrontation. Words were exchanged. From the solicitor's perspective, Stenstrom didn't belong there. He told him, in so many words, that he could either back down or be arrested. Stenstrom didn't back down. Police wandered over. A deputy sheriff, Mike Donohue, who knew Stenstrom, tried to calm him.

"Greg, let's step aside for a minute," he said.

They moved into the building's downstairs lobby and Donohue told Stenstrom that he would have to leave. Aware that his entourage was recording the scene, Stenstrom stood his ground—video of a Trump poll "watchdog" being refused access to a counting center would be useful.

"Mike, I'm not leaving," he said. "I don't mind getting into a fight. I have a right to be here. I'm not going, and you can't make me go unless we get into a fight. I'm willing to get into a fight."

"Well, we don't want to arrest you, and we don't want to get into a fight," said Donohue. He suggested that if Stenstrom believed he was lawfully entitled to enter, he ought to get an attorney.

That's when he had called Hoopes. She heard how upset he was. From the brew pub she started making calls, and a few hours later, John McBlain showed up at The Wharf. The attorney was a notable, well-liked, and respected figure in Delco. He had served as chairman of the county council years earlier and knew personally many of those supervising the election. His intervention was immediately effective. In the interests of keeping the peace, Martin agreed to add Stenstrom's and Hoopes's names to the list of certified Wharf observers. It was now late in the evening, about eleven. Stenstrom would later make much of the fact that he had been barred from watching the count for hours, leaving out the fact that authorized Republican observers had been present throughout.

Escorted upstairs, he was immediately, predictably, alarmed. The counting floor, a huge open space, was alive with activity. The big BlueCrest machines hummed. Workers moved in all directions. Elevators opened and closed, disgorging carts with boxes and tubs of ballots in various stages of processing. Although he was new to all this, it nevertheless struck him immediately as wrong. He knew there were more than a hundred thousand mail ballots, which was a lot, but in his opinion, they were not sufficient to explain this much bustle. He concluded he was watching, as he would later put it, "Kabuki theater," a stylized performance designed to confuse all but the expert eye. Stenstrom considered his eye expert, and he was not fooled. The commotion was designed to distract him from the introduction of fake Biden ballots. He wondered where the real ones were hidden.

He called a contact who, he was told, was in the room with President Trump. Stenstrom reported his alarm, but his contact was untroubled. He was happy with the early numbers from Pennsylvania, as was the president.

"Look," said Stenstrom, "I'm sitting here. I'm watching this."

"Greg, relax. We're six hundred thousand votes ahead."

"Well, I hope you have a good plan B," Stenstrom said and repeated his prediction from months earlier, "because tomorrow morning, you're going to be one hundred thousand behind."

One of the things that most disturbed him was the way outer envelopes were being separated from the inner ones. Opened outer envelopes ended up in bins, while the ballots themselves, each inside the unmarked inner envelope, were wheeled off to the scanners. As he saw it, this destroyed any chance for a detailed audit. If outer envelopes, with their identifying bar codes and signatures, were not kept with ballots, how could anyone later prove the votes were authentic?

The separation was, of course, necessary to ensure the ballot's secrecy. By design, no one could reconnect inner envelopes with outer ones, but you could make sure that no extra ballots had been introduced. At the end of the counting, the number of ballots cast could be compared with the number of scanned envelopes. There were two ways of doing this: against the scanned images in the machines and against the opened envelopes themselves.

Nevertheless, the practice seemed nefarious to Stenstrom. It was, as he would later authoritatively put it, "forensically destructive."

He also became increasingly agitated by the way he and the other observers were roped off, too distant to actually inspect the envelopes. Whereas the others watching trusted that the envelopes and ballots before them were the real thing, Stenstrom, of course, did not. Worse, there was a rear area where he could catch only occasional glimpses of what was going on. The counting floor was open in front, where the machines were working, but there was a wall behind them, and behind the wall were tables where he could see, when doors swung open, workers examining ballots. He was told that this was where envelopes were "pre-canvassed," inspected for tears or irregularities before being fed into the sorting machines. Nothing was being done to them. There were cameras that provided a live feed of that action on nearby screens. Also in that rear area was a locked closet. He asked to be taken back to inspect both but was denied.

McBlain again interceded, discussing the matter with Martin, but this time he couldn't get the county solicitor to budge. Both parties had agreed to the observation rules beforehand. As far as Martin was concerned, it was too late to be making changes. The work was in full swing. McBlain next sought out Gerry Lawrence, chairman of the county's election board, looking for a compromise.

"If you won't let them stand there, why don't you take some representatives of both parties back and give them a tour?" McBlain suggested. The whole process was new, he said, and it was reasonable for the poll watchers to want to see the pre-canvassing for themselves. That suggestion was accepted, but it was now after one in the morning, everyone was exhausted, and the count was about to be paused until morning. Lawrence suggested that they wait until then.

To anyone operating with the assumption that the count was proceeding honestly—as did McBlain—it seemed a perfectly reasonable solution. It did not satisfy Stenstrom. If a crime was being committed, you didn't wait around for a convenient time to catch the perpetrators in the act!

"Why not now?" he asked McBlain.

"Because they are going to shut down the count."

"I don't care," said Stenstrom. "Let's go get an injunction because I want to go back there now. I don't care if it's three in the morning, four, or five. Go get the injunction. These ballots are not real. They are hiding them for a reason."

McBlain said it would take four or five hours to get a court injunction anyway, so why not just wait until morning?

Stenstrom wasn't happy about it. He called Hoopes to vent about the hidden "back room," a classic trope in stories of political chicanery, conjuring up visions of cigar-smoking political bosses manipulating the vote behind the scenes. The expression would stick.

GEORGIA

The machine loomed, enormous. Lawrence Sloan, a *Star Trek* enthusiast, thought of it as one of the show's shuttlecrafts. It surrounded him. He piloted it.

The job had given his life a rhythm over the past few weeks. He got up at four in the morning, which was too early for breakfast. Instead he downed three bottles of water in succession, then caught a train across Atlanta to the State Farm Arena. There, like shuttlecraft in their hangar, the machines waited in a cavernous room where the ballots were collected. Taking a seat at his machine, Sloan fed it the intact envelopes; it deftly sliced open both the outer envelope and the inner one. He would then extract the inner one with its secret ballot. He did not remove the ballot—that was somebody else's job.

The election workers were a diverse lot. Sloan was in his mid-thirties and black. His favorite colleagues were a young anarchist woman and an older conservative man who had nothing in common but the election work. It struck him as a peculiar American nexus.

The mood felt electric on Election Day. When Sloan wasn't at his machine, he visited polling places to help out, and he could feel the engine of democracy move into hyperdrive as he watched people turn out to vote. As the hours stretched, local restaurants dropped off snacks and drinks. The older conservative man looked wistfully over toward the food at one point. He was too busy to leave his station. "Are they giving out fish tacos?"

The anarchist came to his rescue. "You're going to get some!" she said.

It made Sloan laugh. He said in mock solidarity, "We're going to destabilize the system! Everybody's getting fish tacos."

This is so weird, he thought. *America is so special and amazing.*

Sloan considered himself "neuro-atypical." His mind skittered across subjects in quirky ways. When he saw pickup trucks pull up to the voting site to drop off pallets of Gatorade and bottled water, chicken sandwiches, and fish tacos, he envisioned the election process as a utopian potluck dinner.

This is what it was meant to be, baby, he thought. *Let's just turn Election Day into Thanksgiving/voting. How about that? We just eat and vote. If we do that, everybody's going to show up.*

Outside the election center, cable news pundits and politicians argued and clashed. Inside, there was just the work. Sloan and his colleagues started their days before sunrise and finished them too exhausted to follow current events. They spent so many hours together that they developed a familial closeness. All kinds of Americans—every age, color, political view—came together for this common purpose.

It really ought to be a holiday.

He had to remind himself to pay attention to the machine, with its sharp blade.

WISCONSIN

In Fond du Lac, a small city that wraps around the lower edge of Lake Winnebago, Rohn Bishop hosted a celebration on election night at Republican Party headquarters.

Inside a big, low, square building just two blocks south of the lakefront, about sixty people watched as Fox News reported the election results. The windowless, fluorescent-lit room was decked with Trump banners, small American flags, and movable wall panels studded with campaign buttons. Bishop had scaled down the usual hotel ballroom postelection gala because of COVID concerns, and he provided free masks, which no one used. He'd also arranged for an open bar, which people did use. Congressman Glenn Grothman, who was up for reelection, had provided free pizza. The mood was festive. All the local Republican candidates were winning, and so was Trump at first. Then when Fox called Arizona for Biden, a chorus of boos went up, and Bishop could see trouble ahead; he knew the Arizona result suggested danger for the president everywhere. Mail ballots were going to swing heavily to Biden—Trump had helped ensure it.

Bishop wasn't happy about it. Few had invested more in Trump's reelection or cared more. The campaign season had so traumatized him that he'd checked into the hospital in September with what was diagnosed as an anxiety attack. Now, despite his misgivings about the president's chances, he could not help but feel relieved. The polls had closed, and at least for a while, his political work was done.

Bishop was GOP chairman in Fond du Lac County, flat farm country that unrolls green and lake pocked to the west and south of Green Bay. He was leery of Trump's chances statewide and nationally, but he had done his job. Trump was going to carry his patch of Wisconsin handily—by about 26 percent, with about 62 percent of the vote. Bishop felt impatient for the Associated Press to declare Grothman's victory so Bishop could get all of his winning candidates on stage at once; but for whatever reason, the news service had not, and Grothman was superstitious about taking a premature bow. AP or no AP, Bishop downed a celebratory beer.

Upbeat, popular, and garrulous, Bishop had a high-pitched nasal voice that was surprising from a man of his bulk. He was broad shouldered, big bellied, with a wide, florid face, big dark-rimmed glasses, a cleanly shaved dome, and a thick red-brown beard. He managed the detailing department of a GM dealership in his day job, but everybody in Fond du Lac knew his passion was politics. He was the face of the Republican Party here.

In at least one respect, Bishop may have been the most authentic Republican in America. Because it was in Fond du Lac County, according to local lore, that the party got its start. In 1854, a group of antislavery former Whigs and members of other parties had met in Ripon, inside a little white schoolhouse. They had formed a new political organization, adopting the name Republican. Other meetings in other states made similar claims, but the Ripon schoolhouse had been preserved as a historical shrine, and the county laid claim to being the GOP's taproot.

Bishop lived in nearby Waupun, a biggish town of clapboard houses on neatly manicured lots, where no one had ever questioned his party bona fides. His whole life was wrapped up in his Republican identity. One of his grandfathers volunteered for Robert Taft at the party's convention in 1952 because Dwight Eisenhower "wasn't conservative enough." His other grandfather worked for the party in nearby DuPage County,

Illinois. He proudly notes that the river that runs near his corner lot is the south branch of the Rock River, which, downriver in Illinois, Ronald Reagan once patrolled as a lifeguard. He named his two daughters after eighties conservative icons—Reagan and Maggie, for Britain's Maggie Thatcher. Beneath the stars and stripes that fly over his driveway is a red 2006 Pontiac with the license plate GOP 4ME. His family calls his favorite pastime, simply, "Republican-ing," which includes riding on the party float in as many as nine annual county parades while waving, as his daughters put it, "like a princess."

Bishop also holds baked-in Republican views. He watches Fox News and sees Democratic priorities as creeping socialism. But he has the personality to transcend differences of opinion, even in the darkest dens of Democratic orthodoxy. Invited in 2019 by a Columbia University professor to a series of interview sessions in New York via Skype, he likely failed to alter a single opinion on the liberal campus about abortion or gun rights, but according to the professor, "they loved him."

For Trump, Bishop's house had been campaign central. On a patch of lawn between his house and his neighbor's garage, he'd set out Trump signs a hundred at a time, inviting supporters to drive up and take as many as they liked. He registered new voters and trained campaign workers at the picnic table in his backyard, where volunteers downloaded the Trump campaign's canvassing app and used it to find fellow Republicans. As they learned how to address potential voters, Bishop served coffee and juice.

Despite the president's popularity in Waupun, Bishop had seen signs that it was slipping in Wisconsin overall. The president's victory over Clinton in the state had been narrow, less than 1 percent. More and more, Wisconsin's people were concentrated in Green Bay, Milwaukee, and the state capital of Madison. When Bishop had driven an hour southwest to do door-to-door work in the reliably Republican suburb of Mequon, just north of Milwaukee, he'd seen "Biden" and "Black Lives Matter" signs on front lawns, which shocked him. This was not his grandfather's Wisconsin anymore.

And as far as Bishop was concerned, Trump had hurt himself badly by discouraging people from voting by mail. When the president had suddenly inveighed against the practice, it came as a surprise to the state's Republican leaders. Not long before, they had mailed pamphlets to every GOP voter in the state encouraging it, with a picture of Donald Trump on the front giving two thumbs up. Now he was telling Fox News, "I think mail-in voting is going to rig the election, I really do," later tweeting that it would produce "the most CORRUPT ELECTION in our Nation's History!"

Bishop countered by urging that the president's comments be ignored.

"It's such a bad idea to scare our own voters away from a legit way to cast their ballot," he tweeted.

That discordant note from the president's own party in America's heartland drew some national press attention, which Bishop found both startling and troubling. A hail of criticism followed. Here he was, the nation's most authentic Republican, a man who considered himself more pro-Trump than Trump, accused of being a "Never Trumper"—all for trying to help get the guy reelected!

"As local party chairman, your job is to help get our candidates elected," one critic wrote. "I am not saying that you are wrong about some of Trump's tweets, but Joe Biden is a greater threat to our future. Focus."

Which, as far as Bishop was concerned, entirely missed the point. If the idea was to win, it was Trump who had lost focus.

"So, basically you're saying I'm right but shouldn't say it out loud?" Bishop responded. "I'm going to vote a Republican ticket and have already put up nearly 100 Trump signs in [the] Waupun area, but I want it noted when I think a presidents (sic) behavior is wrong, or when I disagree with him."

A local Wisconsin news program invited Bishop on to explain himself.

"I think the mail-in absentee voting can actually help Republicans in a state like Wisconsin," he said. "We have early voting [by mail] for two weeks. So why give big metropolitan areas where the Democrats are more concentrated fourteen days to vote while only giving the Republicans one day to vote? . . . I think urging Republican voters who live in those more rural areas to get their ballot in the mail . . . is a good way for us to reach voters. And any vote we can bring in, in what I think's gonna be a high-turnout election's a good thing for us."

He defended the voting system in Wisconsin, which he had witnessed up close for years. As a young man, he'd tended to believe stories of widespread voter fraud, but his familiarity with the process had taught him that it would actually be very hard to fix an election. Instances of fraud were rare, almost always insignificant, and committed by both sides. Whipping up fears among conservatives would just discourage them from voting.

In the primary that spring, "a lot of people did [vote by mail] for the first time ever. And they found it convenient and easy to do. . . . My nightmare scenario is, there's another uptick in this virus, like a second wave come election season, and you have maybe, like a lot of our Republican-base voters are older, and what I would hate to see is for those voters to be scared to go to the polls to vote, but they're also scared to cast an absentee ballot via the mail because of the president's tweets. And then they don't vote at all! Because, then not only is President Trump not getting that vote, neither is my congressman, my state senator, and my state assemblyman."

Like the audiences at Columbia University, his listeners were unpersuaded. More criticism followed from his own people. Some passed word that the White House was not happy with him. Bishop was used to being criticized. Democrats were after him all the time. If they weren't insulting him, he figured he was doing something wrong. But here he was, trying to help Trump, lending his considerable local expertise, and getting vilified for it!

And there was no doubt that he was right. He didn't have to wait for the election results in Wisconsin to prove it, as they would. Bishop knew what he was talking about. People who knew and respected him, after hearing him out, would say, *Okay, I get where you are coming from; that makes sense.* But he couldn't have that kind of talk with all his new critics. And increasingly, he found, even those who would hear him out simply responded, *But Trump says....*

He had contradicted the Oracle. It didn't matter that he made sense. Heresy was heresy.

Other state Republicans found themselves in the same boat. Dean Knudson, a longtime Republican leader and former mayor of Hudson, a small city at the westernmost edge of the state, across the Saint Croix River from the twin Minnesota cities of Minneapolis and Saint Paul, had angered Trump supporters a week before Election Day by giving them good advice. He urged them to mail in their ballots promptly. Knudson was one of the state's most respected election experts.

Appearing on a local TV program, *Western Wisconsin Journal,* he was asked by the host to comment about the recent "controversy" stirred by Trump's assault on mail voting. Knudson didn't argue. He simply urged Wisconsin voters who planned to vote by mail to send their ballots early so that in the event they made a mistake, clerks would have time to contact them for a correction. He said there was no substantial difference in voting by mail or in person.

After that, he became, like Bishop, a target for angry Trumpists. Knudson laid low, but Bishop fought back.

After a shock jock in Green Bay aired a segment condemning him, Bishop had angry people phoning him from all over northeast Wisconsin. He ignored most, but every once in a while, he picked up. An irate Green Bay caller—Bishop had mistaken the number for his Trump poster supplier's—shouted at him about mail ballots until he'd run out of breath. Bishop interjected, "Well, hold on. You're listening to this radio show up in Green Bay, aren't you?"

The caller admitted it.

"Well, the guy [Joe Giganti] doesn't really know what he's talking about," said Bishop. He defended his position on the importance of mail ballots, explained all he had been doing to help Trump, and by the time the call ended, the man had apologized.

But that was rare. It was hard not to respond to some of the things people posted in his Twitter feed. It got to him. In early September, he noticed his heart racing strangely. It worried him. He'd had an ear issue earlier in the summer, and when he went back for a checkup, the doctor noted that his blood pressure had shot up.

"Hey, it's the middle of an election year," Bishop said and laughed it off. But his mom told him that high blood pressure ran in the family. He started worrying about it.

Not that he didn't already have enough worries: the election stress, the criticism, planning for his wife's birthday and their anniversary in the same week. . . . The final straw was a call from the state GOP chairman, who complained that internal polling showed weak numbers for Trump in Fond du Lac County. This made no sense to Bishop. His county was full of farmers, people who wouldn't vote for a Democrat if the GOP put up a dead man. But now the party questioned his performance as county chairman.

That's when the heart started to flutter. Normally, he didn't notice his heart beating in his chest, but now it went so fast that he could hardly focus on anything else. It would stop and then start up again. The more he worried about it, the more it happened. Finally, sitting behind his desk at the dealership, there came an attack so strong that he drove to the emergency room on his lunch hour. Doctors hooked him up to an IV, gave him a calming drug, and ran some tests. Only when the results came back normal could he breathe easily again. He went home with anxiety medication, took a few days off, and resolved not to let things get to him so much.

So the clean sweep of local candidates on election night felt like vindication. Bishop finally coaxed Grothman on stage with his other local winners without the AP's blessing, and there were happy speeches.

But Trump's numbers continued to fall, just as he had feared. And he was not the only Wisconsinite to see what loomed. Joe Handrick had been the state GOP's go-to elections guru for thirty years, ever since he had started in the legislature in 1994 as a representative of Minocqua in the north woods in the woodsy ceiling of the state south of Lake Superior.

Handrick had made an art of state elections. In recent years, he had begun crowdsourcing data, using Twitter and Facebook, asking his followers to post exactly where and when they had posted their ballot, and what number voter they were at that polling place. This gave him a detailed sense of turnout across the state throughout the day. By mid-morning on Election Day, he could tell that turnout was heavy, much higher than in 2016, which spelled trouble for the president. He could see where most of the votes were coming from, the cities, and knowing that late-reporting mail ballots would strongly favor Biden, he confidently predicted Trump's loss on Twitter. There was immediate dismay—the tweet equivalent of a statewide groan—and pushback. Many of Handrick's followers refused to believe it. And as the numbers began to prove Handrick's prediction, disbelief turned to anger and accusation. Handrick saw perfectly well how it had happened, but shocked Trump supporters labeled Biden's lead, without reason, as fraudulent.

Handrick would answer, "Well, let me explain again." The results were entirely predictable. They did not reflect an illegal pattern or even an odd one. But expert or no expert, people didn't want to hear it. Finally, he gave up. He heard again and again how one hundred thousand votes had mysteriously "showed up in the middle of the night in Milwaukee," which he knew to be completely untrue.

ARIZONA

Marko Trickovic, a self-professed patriot and ardent Trumpist, felt sure he'd caught something big. On Election Day, he learned that poll workers in Maricopa County were handing out Sharpies, felt-tipped markers, to voters and urging them not to use ballpoint pens to mark their ballots. Why would they do that? Armed with energetic suspicion, this riddle birthed the notion that voting machines could not detect ink from Sharpies; so poll workers, see, aiding Biden, were pushing them on unsuspecting Trump voters—it isn't clear how they would know who they were—so that their votes would not be counted.

Trickovic took this conjecture seriously enough to begin handing out ballpoint pens to waiting voters at an East Valley polling place, warning them not to use Sharpies. After sheriffs stopped him, he shot a short video of himself interviewing a masked young woman in a floral top and green sweater as she emerged from a polling place. This may or may not have been scripted.

"Explain one more time," he asked the woman.

"There were two people in front of me that used a Sharpie that was given to them by the poll workers," she said. "It did not read their ballot, and they fed it in there twice. I used a pen . . . and it read my ballot."

"So what they're doing is, they're telling people to use the Sharpies; that way, those votes aren't counted?"

"Yes," the woman said.

"That's exactly what's happening."

"Yes."

"So there was other people that were in there voting with their pens, and they literally went around and they were yanking pens out of their hands?"

"Yes. They tried to do that to me, and I took their Sharpie and I hid it."

"So the ones with the Sharpies are not being read at all?"

"No."

"None of those ballots are being read."

"Of course not."

"So they're doing it because they are trying to skew all of the votes in there . . . that's exactly what's going on . . . We know that, and we've been telling them, you need to use a ballpoint pen, not the Sharpie. . . . So people are coming here to vote for Donald Trump, and those votes are all getting invalidated."

There was no indication that Trickovic checked this out. He might have asked someone who knew something about the machines. Instead, he posted his accusatory video, and it went viral. Outrage spread. A lawsuit was promptly filed claiming that Sharpies had fouled the election.

Arizona attorney general Mark Brnovich announced an immediate inves-tigation. This lasted for a day. Brnovich checked and found that Dominion machines counted Sharpie-marked ballots perfectly. The lawsuit was withdrawn by the plaintiffs.

But Trickovic's story lived on. Fantasy and fact share footing online, and where all information is weightless, you can choose to believe what you wish. Like Leah Hoopes in Pennsylvania and Lynie Stone in Arizona, Trickovic had approached Election Day convinced, egged on by Trump himself, that Democrats were going to pull a fast one. And here he'd found something that fit the narrative. Where Hoopes and Stenstrom saw a conspiracy to exclude poll watchers and where Stone had spotted the hand of Satan in a spreadsheet, Trickovic had discovered . . . Sharpies!

The video briefly made him a star. TV and radio shows sought him. His video racked up views. Word of "Sharpie-gate" spread everywhere, and of course, many believed.

Trickovic was a fit young man with a scruffy, sculpted beard who posted pictures of himself on Facebook wearing wraparound shades, "patriot" T-shirts, and dressed in battle kit like special-ops soldiers in movies, with a scoped automatic weapon strapped to his chest. He stared out resolutely, camera ready, if not actually combat ready.

On election night, he gathered with hundreds of like-minded Trump-ists outside the Maricopa County Recorder's Office.

"Count the vote!" they chanted.

"Where are the votes?"

"Count those damn ballots!"

"Get this over with!"

"Why aren't you counting?"

Inside, of course, they were counting like mad. There was a vast pile of mail ballots to process, which in Arizona required a two-tier identification procedure. Citizen boards—forty boards of 120 people—opened every envelope at tables with a Republican observer at one end and a Demo-cratic observer at the other end. If anyone in the parking lot had knocked on the door and politely asked, Rey Valenzuela, the county's election director for the past three decades, would have been happy to explain that he had not been allowed to start counting until the polls closed.

But the crowd outside appeared to be having fun. It didn't seem much interested in having the thing explained.

Sharpie-gate was just the latest headache for Clint Hickman, then the chairman of the Maricopa County Board of Supervisors and a Republican and Trump supporter. He had been on the board for seven years when it became his turn to serve as chairman in 2020, for the second time (the position rotated annually). This turn in the top chair came just in time for a doozy of a year. There was the pandemic and a national election. He had done his level best to prepare, but as a famous Republican once said, what we should most fear is not the unknown but the "unknown unknowns," the things that bite us completely out of the blue.

Hickman had actually thought about Sharpies. He had concerns about them early on but not for the reason Trickovic did. Ink from Sharpies tended to soak through the two-sided paper ballot, registering inadvertent choices on the flip side and confusing the count. That's why, for years, the county had urged voters not to use them. But this year, Maricopa had leased state-of-the-art Dominion voting machines, which used different ballots. Sharpie marks still soaked through, but the layout of the ballot's flip side had been designed to prevent the earlier problem. So now Sharpies worked fine. The board produced a one-minute video to explain why, but apparently few watched it. Fuzzy misgivings about felt tips remained, which probably fed Sharpie-gate. In any event, neither Hickman nor anyone else had anticipated Trickovic's little piece of agitprop.

The video's claim wasn't just untrue. Dominion voting machines actually performed *better* with Sharpie-marked ballots than with those marked in ballpoint. Ink from the pens dried more slowly and tended to gum up the works. This was discovered early on Election Day, so the county had rushed Sharpies to polling places and urged poll workers to encourage their use.

By the end of election night, this was only one of many issues bedeviling Hickman. Maricopa County is, for election purposes, Arizona. It encompasses Phoenix, the state's capital and largest city, and enough of the surrounding desert that its land area is larger than four of America's states. With a population nearing 4.5 million, it is home to more than 60 percent of the state's population. It takes no special political insight to say that as goes Maricopa, so goes Arizona.

Hickman was homegrown, the very picture of white bread middle-American conservatism, with—in an earlier era—surefire leading man good looks. Tall, with blue eyes, sandy hair, and broad shoulders, at fifty-five he still had an appealing, youthful, farm-fed glow. Born into one of the county's biggest businesses, Hickman's Family Farms, an egg producer, his wholesome appearance and bonhomie had made him the clan's corporate spokesman. Well before he ran for office, his face and boyish charm were familiar not just as the voice of Hickman Farms but also for the egg industry. He stood in a white coat and white sanitary cap before conveyor belts moving thousands of eggs in advertising spots and in promotional videos and had even made appearances on broadcast TV—segments on the reality show *Dirty Jobs* and on *Sesame Street*. His fame had helped him win election to the county board of supervisors in 2013, a political position in Arizona that rivaled any office in Phoenix or the state. Hickman had grown up admiring those who served on the county board. He had been slightly awestruck as a kid when one of them coached his Little League team—"almost like a governor coaching my team."

COVID was still beneath the horizon when he'd started his second turn as chairman, but soon it plunged him into the minutiae of public health policy. The infection rate and death counts alone posed a defining challenge, but with primary and general election dates looming, Hickman's board work became all consuming. Given Arizona's pivotal role in national politics and Maricopa County's pivotal role in Arizona, he knew the whole world would be watching. Weighing the need for social distancing and hygienic precautions, the board decided to simplify matters by consolidated voting centers instead of opening the usual hundreds of precinct polling places. To handle the higher volume at the concentrated centers, the county leased Dominion voting machines, which operated twice as fast as its old ones—slow reporting of results had riled voters in previous years—and like everywhere else, they were going to be getting a lot more mail ballots this year. With Trump raising suspicions about mail voting, Hickman made sure that the county advertised the results when the newly leased machines passed mandated "logic and accuracy" tests.

All this they had foreseen. Distrust. Health protocols. Machines for the mountain of mail ballots. But then, there was the unknown unknown: Marko Trickovic.

2

The Count

Fox News coanchor Bill Hemmer stood before the big electronic board in the final minutes of election night. Polls had closed all over the country, and the count was under way. States that already had been declared for Biden were colored blue, those for Trump red, and those undecided white. As the network's decision desk called them, the white states changed color one by one.

Hemmer explained how strong Trump's numbers looked in Wisconsin, which was still white, tapping it to call up a closer look at the state. The map broke the state down to the state's seventy-two counties. He zeroed in on Kenosha County in the state's southeasternmost corner, birthplace of Orson Welles.

"[Trump] is going to easily win this county," Hemmer said. "It's not a ton of votes, but it's a point to be made about the message that he has carried to the upper Midwest."

This news held with the general trend and found a welcoming audience at the White House, where Trump watched Fox News upstairs in the residence. Downstairs in the Map Room, his campaign manager, Bill Stepien, watched, too, with campaign staffers and assorted supporters. They had four TVs going.

Hemmer next tapped the state of Arizona, still white on the country map, to pull up a closer look at the state. It showed a developing patchwork of counties colored red and blue, according to the current margin in each. The legend at the top of the screen showed Biden with 53.6 percent of the Arizona vote overall, Trump with 45.1 percent.

"If you look at the numbers right now and drill down . . . [Trump's] got some ground to make up. . . . If Joe Biden were able to hold onto this, and he's doing pretty well in Maricopa County so far, a lead by ten points . . . right now Joe Biden has the lead."

He tapped the screen to switch to the countrywide view, and when he did, the state of Arizona suddenly showed blue. At first, Hemmer didn't notice. When he did, he was startled.

"What is this happening here?" he asked, pointing. "Why is Arizona blue? Did we just call it? Did we make a call in Arizona? Let's see," he said, tapping to call up the state map again. The legend at the top showed a check next to Biden's name.

"There's a check mark," he said. "Did our decision desk make it? Arizona. Eleven electoral votes."

"Yes," said Martha MacCallum, across the room at the anchor desk. "We can con . . . I believe we have a yes."

"If you lose Arizona, where do you win now?" asked Hemmer.

"Time out," said coanchor Bret Baier. "This is a big development. The Fox News decision desk is calling Arizona for Joe Biden. That is a big get for the Biden campaign."

There was stunned silence in the White House war room. People started crowding in to see for themselves. Stepien's phone rang. The voice of the president was loud in his ear.

Trump screamed, "What the fuck is Fox doing? Call Rupert! Call James and Lachlan!"

When the call was placed, he demanded, "Reverse this!" and when the network wouldn't comply, his immediate reaction was, "This is a major fraud."

The result was surprising and very significant—Arizona was a swing state. It was also, at least in modern times, unprecedented. Every Republican candidate for president (except for Bob Dole in 1996) had carried the state since 1952. There were plenty of legitimate reasons for the flip, but only "fraud" registered with Trump and his followers. He had primed them for it.

PENNSYLVANIA

Eager for their promised tour of The Wharf's "back room" on Wednesday morning, Delco's Leah Hoopes and Greg Stenstrom showed up at eight-thirty. Early that morning, Trump had demanded that the counting stop, but it proceeded everywhere.

At The Wharf, no one in charge seemed to be aware of the deal GOP attorney John McBlain had struck the night before, and he had not yet arrived. So Hoopes and Stenstrom remained unhappily confined to the prescribed observation pen with the other election watchers.

Stenstrom began to raise hell. The night before, he had reluctantly agreed to put off his demand to inspect that "back room," with a promise that he'd get a look as soon as the count resumed. Here they were counting again, and he was still barred from seeing it. He got into it again with solicitor Martin, neither man again willing to back down. Quite apart from the mysterious "back room," they still stood twenty feet or more from the nearest action. The BlueCrest machine whipped through envelopes so fast, they blurred. Hoopes wanted to be close enough to actually inspect individual ballots and envelopes, even though such a process might take months. Their suspicion that a crime was in progress was rooted, ultimately, in unhappiness over the county's recent political flip. In winning a majority on the county council, Democrats had gained a two-to-one advantage over Republicans on the bipartisan board of elections. For Hoopes, this meant the election process itself was tainted enough to entitle her or any other disaffected citizen to, in effect, inject themselves directly into the counting, to join in the screening of every ballot.

This inability to inspect mail ballots closely was an issue throughout the country, and unlike the many completely unfounded concerns that would be raised, there was some justification for it. Allowing unrestricted mail voting had introduced a fundamental change. Prior to the pandemic, the number of mail ballots was always small, no more than a few dozen in most precincts. These were from residents living out of state, military personnel stationed elsewhere, or from those too infirm to visit a polling place. Opening and counting them had been a minor task on election night. They were shipped to local precincts, where they were read aloud before observers from both parties who could object if a ballot looked suspect. Few did. By allowing mail voting across the board, in deference to the COVID threat, the sheer volume of these ballots made the old method of observation obsolete. Opening and scanning them had to be automated—hence, the BlueCrest machines. The kind of close inspection Hoopes wanted was no longer practical in Delco and other large automated counting centers.

Automating the count did not sacrifice verification, however. The machines scanned every envelope for identifying information and recorded its image, and saved them all. Every ballot was likewise recorded and saved. The machine count was verifiable in both computer memory and with physical ballots and envelopes. Doing so would be a laborious undertaking, but if statistical reviews raised suspicions, say, about a sudden sharp increase in Biden or Trump votes in an unlikely place, or if the ballot count failed to match the envelope count, then there were multiple ways to check. In some jurisdictions, such audits were mandatory, and in many after the initial 2020 count, officials undertook them without any statistical indication of error or fraud.

To closely observe the count as Hoopes wanted would have necessitated a return to hand counting mail ballots. With so many, the process might well drag on until well after Inauguration Day, especially with both parties haggling over every ink mark. And why stop with just Democratic and Republican observers? Hoopes and her Watchdogs had not been satisfied with the officially designated GOP observers at The Wharf. She wanted her Trump Watchdogs to see for themselves. If they were let in, as they had been, why not disaffected Democrats? Why not any other group with its own ax to grind? With a hand count and with the inclusion of every group that demanded access, one could imagine an ultimate participatory vote count that stretched until the next Election Day.

The root of this absurdity was distrust. Democracy depends on a modicum of trust. After each election, the winning party is empowered to govern until the next vote, which it is empowered to manage. This requires an acceptance by all contenders that they are fellow citizens, no matter how much at odds, invested in something bigger than the issues and personalities of the moment. There were built-in safeguards to prevent the party in power from subverting the next contest. In Delco, an appointed member of the minority party sat on the three-person election board to sound the alarm or object if the others weren't playing fair, or to push contested issues into court. Judges settled disputes. To reject this time-honored process was, at heart, a rejection of democracy itself. Until there appears on earth a society in perfect harmony, democracy must settle for majority rule, which requires . . . this modicum of trust.

Trump's persistent cries of fraud hammered away at that trust. It's not clear that he understood exactly what he was doing. He had always been propelled by an unshakable belief that he was right. It was how he approached everything—marriage, business, politics. He did not burden himself with details. He hired people for that kind of thing. Sometimes he even listened to them, but ultimately, he trusted his own gut. If they disagreed with him, he fired them. He did not question himself and bulled through those who did. The approach had served him well through sex scandals, bankruptcies, and political setbacks. His surprise election to the nation's highest office was the ultimate affirmation. As "Hail to the Chief" played and soldiers snapped to attention, there is little wonder his faith in his own judgment grew larger still. He believed a majority of Americans stood behind him because his gut told him so. His enthusiastic rallies affirmed it. He believed he simply *could not lose* in a fair election. This was not some hidden conviction. He said so clearly and repeatedly. So when the numbers began to mount against him late on Election Day, the answer came plain enough. His victory, the one he had seen on the TV screen with his very own eyes, the will of the people, the very cornerstone of democracy, was being stolen.

Hoopes saw it that way, too. Like Trump, she had gone into the contest convinced that it was rigged. Her Watchdogs were not just invested in observing the process. The president had summoned them to action. They came to catch Delco's "lying hacks" in the act.

But right now, she was stymied. Hoopes left the counting center to record a video sitting in her car outside The Wharf. It was a sunny morning. She had her hair pulled back and wore big mirror sunglasses and vented her exasperation.

"I don't even know where to begin right now," she said, looking sad and bewildered. She turned her camera to show The Wharf's impressive pillared facade and then talked about the agreement to view the "back room" that had not been honored.

"There are a ton of questions. There is no observation going on in this back room, and so they are bringing in ballots and nobody has . . . even bipartisan observation, and there's also no security cameras in the back room! . . . Okay, Delaware County people, you are seeing the mechanical part of how they sort the ballots, you're not actually seeing what's going on in the back room. What I'm here to say is, there's a problem with that. Big time. I am not leaving here until we get answers."

Attorney John McBlain finally showed at about eleven, and at that point, Stenstrom and Hoopes and the other observers were led out onto the main floor of the counting area and given about a half-hour tour by the county's clerk of elections, Laureen Hagan. Stenstrom peppered Hagan with questions until an assistant county solicitor, Manly Parks, put an end to it. He said the elections clerk had better things to do. Neither Stenstrom nor Hoopes was satisfied. They had still not seen the "back room." Stenstrom protested again. Martin again stood firm. Again, it grew heated.

"This is crazy," Stenstrom finally told McBlain. "I need you to go down [to the county courthouse in Media] and get an injunction right now, okay? Get us into that room. That's where the action is. That's where any fraud that could potentially happen is happening. I need to get into that back room."

McBlain took it up with Parks, who said, "Nothing is going on in that back room."

The attorney pushed back.

"I don't know what it is, but somebody is doing something, and we should be able to take a look and see."

"We are not doing that," said Parks.

So McBlain next consulted with his client, not Hoopes and Stenstrom, but the county Republican Party. To that point, the organization had backed these two maverick observers. With their blessing, McBlain filed a petition for a court order.

It was one of a flurry of lawsuits being filed by Trump's lawyers all over the country. In Michigan, Georgia, and Pennsylvania, his lawyers demanded that the tally stop until his observers were given more access to the counting. They wanted to be close enough to inspect ballots. None of these efforts would succeed—none had any firm legal basis—but all did spread the notion among Trumpists that the vote count was being hidden from the public's gaze. They fed doubt.

Hoopes again retreated from The Wharf to sound the alarm with a video on her Facebook page. She urged her friends to spread the word. She said she was contacting members of the local news media.

"I can honestly say that I have never been more disgusted in my life with the lack of transparency," she said, noting that both Republican and Democratic observers were being denied access to the "back room."

Throughout that afternoon, Stenstrom and Hoopes stayed with the other observers watching the machines hum on and paper being carted off in different directions. As the Trump lead steadily eroded, their anger and frustration mounted. This was evident to the election workers toiling around them, who felt themselves eyed with suspicion. It was not a comfortable feeling. Immediately behind the area where Hoopes, Stenstrom, and the other observers were confined were the offices of IT managers. At one point Wednesday, one of them noticed a box filled with about two hundred unopened mail ballots that had been left, apparently by accident, under a table in his office. He wanted to move it across the counting floor to place it with the other unopened ones, but he was afraid to draw attention to himself.

"These people are going to go nuts if they see me carrying a box of ballots!" he complained to an election supervisor.

"Let me go over there," the official said, "and I'll start talking to Leah and I'll get her agitated."

He walked up to Hoopes and, raising a clipboard, said that they were rechecking to see if she and Stenstrom belonged. This provoked the expected response, and in the ensuing dustup, the IT manager scurried across the room with the box unnoticed.

It was not until nine thirty that evening that McBlain secured a court order from Judge John Capuzzi, a jovial, bald, bull-necked jurist with a known conservative bent. The judge had no sympathy for county efforts to enforce pandemic safeguards. At the hearing, he said he didn't want to even hear the word "COVID." When the county offered to move all of the pre-canvassing activity from the back room to the front, where it could be better seen, McBlain accepted. He then pressed for access to the locked "back room," which was in fact a storage closet that held unopened ballots awaiting processing. They were locked because the law required them to be secured. Capuzzi ordered that election observers be allowed to enter the closet and inspect it for five minutes every two hours. That way, they could periodically eyeball the number of ballots remaining to be counted. They were forbidden to touch the ballots.

McBlain felt pleased. As far as he was concerned, the solution resolved the complaint. Stenstrom considered it obscene, a complete cave-in. He now had his doubts about McBlain. Whose side was he really on?

In Erie, at the opposite end of the state, postmaster Rob Weisenbach knew the stakes. If you could shrink Pennsylvania to its political essence, it would look like Erie County, on the southern shore of the lake that shares its name. It's a snow globe version of the whole, with red rural areas anchored by a blue city, separated by purple suburbs. As Pennsylvania is to the nation, so Erie County is to the state: a swing county in a swing state.

So the stakes were high. Weisenbach could see that in the most literal sense; it seemed every yard before every house was staked with political signs. As postmaster, he also knew that in the midst of a historic pandemic, many voters would mail in their ballots and that these would likely lean toward Biden. But parsing political odds wasn't his job. His job was to deliver the mail, and ballots were among the most precious of all American correspondence.

He streamlined the process, instructing his carriers to collect ballots on a special table in the post office and then take them in batches directly to the Erie County Board of Elections. He arranged for his staff to meet with mail carriers from surrounding facilities so they could more efficiently gather and deliver ballots. The effort was herculean and had prompted public praise from the chairman of the elections board.

Its press release said, "Rob stayed in contact with the Election Board Office coordinating mail pickup and extra trips with overnight ballots; with 49,218 mail-in ballots this year—the most in any election—postal workers were under enormous pressure. They should be proud."

A job well done, Weisenbach thought, and so the day after Election Day he stayed home and rested. He took a phone call from a reporter, something he rarely did, but maybe it was a follow-up on the kind words from the elections board.

Instead the reporter said, "There's a whistleblower inside your office that says that you have been ordering employees to backdate ballots to November 3, from November 4th and 5th."

This shocked Weisenbach. Ballots postmarked after Election Day were not to be counted. So the implication was that Weisenbach's post office conspired to sneak likely Biden votes into the count.

"That's untrue. And I don't talk to reporters like you."

"Okay, but we've had multiple sources say that this is happening."

Weisenbach hung up. *What in the world?*

Later that day, an online video streaked into his world like a digital comet. The "multiple sources" seemed to be one: Over dramatic music, an interviewer questioned a man who wore a vest bearing an unmistakable logo: the blue eagle of the US Postal Service.

"I work at the post office in Erie, PA," the man said.

The video's maker had blurred the man's face and distorted his voice, which had the paradoxical effect of erasing his identity while also giving him credibility with a public accustomed to investigative journalistic techniques. This man was clearly in danger. Surely, he was about to reveal something dark and hidden.

"This morning, I was casing my route, and I saw the postmaster pull one of our supervisors to the side," the man said. Carriers "case" mail by organizing it at a station before making their rounds. "And as he was pulling the supervisor, it was really close to where my new case was. So I was able to hear, to listen in. And I heard him say to the supervisor that they messed up yesterday. So I was like, oh, what did they mess up on?"

The interviewer wore a grave expression, the look of a man about to extract a thorn from America's paw. His name was James O'Keefe and he ran Project Veritas, a group of self-styled "guerrilla journalists." He had often been accused of conducting misleading investigations, making wildly false accusations, and deceptive editing. In 2013, for instance, a court ordered O'Keefe to pay $100,000 to a former employee of the community reform group ACORN, after Project Veritas used hidden cameras to falsely claim the employee was willing to help O'Keefe smuggle underage girls into the country for prostitution. In 2017, Project Veritas tried and failed to mislead the *Washington Post* into publishing a false story about Judge Roy Moore, a Trump supporter; the paper instead discovered that the woman posing as a sexual victim had recently opened a GoFundMe page that read, "I've accepted a job to work in the conservative media movement to combat the lies and deceipt [sic] of the liberal MSM." Scholars have described Project Veritas as a "flak mill" and "disinformation outfit." And O'Keefe was funded, in part, by the Trump Foundation.

His video was compelling.

The disguised mail carrier alleged his postmaster had schemed to backdate late ballots so they could be counted. Only ballots postmarked by 8:00 p.m. on November 3 could be. The postmaster had collared an underling to chastise him for bungling one of the ballots.

Disguised man: "He told the supervisor that they had postmarked one of the ballots the 4th instead of the 3rd. Because they were supposed to put them for the 3rd."

"Why was he upset?"

"Because, honest to God, he's actually a Trump hater."

Then the man reiterated his accusation: "All these ballots that are coming in today, tomorrow, yesterday, are all supposed to be postmarked the 3rd."

"Do you believe that order still stands?"

"Yes, I—no doubt, considering that they still want us to pick up ballots tomorrow."

Many questions might have been asked at this moment. What did the man overhear, verbatim? Are there other possible interpretations? What is the normal postmarking process, and who actually makes the mark? And so forth.

Instead O'Keefe put up a photo of Rob Weisenbach's face on-screen, along with his name.

"Rob, the postmaster?" O'Keefe asked.

"Yes."

The video cut to O'Keefe alone, holding a phone. His brow furrowed. On camera, he called Weisenbach and the postmaster answered.

"There's a whistleblower inside your office that says that you have been ordering employees to backdate ballots to November 3, on November 4th and 5th," O'Keefe said.

Weisenbach's voice came over the speakerphone.

"That's untrue. And I don't talk to reporters like you."

"Okay, but we've had multiple sources say that this is happening."

The line went dead, and O'Keefe looked into the camera. "He hung up the phone on me."

Shortly afterward Weisenbach's social media flooded with harassment and threats. And interview requests, not just from the Erie paper, but from Fox News, CNN, the Associated Press, and others.

The next day two special agents from the USPS Office of the Inspector General came to interview him. He was, it turned out, not a Joe Biden supporter. In fact, he was a big fan of Donald Trump. He had voted for him. He had a big Trump banner at home and a Trump-logo mask. He had simply set that aside and done his best to make sure every vote arrived on time.

The investigators found no initial evidence of a fraud conspiracy, but they did find a man under siege. Even as they interviewed the postmaster, O'Keefe's video raced around the world, stirring the anger of millions of Trump supporters who now had a name and a face to hate. After the special agents interviewed him, a postal inspector followed him home so he could collect his family for their safety.

At home, Weisenbach pulled his red Jeep into the driveway. Everything appeared peaceful at his cream-colored, two-story home. His wife and dog waited inside. As he stepped from his car, though, a man appeared behind him, screaming. The postmaster kept fit—his close-cropped hair gave him the bearing of a military officer—but this stranger stood about six feet tall, in his late thirties or so, wearing a heavy winter coat. He'd been hiding somewhere, watching and waiting. Now he approached, holding up a phone in one hand, as though making a video. "I need to talk to you," he said as he closed in, and with the other hand he reached into his coat pocket.

Weisenbach dived into the back seat of another family vehicle, locking the door behind him. He dialed his boss. "I got this crazy man in my driveway!" he said. "Help me!"

Outside the vehicle, the man ranted for him to unlock the doors. "Get out here! This is *wrong!*"

Weisenbach's wife watched through a window of their house, terrified.

The postal inspector pulled up now, and through the window of his car he shouted for the man to leave. The man moved from the driveway to the street immediately behind Weisenbach's vehicle. He continued to shout at the postmaster to get out of the car. A neighbor, a Pennsylvania state trooper, heard the commotion and came over to tell the unknown man to leave. The man ignored him.

Local police arrived and blocked the street with two patrol cars. Then they stepped from their cars with weapons drawn. One tapped on Weisenbach's car window with his gun, shouting, "Get out!" Still holding his weapon, he pulled Weisenbach from his vehicle and laid him on the ground at gunpoint.

Police told the interloper to leave, and he did. Then Weisenbach did as well; he packed some clothes and drove with his family to a hotel hours from Erie. Word of his alleged fraud, though, outraced him. Senator Lindsey Graham of South Carolina called on the Justice Department to investigate the allegations of fraud in Erie. The Trump campaign filed suit in federal court to stop certification of Pennsylvania's election.

"It has been reported by Project Veritas," the suit read, "that carriers were told to collect, separate and deliver all mail-in ballots directly to the supervisor. In addition, Plaintiffs have information that the purpose of that process was for the supervisor to hand stamp the mail-in ballots."

In the meantime, O'Keefe and his source made a couple of maneuvers. The mail carrier, Richard Hopkins, signed a legal affidavit describing Weisenbach's alleged fraud. And at Project Veritas's suggestion, he said, he opened an account at the crowdfunding site GoFundMe. This fit a pattern among O'Keefe's sources, who often opened crowdfunding pages within days or even hours of their stories going public, and which O'Keefe and Project Veritas then pumped on social media. In Hopkins's case, total contributions shot past $100,000 immediately and showed no signs of slowing.

"The #VeritasArmy has stepped up big time. Thank you," O'Keefe tweeted, along with a link to the GoFundMe page. "Richard deserves our support. Hero."

The special agents who had interviewed Weisenbach now returned to the Erie post office. This time, they had questions for Hopkins, the mail carrier.

MICHIGAN

Pandemonium broke out in Detroit.

Election Day itself had passed without any real trouble, but the next morning during the vote count, it became clear that Biden would overtake Trump. Republicans panicked. The chair of the Michigan GOP, Laura Cox, started calling pro-Trump activists, urging them to head toward the TCF Center in downtown Detroit, a central site for counting absentee ballots.

That set off a technological call to arms. Unlike historical political movements, when organizing and mobilizing a large popular response took planning and time, in Detroit the call came at digital speed. In nearby Livingston County, the Republican Party posted to its Facebook page:

Urgent & important!

We just got this urgent message from Wayne County Michigan Trump field director.

"Come to TCF Center 1 Washington Blvd, Detroit, MI 48226 (Room 260) help needed to protect our lead, will get you credentialed upon arrival. Tell others."

35,000 ballots were suddenly found at 3:00 a.m. in Detroit. We need YOU to help us defend the vote and help President Trump.

Like · Comment · Share · Favorite

In Michigan, private citizens called poll challengers observe the vote count and can object to the validity of a mail-in ballot and its handling. At the TCF Center, each party was allowed 134 challengers. A full complement of Republicans had already entered the building. How new arrivals might "protect our lead" was left unclear.

A group called the Wayne County 11th Republican Committee posted:

> EMERGENCY HELP IS NEEDED AT TCF PROTECTING THE REPUBLICAN LEAD RIGHT NOW!!
>
> Like · Comment · Share · <u>Favorite</u>

The call proliferated across social media, and soon a crowd gathered outside the TCF Center. They arrived convinced that, as Mike Roman, Trump's director of election day operations, had tweeted, "The steal is on!"

As pressure built outside the center, inside election officials realized they had a problem. Tension among vote counters and poll challengers had mounted throughout the day as the tally for Biden rose. That tension was exacerbated by subtexts old and new in Detroit. Strife had long simmered between the majority-black city and Michigan's white Republicans. And now, as a pandemic swept the land, new protocols led to shouting and interventions by police. And the center grew overcrowded: Contrary to social media suspicions, officials had allowed *too many* poll challengers, about two hundred from each party. To stay within the law, they needed to reduce that number to 134. So they locked the center's doors, and as excess poll challengers left during the afternoon, new ones weren't allowed in for either party.

The crowd outside interpreted this as confirmation Republicans were being excluded, and the atmosphere grew volatile. Protesters pounded their fists against the center's windows, shouted slogans like "Stop the count," and made videos of the counters inside. Counterprotesters began to gather, shouting, "Count every vote." Rumors spread of subversion and sabotage, of fake ballots smuggled in by a hand-pulled wagon and later by industrial van.

The chaos outside grew so fevered that election officials started taping paper over the windows as protesters pounded on them. The mob outside intimidated vote counters, officials said, and taking pictures of the ballots risked violating voters' right to privacy. Regardless, poll challengers from both parties freely roamed the center, observing the count.

The protests spilled over into the next day, when Trump addressed the nation from the White House. He amplified the rumors circulating in the crowd outside the TCF Center and said Republicans were "denied access to observe any counting in Detroit."

None of it was true.

In Antrim County, Sheryl Guy faced what seemed like a Gordian knot of numbers and ballots and tape and machinery and *technology*.

She took down the published numbers and tried to regroup. But by now, the world had noticed something was off kilter in Antrim County. On November 6, the *New York Post* published a story that began, "President Trump's supporters are pointing to a small Michigan county as evidence that vote-counting software used in the state may undercut Trump's number of votes."

The days that followed were a blur of meetings and calls with county attorneys and software programmers, and through the haze, a thought gradually dawned in Guy's mind: *I did this. It's my fault.*

When she added that last-minute candidate for village trustee to the ballots, she should have updated the counting machines with the new parameters. But she hadn't. So when the numbers started rolling in, they dropped into the wrong columns. A little over two thousand Trump votes had been shifted to Biden's column. Her error.

Then when she had tried to fix the issue, entering the correct numbers directly into the central computer, she hadn't zeroed out the mistaken ones. So she had published a stack of both wrong and right totals.

"It's a horrible mistake," she told the county's attorneys. "I own it." She said the same to people who called the office to complain, to her neighbors, to the county commissioners.

At last, the night of November 6, the team of people working on the problem had stripped away all the compounded mistakes—they rescanned all ballots—and published the correct tally of votes: a win for Trump, by 3,800 votes. The county board of canvassers examined the results and certified them. The system worked as intended. The mistake had been noticed immediately. It had been investigated and corrected. It seemed, that night, like the end of a terrible episode in Guy's public life.

That was her greatest miscalculation. The plot about to unfold in out-of-the-way Antrim County would render her a pariah in the community she'd called home since birth, and tear at the social fabric of Antrim itself. It would threaten to overthrow the election of the president of the United States.

And it turned on a single ballot in Antrim County: a vote for the local marijuana shop.

NEVADA

When it became clear that the count was going to drag out for a few days, intense interest focused on the places where the whole contest might turn. One of those was Nevada, and more precisely, Clark County—Las Vegas and environs—where the bulk of the state's people lived.

That county's registrar of voters, Joe Gloria, held the first of what would become daily press conferences before the election center in North Las Vegas on Wednesday afternoon, November 4. These would turn him, in the coming days, into a public figure, which he quickly discovered is not always a good thing. A roly-poly man in glasses, with short brown hair, the round lower half of his face wrapped in a blue mask that strained to reach his ears, he wore a purple shirt with the emblem of Clark County over his left breast and "Registrar of Voters" in gold script on his right. He knew that a lot of people waited for his news. He stood somewhat prissily, with his hands joined before him at the waist, big arms enclosing his broad purple belly.

"The purpose of bringing you here today," he said, beginning in his formal, roundabout way, "is to give you some information related to when we will be able to report accurate numbers as to what we received on Election Day through the mail and also through our mail ballot drop-off boxes. We are working feverishly to get all of that counted so that we can make an accurate report."

Impatience for Clark County results was coming from both political sides. The election nationwide was still close, although Trump's chances were dimming. His camp needed the state's six Electoral College votes and still had a shot. By far, the bulk of those remaining would come from here. Meanwhile, Nevada Democrats wanted their state to be the one to lift Biden over the top, which would only happen if Gloria announced before Pennsylvania did. Under Nevada law, he had nine days to finish the count. He was going to beat the deadline, but he wasn't going to speed things up just to mollify everyone's impatience.

Even more than most states, Nevada is politically schizoid. Most of its vast territory was colored red but was only sparsely inhabited. Seventy-two percent of the state's citizens were crowded into Las Vegas in southeast Clark County and Reno in northwest Washoe County. These were, predictably, Democrat and not just mildly so—the party's most leftist national candidate, Bernie Sanders, had run a close second in Nevada's 2016 primary. This made for an especially volatile rural-urban mix. In 2016 Hillary Clinton had won the state narrowly, by just 2.4 percentage points. So with early reports from the red counties favoring Trump, Republicans were eager to slam the door. A lawsuit to stop mail voting had failed in October. Now the Trump camp prepared a lawsuit to stop the count, claiming that the counting machines for mail ballots were faulty—it would be promptly dismissed, there being no evidence to support the claim. The machines were working "feverishly," as Gloria put it, but the process took time. The longer it dragged out, the more anxious and annoyed everyone grew.

Gloria understood. He was used to his county being on the hot seat in these contests. He'd started as an entry-level staffer in the registrar's office almost twenty years earlier, so he knew the state and its politics well enough. He steered clear of them. He was a registered Democrat, but his commitment to the vote was professional, not personal. He was less interested in the outcome than in showing that he and his people were pros, that they could perform the count quickly and accurately. Part of that—earning the public's trust—meant being forthcoming about what was going on. Gloria was no practiced mouthpiece. He had been hoping that someone higher up the chain, someone like Secretary of State Barbara Cegavske, would step up to be the face of the vote count, but that hadn't happened. So he reluctantly shouldered the task himself.

He opened his first appearance before the mics by announcing that he would be holding a daily press briefing at ten in the morning, "from now until we're done with the counting process." The idea was to promote transparency "and to give the media an opportunity to ask any questions related to details for our mail ballot process."

He then opened it up for questions.

"Joe, at this stage, how many do you have left to count?" a reporter asked.

Gloria started to answer when an angry stout man with wild gray hair, wearing a pale blue surgical mask rendered useless by being pulled down below his mouth and a sleeveless T-shirt with the words "BBQ/ Beer/Freedom" on the front, stepped up from behind him and started screaming.

"The Biden crime family is stealing the election! The media is covering it up! The Biden crime family is stealing this election! The media is covering it up! The Biden crime family is stealing this election! The media is covering it up!"

The man appeared to be expecting someone to tackle him, and when no one did, his coherence sputtered. This did not stop him.

"We want our freedom for the world! Give us our freedom, Joe Biden! Biden's covering up this election. He's stealing it!"

Exhausted, he stalked off.

Gloria had stood watching throughout, turning politely, arms still folded across his belly. When the shouter departed, he stepped back up to the mics.

"Where were we?" he asked. "What was the last question?"

Gloria didn't show it, but the heckler had rattled him. His daily briefings would be moved indoors and with tighter security.

The incident put Gloria's masked face on the national news. He was contacted by people he hadn't heard from in years. His wife's family in Mexico caught him on Univision. They were thrilled.

GEORGIA

The morning after Election Day, John Porter stopped at a RaceTrac gas station at the foot of Kennesaw Mountain for a Coke Zero. He was chief of staff to the lieutenant governor, and had stayed up almost all night following election results. Now he needed caffeine. He had just climbed back into the driver's seat of his white Ford truck when his phone rang, and he set aside his drink—his boss, Geoff Duncan, was calling with the news that Trump, as it looked to him, had the contest locked up.

"Geoff, I am not so sure," Porter said. "Let's just hold tight. You know? Just keep our heads down. Let's see how this plays out."

The strain of the presidential election in Georgia was heightened by the possibility of runoff races for Senators Kelly Loeffler and David Perdue. Both were Republican incumbents, which in Georgia traditionally meant certain reelection, but so far neither had secured a majority of the vote. If that remained true, then a runoff election loomed in January between them and Democratic candidates Raphael Warnock and Jon Ossoff. The outcome of those contests would determine the balance of power in the US Senate for at least the next two years.

Trump's first legal salvo in the state was a weak one. On November 4, his campaign filed suit in Chatham County, based on a poll watcher's allegation that late ballots were being counted with on-time ballots. The next day, Superior Court judge James Bass listened to more than an hour of argument and testimony, delivered via video calls.

The county's lawyers had shown that each ballot was time-stamped as it arrived. No late ballots had been counted.

As Trump lawyer Jonathan Crumly answered, he looked down and swiped a couple of times at his phone. If he was looking for a good counterargument, he didn't find one. Gray-bearded Judge Bass didn't waste time. He said, "After listening to the evidence, I'm denying the request and dismissing the petition."

Even as he spoke, he leaned forward to switch off his video camera.

Lawrence Sloan's machine cut him.

In the two days since the election and after many thousands of repetitions, the blade on one of the envelope slicers he piloted in the Atlanta counting center had drifted slightly out of calibration. If a voter had ignored instructions and included extra material in the envelope, which people did all the time—personal letters, a driver's license, a check intended to pay their electric bill—the machine didn't slice cleanly.

It made a mess of the envelope unless the operator snatched it out with quick fingers, sometimes getting a nip from the slicer. Sloan had volunteered to man it. He was so good with the cutting machines that he had trained the others how to use them. And with his atypical brain, he had come to see the machines almost as people, each with its own personality. As he saw it, this one just felt cranky and needed a little extra attention.

The warm, collegial atmosphere of Election Day had pressurized in the days since. "STOP THE COUNT," Trump tweeted Thursday morning. His campaign operatives were determined to at least slow things, because as the count dragged on they spread more suspicion and the volume of protest grew louder.

At the counting center, a horde of people now stood outside with their phones, recording and livestreaming the comings and goings of otherwise anonymous election workers. Official observers from each party played an important role, helping to guarantee a fair accounting, but now a large swath of the public didn't trust anyone "official." The observation had become unofficial, omnidirectional, constant, and hostile. Sloan felt like the audience was rooting for them to fail.

It was unnerving. Sloan tried to shrug it off.

"Just don't pay attention to them," he told his coworkers.

In the wee hours of Thursday, November 5, in the back stretch of a twenty-hour shift, the misaligned blade on Sloan's machine encountered an envelope with extra material in it and started to tear it. Sloan snatched it out, but not before it nipped his fingers.

He'd had enough. He snatched his hands back, punched the air, then sat dejected and shook his head. He raised a middle finger to flip off the machine. He took the extra material—the paper instructions voters are meant to throw away—balled it up, and tossed it aside. Then he leaned in close to the machine, and from behind his gray mask, he whispered murderous threats.

"Oh, fuck you," he said. "Do not do this to me right now; it is too fucking late. We have a better relationship than this."

Then he carried on with the work.

Several hours later, as the East Coast started to wake up, he got a message from a friend: *Have you seen this video?*

The link showed Sloan's spat with the machine. Someone had recorded it, added narration, and posted it.

"I wonder what's going on here," the narrator says. In the video, Sloan punches the air. "This dude has a fit about something." Sloan raises his middle finger. "And then flips off a ballot." Sloan tosses the extra paper. "And then crumples it up."

It didn't matter that Sloan, opening the outer envelope, had no idea how the ballot was marked. Or that, unlike the small piece of instructional paper he threw away, the ballot inside the secret inner envelope was an unwieldy 8.5 by 19 inches.

The narrator concludes, "If that's not voter fraud, I don't know what is."

Sloan watched the video, then walked over to his supervisors and showed them, but there was little they could do. It was rocketing around the globe, yet another *documented instance* of what the protesters hoped to find.

People swallowed it whole, and not just anonymous Twitter users.

David Shafer, chairman of the Republican Party in Georgia, retweeted it.

"Lawyers for the Georgia Republican Party," he said, "have demanded that the Fulton County Board of Elections investigate and explain what is happening in this video."

Trump's son Eric retweeted it, adding sarcastically, "Nothing to see here."

Donald Trump Jr. retweeted it, adding, "WTF?"

More than five million people watched the clip on Twitter alone. Some called for Sloan's imprisonment. A deluge of messages came from concerned friends and family. He told his supervisor he needed a break. He left the counting room and walked into the arena's parking deck. He lit a cigarette. *What had he gotten into?*

He called his brother, who said, "I've seen it. But you'll be all right."

Around a corner came a small caravan of pickup trucks and a work van, adorned in Trump flags and homemade Trump logos. Sloan said a quick goodbye and pocketed his phone. The truck drivers started honking their horns and veered in his direction.

Sloan turned and started to run.

On Friday, Secretary of State Brad Raffensperger held a press conference. He stood before a tangle of television and radio mics at the foot of white marble steps in the Georgia capitol and in his characteristic unruffled tone said, "Out of approximately five million votes cast, we will have a margin of a few thousand."

The race was too close to call and would likely require a recount. Beyond the capitol building some people celebrated while others protested. Raffensperger gestured with long, slender fingers and continued dryly, "The stakes are high, and emotions are high on all sides."

At that point a smaller, faster-moving man stepped to the podium. Silver-haired Gabriel Sterling is the chief operating officer for the secretary of state's office and acts as Raffensperger's right hand. He whipped off a mask decorated with the state flag, and for a moment he resembled the bulldog mascot of his alma mater, the University of Georgia.

"Just to preempt a question, because I know it is going to come up: Are we seeing any widespread fraud?" he said. "We are not."

This was not coming from a Biden supporter. No one could accuse fifty-year-old Sterling of tilting any way but rightward. Republican politics have given structure to his entire life. His parents were both teenagers when he was born, and they divorced when he was just a few years old. They moved around a lot, and as a boy he discovered a knack for argument and self-determination. He had skipped first grade, so he was always the smallest kid in class and he learned to look out for himself.

He called the GOP the "daddy party," the one who told you the truth whether you wanted to hear it or not. It was the party of personal responsibility, the party that wouldn't let the government freely spend other people's money. Sometimes that meant saying no to what a lot of people wanted.

When he was thirteen, he moved from Atlanta city schools to Fulton County schools, where the high school had a program for smart kids. He wasn't in it. He approached an administrator. "Hey, I'm supposed to be in the Talented and Gifted program," he said.

The administrator asked, "Well, who's recommending you?" Sterling said, "I'm recommending me."

It worked.

In high school, teachers weren't quite sure what to do with the headstrong, conservative kid except maybe try to break him like a colt. So when it came time for students to argue on behalf of a country in international affairs, for instance, teachers assigned him Nicaragua and Vietnam. In college, though, the administrator of a leadership program pulled him aside and said, "You can go places." And he did. By the time he finished college, he was state political director for the Bush-Quayle campaign, at age twenty-one.

Now, three decades later, Sterling understood election machinery the way a veteran mechanic understands the inner workings of a familiar car. They may run smoothly or malfunction, but for him they held little mystery.

A few days after the press conference, midday on the 9th, Sterling got a text that puzzled him. It came from a friendly staffer with Senator Loeffler's campaign. A fellow Republican. It contained a formal-sounding statement that started, "Today, Senators David Perdue and Kelly Loeffler issued the following statement calling on Georgia Secretary of State Brad Raffensperger to resign."

Sterling texted back, "Ha ha, very funny."

"No, this is getting released in five minutes," came the response.

Sterling's eyes drifted down the rest of the statement. It offered no specific criticism of Raffensperger and cited no wrongdoing. But it sprayed incendiary language like gasoline: "The management of Georgia elections has become an embarrassment for our state. Georgians are outraged. . . . The Secretary of State has failed to deliver honest and transparent elections. He has failed the people of Georgia, and he should step down immediately."

Sterling shot back, "Are you f—ing kidding me?"

At that same moment in Sandy Springs, on the north side of Atlanta, Deputy Secretary of State Jordan Fuchs sat in a salon chair with her blond hair fully wrapped in foils. Having her hair done felt like both a luxury after more than half a year of pandemic and an act of defiance in the face of her sexist critics in Georgia politics. She had taken some shots.

For instance, Atlanta-area lawyer and conspiracy theorist Lin Wood had recently tweeted to his wide following, "Do you believe @JordyFuchs age 30 with 1 year of government experience should have negotiated Dominion deal & thereafter essentially run GA Sec. of State Office? . . . Something ain't right in GA."

The message required a little decoding for the uninitiated, but Fuchs knew exactly what it meant. The reference to a "Dominion deal" referred to one of the latest theories about voting fraud to gain traction. Dominion manufactured voting machines and software used in Georgia and twenty-seven other states—including Arizona and Michigan, as we have seen—to scan, record, and count ballots. Based in Toronto and Denver, the company was a contentedly successful enterprise little known outside the worldwide election industry. It was the second largest supplier of voting machines in the United States. As beleaguered county clerk Sheryl Guy struggled to resolve issues with her Dominion machines in Michigan, the bizarre conspiracy theory clearinghouse QAnon had begun promoting the claim that Dominion was part of an international scheme to either delete millions of Trump votes or switch them to Biden—the story varied. Trump's campaign had quietly vetted the allegations just days after the election and found them to be completely false. Staffers circulated an internal memo to that effect, but Trump and his surrogates continued making the accusation. Plucked from the outermost fringes of The Steal movement, it made headlines when the president gave it his nod of approval. He retweeted that Dominion machines had "glitched" in favor of Biden.

In denigrating Fuchs, Wood had gone further than insinuating she dealt in corrupt voting machines. He wrote that she "has admitted publicly on Facebook that she was at one time a practicing witch. Yes, a Wicken. I do not respect that belief."

He had unearthed, somehow, an account of a Gwinnett County school board hearing dating back almost a quarter of a century to the publication of the first Harry Potter book. Several local middle school children testified of the dangers of the British novel about a boy wizard, and Fuchs's parents, severe fundamentalist Christians, had made her join them. She had testified that reading the book had made her want "to perform spells, curses, potions, hexes and vexes just like Harry."

So she had now become, according to this critic, a "Wicken," by which he surely meant "Wiccan."

In truth, Fuchs was now a grown woman with a big job, a savvy Republican political thinker, and a faithful Christian who just wanted to color her hair in peace. But midway through the process her phone erupted with calls. With apologies to her hairdresser, she answered one from Sterling, who told her about the senators' statement calling for their boss's resignation.

"I can't believe they did this," Sterling told her.

Fuchs also felt baffled, but for different reasons. If Loeffler and Perdue hoped to win their upcoming Senate runoff races, she calculated, they had just crushed their odds. Why?

She called a political consultant working for Perdue.

"This is a mistake," she said. "Who made this decision? I mean, this has just literally cost you the US Senate race. Not because Brad is going to retaliate. It's going to simply take you off message."

They had attacked a prominent member of their own party and, worse, undermined faith in elections *as they were campaigning for reelection.* Why would they do such a thing?

The consultant could offer no insight. Perdue and Loeffler had been in a private meeting with President Trump. They had not consulted anyone else. Apparently, the president had insisted.

PENNSYLVANIA

At The Wharf early Thursday, the pre-canvassing tables had not yet been moved to visible areas in front, as promised.

That morning, officials had at last escorted Leah Hoopes to the rear area and allowed her to watch for a few minutes from a distance. No one had yet been let into the locked closet. Stenstrom again confronted the sheriffs, who by now had donned riot gear. McBlain arrived to calm him and explain the deal. He assured him that the pre-canvassing work in the back room would be shifted forward, "so there will be no ballots in the back room and no reason for you to go back there."

"Well, that's not going to work for me, John," said Stenstrom, who remained concerned about the storage closet. "We are going into that fucking room, okay?" He wanted McBlain to lead a charge into the area. "Or I'll go get another order from another lawyer."

That sounded fine to McBlain. He and the county Republican Party had done all they intended to do for Greg Stenstrom. The sheriffs and election officials at the counting center were also fed up with him and weren't giving an inch further. Nor was Judge Capuzzi. When Stenstrom called his chambers, irate, a clerk answered. Stenstrom wanted the judge to command the counting center officials directly to obey his order. He offered to walk his phone over to them.

The clerk told him that the court order had been made in response to a filing by the county's Republican organization, not by him. If he now wanted to intervene, he needed his own attorney.

"I recommend that you seek counsel," she said.

Stenstrom, with little patience for the legal niceties, said McBlain had been sent by *him* and that he had been acting as *his lawyer*. It didn't help that the lawyer had split.

"I recommend that you seek counsel," the clerk repeated.

No matter how loud he got, her response was the same.

"I recommend that you seek counsel."

Stenstrom was infuriated. The clerk eventually hung up on him, or thought she had, because Stenstrom could still hear her on the other end. And what he heard was laughter. The clerk and a male voice—he presumed it was the judge—were laughing at him!

This was fuel to the flame. Stenstrom exploded. Abandoned by his attorney, treated as a joke by the judge, he now felt entirely convinced that everyone was in cahoots. This fix wasn't just a Democratic crime; it was the work of both parties! He was a big, loud, very angry man.

At this point, Dr. Jonathan Briskin, an observer representing a county association of Democratic lawyers (he was both a physician and an attorney) stepped up. The doctor was troubled by Stenstrom's rage. Briskin had been observing elections in Delco for years and regarded his role as strictly nonpartisan. He saw nothing untoward in the ongoing count. By now, the pre-canvassing work was being moved to the front, as promised, but the storage closet was still locked and unviewed. He also didn't see any harm in letting Stenstrom look wherever he wanted. So, to be nice, he intervened.

"Look, the court order says we're supposed to have access to this," he argued to election supervisors, referring to the closet. "I have been here for four hours. Could you please take me and whoever else is permitted, including this guy"—gesturing to Stenstrom—"into that room?"

It worked. Briskin and Stenstrom were escorted there. In it, they found boxes of as-yet uncounted, unopened ballots. McBlain had been told there were about seven thousand of them.

This is not what Stenstrom saw. Once more, he felt shocked. His count, estimating about five hundred envelopes per box, reached fifty thousand. Briskin, standing alongside, considered that a wild exaggeration, but he was not about to argue with Stenstrom. Later, the estimate would swell to seventy thousand. Stenstrom was convinced that what he saw before him were, in fact, the real mail ballots, the ones filled out by actual voters. Those being flung around on the spacious counting floor and fed into the giant machines, those were fake—ballots filled in for Biden in advance to ensure his victory.

Further confirming this suspicion, for him, was his belief that at that point—midday Thursday, November 5—all mail ballots had been counted and reported. So what were these doing locked in a closet? It was, as far as he was concerned, a smoking gun—no wonder the Democratic election officials had fought to keep him out!

Except Stenstrom was wrong. The count was not over. It would continue through that day, the next, and most of the next, ending on Sunday evening, the 8th. The number of ballots in the closet would gradually diminish over that time, but some remained even after Sunday. These were postmarked prior to Election Day but had arrived after the voting deadline. The county had been ordered to hold them until it was determined whether they would be counted.

None of this would dissuade Stenstrom. The closet remained, for him, clear proof of what he had expected to find. And it wasn't the only thing. When he had been on the phone butting heads with officialdom, Hoopes had shown him a picture. She had captured Jim Savage, the county's voting machine warehouse supervisor, arriving with a clear plastic bag filled with USB drives. This was patently improper! What was he doing if not baldly delivering more false Biden votes? Savage had been a Bernie Sanders supporter, which marked him, in Hoopes's eyes, as the worst of the worst.

Each voting machine in the county contained a USB drive that backed up the machine's memory. Proper election procedure called for these drives to be removed from the hundreds of machines and delivered to the counting center packaged with the actual paper ballots in order to ensure chain of custody. So what was Savage doing with this baggie of random USB drives? With the numbers climbing in Biden's favor, the answer seemed plain.

The county had another explanation. It seemed that not all of the machine operators at its 428 polling places had followed instructions. Some had failed to remove the USB drives from their scanning machines on election night. So some bags of paper ballots had arrived without them. Savage had retrieved them. It happens every election. It was a departure from procedure but hardly critical because the USB drives were just backups. The real count was stored, along with a scan of every ballot, in the machine's memory. Beyond that were the actual, physical ballots.

This explanation, of course, did not fly with Stenstrom and Hoopes. Ballots locked in a closet? Savage delivering USB drives from nowhere? The Biden count climbing? How dumb did the Democrats think they were?

There was more, for those with eyes to see. A group of no-doubt progressive student volunteers from nearby Swarthmore College were observed at a long table actually *filling in* ballots by hand. A craftily edited video of this was uploaded to social media, presented as proof that Democrats were filling in false ballots.

Of course, for this there was also a benign explanation. Ballots rejected by the scanning machines were, according to established procedures, being hand-copied so that they could be entered and counted. After objections were raised, a Democratic observer was placed at one end of the table and a Republican observer at the other, witnessing that the votes were faithfully copied.

Valerie Biancaniello started getting calls from Hoopes at the counting center on Thursday.

"Me and Greg are down here," she said.

"Greg?"

"Greg Stenstrom."

Biancaniello remembered the name because Hoopes had contacted her about getting him listed as a poll watcher, even though there was some question about whether he actually lived in Delco. Biancaniello, as the liaison between the Trump campaign and the county's GOP, had gotten him certified.

"There's fraud. The feds are coming in," Hoopes told her.

"Explain to me why the feds are coming."

"We called them," said Hoopes. "Greg has connections."

Still unhappy with their access and having worn out their welcome with the county Republican organization, Hoopes and Stenstrom wanted Biancaniello to intercede. With a long history in Republican politics, she had been asked the year before by Tom McGarrigle, the county Republican leader, to take the lead for Trump locally because, as she remembered, he told her, "the Trump people are a little unhinged." An enthusiastic Trumpist herself, Biancaniello had felt insulted. She had worked so hard for him in 2016 that she had been named the campaign's top grassroots organizer in Pennsylvania. A tall, slender, dark-haired, carefully put-together woman from her long, colored nails to her high heels, Biancaniello's Facebook page featured her posing on the tarmac before a Trump-Pence bus and Air Force One. She was the local Trump

Lady. She shrugged off McGarrigle's affront, having long ago learned to roll with the punches in politics. Although sanguine about the president's chances for reelection, she had no illusions about his chances in Delco. Trump had taken only 37 percent of the vote there in 2016. She believed that with lots of committed nuts-and-bolts, door-to-door campaigning, she might be able to up his margin by 5 or 6 percentage points, but Biden was going to win the county.

Hoopes explained how they had gone to court to gain better access but that even after the court order, they still couldn't see all they were entitled to see. The Steal was under way.

"Not being able to see does not mean fraud," Biancaniello said. "We have to be reasonable here. I'm not saying there isn't fraud, and I'm not saying there is, I'm just saying we don't know."

This was a lot less than her candidate was saying.

She knew Hoopes had not observed an election before. She saw her as someone who had shown little interest in the details of electioneering. Still, she took the charge seriously. Biancaniello was herself scheduled for a shift at the counting center that evening. She told Hoopes to "sit tight" and then contacted a lawyer working for Trump, Britain Henry, telling him that Delco's center had been "flagged," meaning there was suspicion of fraud.

When she and Henry arrived, Stenstrom began shouting at her. She told him to calm down.

"You don't speak to me like that," she said. "I brought a Trump lawyer."

"You didn't get the Trump lawyer; *we* got the Trump lawyer," he insisted.

"Okay, *you* got the Trump lawyer," she said.

Stenstrom told her about the fifty thousand unopened ballots locked in the closet.

"You're yelling numbers at me, but what do they mean?" she complained. "Make sense of it to me. Can you prove fraud?"

When the next court-ordered five-minute closet tour came around, Biancaniello went in. She saw racks, most of them empty, but a small number of ballots still in boxes. There were nowhere near as many as Stenstrom claimed. Walking around, she spotted a few marked Springfield and Marple, two county townships. That interested her, but even if they were not counted, they were too few to turn the election.

When she emerged, Stenstrom was furious.

"Why did you go back there?" he said. "You shouldn't have been the one to go back!"

She was fed up with him. "I don't even know you," she said.

"We've been down here for four days straight," said Stenstrom. "We haven't even gotten any sleep!"

Hoopes also started shouting at her.

"You need to calm down," Biancaniello said. She conferred with Henry and with McBlain, who had returned. Stenstrom had peppered him with angry text messages all day. As she tried to confer with them, Stenstrom kept interrupting.

She told him, "Look, there is no fraud." She said there were not large numbers of ballots in the closet.

"That's not true," said Stenstrom.

"There is no fraud," she repeated emphatically, which further riled Stenstrom, provoked laughter from Parks, the assistant county solicitor, and then from Biancaniello, Henry, and McBlain.

"Do you understand that you can suspect something, but it means nothing if you don't have evidence," she told Stenstrom, reminding him of her own Trump credentials. "If you can find evidence, I'll be the first person to thank you."

She thought that Hoopes and Stenstrom were crazy and told them so. Hoopes left, angry. As far as Biancaniello was concerned, there was nothing shadier going on with this vote count than in any normal election. It was a complex process. There were always mistakes made, and a few people always cheated. But there was nothing big enough to matter. She thought Hoopes and Stenstrom mistook grandstanding for actual political work. As she saw it, a committeewoman's job was not to show up at the counting center just to raise hell.

Biancaniello had the option of filling out an affidavit claiming irregularity, as Hoopes and Stenstrom had, but she declined to do so.

Now Hoopes and Stenstrom were on their own, at least locally. Trump and his team of lawyers and loyalists continued to sound the fraud message loudly from afar, but in Delco, it didn't register. Nearly everyone felt satisfied with the process: Democrats and worse, the local GOP machine, and worse still, the Trump Lady.

Standing alone, against even those who ostensibly shared their goals, might cause some people to doubt themselves. Not Leah Hoopes and Greg Stenstrom. It made their stand feel *heroic*. People made movies about such things.

Stenstrom had formed a clear picture of what had happened in Delco. Tens of thousands of fake Biden ballots had been preprinted and substituted for the real ones. This had happened right under the noses of everyone watching at The Wharf, distracted by the big show officials made of the count—the Kabuki theater. Deviously clever, since Trump's loss accompanied so many wins for Republicans in state races, such as Hoopes's candidate Craig Williams. The party had actually increased its majority in the state legislature. This just confirmed that the GOP had been in on The Steal, too.

Stenstrom, with his background in fraud and security, felt that he was uniquely positioned to see this. If the others could not—no, *refused* to see it—then that told you something right there. The Republicans added betrayal to the crime, but the worst was this Trump Lady with the high heels and polished nails who despite flying the Trump banner and being a Trump delegate and a fervent Trump campaigner for four years had revealed herself to be a disguised "Never Trumper." It all fed Stenstrom's and Hoopes's growing conviction that there really was no two-party system in the county or the country. It was all a sham. The Steal revealed that we lived in a uniparty state. This suggested that, at least in their corner of Pennsylvania, every vote, every government policy, every appointment, every government contract, was prearranged and that, in essence, everybody in a position of power was corrupt. All being paid.

The fact that no one would listen to him and Hoopes, that they had been *laughed* at, showed that this wasn't just about Trump or the 2020 election. It was about a huge, deeply deceptive, corrupt, politically transcendent establishment: *The Swamp.*

Was this not, after all, what Donald Trump had preached for four years?

WISCONSIN

Rohn Bishop had remained at campaign headquarters in Fond du Lac on election night long enough to watch Trump appear on TV to give a rambling, disconsolate "victory speech." It was just before two-thirty in the morning in Washington, one-thirty in Wisconsin. Only a few of the Fond du Lac crowd remained. The president spoke from the White House with his wife, Melania, and Vice President Mike Pence at his side. He didn't look like a winner. He looked bewildered and disgusted. Before a wall of American flags, he saluted the millions who had voted for him and said, "A very sad group of people is trying to disenfranchise that group of people, and we won't stand for it. We will not stand for it."

He spoke about his disappointment in having to cancel a big outdoor celebration because the votes were not being properly tabulated. He said he was "winning Pennsylvania by a tremendous amount of votes. We're six hundred, think of this, think of this, think of this, we're up six hundred and ninety thousand votes in Pennsylvania. Six hundred and ninety. These aren't even close. It's not like, oh, it's close. With sixty-four percent of the vote in, it's going to be almost impossible to catch, and we're coming into good Pennsylvania areas where they happen to like your president, so we'll probably expand that."

He meandered rhetorically through the various states where he said he had either won already or would soon win and then complained, "All of a sudden, I said, 'What happened to the election?' It's off. And we have all these announcers saying, 'What happened?' And then they said, 'Ooooh.' Because you know what happened? They knew they couldn't win, so they said, 'Let's go to court.' And did I predict this, Newt?" He pointed to the former House Speaker Newt Gingrich in his audience. "Did I say this? I've been saying this from the day I heard they were going to send out tens of millions of ballots. . . . This is a fraud on the American public. This is an embarrassment to our country. We were getting ready to win this election. Frankly, we did win this election. We did win this election. So our goal now is to ensure the integrity for the good of this nation. This is a very big moment. This is a major fraud on our nation. We want the law to be used in a proper manner. So we'll be going to the US Supreme Court. We want all the voting to stop. We don't want them to find any ballots at four o'clock in the morning and add them to the list. It's a very sad moment. To me, this is a very sad moment. And we will win this, and, we, as far as I'm concerned, we already have won it."

This is a fraud on the American public. This is an embarrassment to our country. This is a very big moment. This is a major fraud on our nation.

Rohn Bishop looked over at one of his colleagues and they rolled their eyes at each other. This was . . . nonsense. Unlike Delco, where Leah Hoopes distrusted the election process because it was being run by Democrats, Wisconsin's election had been run by Republicans. In fact, the election laws in that state had been overhauled just a few years earlier during the tenure of Governor Scott Walker, a Republican. Bishop had been around for that, had cheered it, and ever since, he had felt especially good about the integrity of the vote in his state.

This election . . . *stolen*? It wasn't just false; it was dangerous. Bishop thought, *This could get ugly.*

Whatever hopes he had that his election travails would ease after Election Day were quickly dashed. He slept for only about two hours after the party, then woke up bright and early Wednesday, running on coffee, playing teacher for his daughters' pandemic in-home virtual schooling. He also did two radio interviews.

He sympathized with Trump's outburst at the White House early that morning but did not agree. He told one interviewer that they had to give the president "a few days" to accept his loss.

"There's enough states outstanding that we're not going to concede anything yet," he said. "But if I was running for president of the United States I'd rather be Joe Biden than Donald Trump at this moment."

Bishop regarded these interviews as a standard wrap-up, but he discovered as the week progressed that the contest remained far from settled for many of those he knew. Saying otherwise riled them up.

His family went to church every Saturday night and afterward repaired to a booth at Tony's Pizza in Waupun for dinner. It was family time. With Reagan to his left and his wife, Jennie, and Maggie sitting across from him, his cell phone began to chirp on the table with another heckling comment from Mike Schwandt, a local Republican who defined himself on his Facebook page as "just a regular, no nonsense, take no crap kind of guy." Schwandt was generally in Bishop's corner, but he had now fully embraced Trump's claims of fraud. Bishop had gone back and forth with him digitally.

His face screwed with annoyance as he read the latest missive. When he looked up, he saw the same expression on his wife's face.

"Just stop reading it," she said.

He put the phone down.

"Yeah, okay, you're not wrong."

But it was hard for him to ignore. He had become the local focus for election outrage. A truck driver called him and screamed at him for helping Democrats steal the election. Bishop wanted to know what had given him that idea. The driver was moving through northern Wisconsin and seeing Trump sign after Trump sign. He hadn't seen any Biden signs. So how could Trump lose Wisconsin?

"Well, do you ever drive your semi in Dane County?" Bishop asked. This encompassed Madison, the state capital, a city of about 270,000 and the second largest population center in Wisconsin, behind Milwaukee. It was also a Democratic stronghold.

"No," said the driver.

Bishop suggested that his sample was flawed.

Strangers were one thing. What really got under his skin were his friends, even his coworkers. He engaged with his colleague Jeff Respalje on Facebook. A mechanic at the GM dealership who had been increasingly vocal about Trump's claims, Respalje had reposted a "news report" that generals would refuse to take orders from Biden as commander in chief. The first mutinous general quoted was Joe Barron, who had died in 1977.

Bishop pointed out this and other clear signs of the article's falsity, to which Respalje made the curious reply, "There's too many fact-checkers already, don't need another one."

Taking a stand on the principle that facts mattered, Bishop had tried to speak to Respalje about it in person at the back end of the workshop where vehicles were hoisted on lifts so mechanics could work underneath. He considered Respalje one of the best workers in the shop. Beneath a Chevy Silverado, Bishop told his friend, "I'm just trying to help because the stuff you're sharing is completely wrong."

Again, Respalje responded, "I don't need a fact-checker." Then they got into it: Respalje, tall and lean with a long, thin beard and a baseball cap; Bishop, bald, burly, and thickly bearded.

"Dude, I voted for the same guy you did," Bishop said. "I'm just telling you it wasn't stolen; these ballots weren't illegally cast. They're not going to be thrown out. There's nothing there."

"You really think Joe Biden got eighty-four million votes?" Respalje asked.

"Yeah."

"No fucking way. He never left his basement."

"Yeah, that's right," Bishop said. "Trump was unpopular enough to drive Democrats to vote for a doormat. Yeah, I don't deny that; but he won and it's legit."

Then another colleague joined in—on Respalje's side. This was a man who had never evinced an interest in politics, but suddenly he was asking whether the state legislature could overturn Biden's win, or whether the state's representatives to the Electoral College might ignore the popular vote, which he had seen reported, and simply cast their ballots for Trump.

Bishop answered the questions, but he could see that nothing he said connected. The fact that he had toiled for a year trying to get Trump elected—he hadn't seen these guys at his training sessions or door-to-door outings—simply didn't matter.

He felt increasingly troubled by the tactics of Trump's ardent followers. When state legislators called for partial recounts in Dane County and Milwaukee, seeking to throw out the votes of those who had voted early and in person, it offended him. The effort went nowhere. Its rationale was that election clerks, following procedures adopted informally years earlier, had used a single form instead of a two-form procedure that was still technically mandated. Bishop saw it as fundamentally unfair, a bald effort to toss out black ballots since both recounts were aimed where most of Wisconsin's black voters lived. As it happened, he had used the single form, too. By this standard, his own early, in-person vote also deserved to be tossed.

ARIZONA

Clint Hickman had sat slack-jawed in front of his TV as Fox called his state for Biden. Republicans had always owned Arizona. Trump had enjoyed a healthy 3.5 percent margin in 2016.

He was still digesting the news when a report came on that the president had immediately claimed fraud. Hickman and the board—four Republicans and one Democrat—had supervised this election! Either they were corrupt, according to Trump, or they'd been had. The results were shocking, but the president's accusation disturbed Hickman.

On Wednesday, he composed a letter to Maricopa County voters:

As members of the Maricopa County Board of Supervisors, we are concerned about the misinformation spreading about the integrity of our elections.

First, vote counting is not a Republican or Democrat issue; everyone should want all the votes to be counted, whether they were mailed or cast in person. An accurate vote takes time. It's possible the results you see now may change after all the votes are counted. This is evidence of democracy, not fraud.

Second, sharpies do not invalidate ballots. We did extensive testing on multiple different types of ink with our new vote tabulation equipment. Sharpies are recommended by the manufacturer because they provide the fastest-drying ink. The offset columns on ballots ensure that any bleed-through will not impact your vote. For this reason, sharpies were provided to in-person voters on Election Day. People who voted by mail could use sharpies, or blue or black pens. Our Elections Department has been communicating this publicly for weeks.

Maricopa County has bipartisan oversight of elections in 2020 with the Board of Supervisors and the Recorder's Office each playing an important role. We would like to thank the hundreds of volunteers, poll workers and staff for being a part of an incredible Elections team. All of us are committed to a fair and efficient count of all votes.

It made little difference. The protests and accusations grew. Hickman was discovering a new, Trump-inspired brand of American politics. It did not respond to argument or reason.

He was as Republican as they came. So was the board of supervisors, which had only one Democratic member, Steve Gallardo, who cosigned the letter. The crowds demonstrating outside the county's election center grew larger and louder nightly. Some of them came conspicuously armed. They frightened the workers inside trying to complete an accurate tally.

Anybody who followed Arizona politics closely, as Hickman did, could see plenty of perfectly legitimate reasons why Trump had lost. Many in Maricopa's fast-growing Hispanic population resented his base characterization of Latino immigrants. His ugly tweets and impolitic behavior had also alienated many of the state's mainstream Republicans—Hickman was the only GOP member of the board who had backed him. Many Arizonians had been disgusted by Trump's ad hominem attacks on the state's beloved late senator and war hero John McCain, the party's former national standard-bearer. These were things astute politicians just didn't do. The Mormon Church, a growing factor in state politics, had urged its followers not to support him. None of these reasons registered with Trumpists. The only cause they could see for his loss was ill-defined fraud.

Hickman took it personally. He knew the things people were saying were, simply, wrong. Provably wrong. None of it mattered. Pointing out error just seemed to make them angrier and more determined.

Marko Trickovic appeared outside the election center Wednesday with hundreds of protesters, filming again, basking in his fifteen minutes of Sharpie-gate fame. A line of armed county sheriffs blocked the election center before them, but despite some weapons on display, the crowd seemed peaceful. Cheerful even. There was conversation and laughter, folks chomping pizza, sipping soda, waving placards, chanting, "Let Them In!" Inside, county workers still made their way through the remaining mail ballots.

"Does this state belong to Democrats?" shouted a man with a megaphone."

"NO!" the crowd responded.

"It was my video that went viral on the Sharpies," Trickovic told a bearded man beside him.

"Oh, yeah! Sharpie-gate!" the man said.

"Yeah!"

"WHOSE STATE?" shouted megaphone man.

"OUR STATE!" chanted the crowd.

There were Trump-Pence signs galore, "Keep America Great," and a homemade sign that said, "Count Every Vote." Another said, "NO VOTER FRAUD."

Speaking through a megaphone, a short, dark-haired young man with a beard and black-rimmed glasses, wearing a green flak vest decorated with a white Iron Cross on a field of red, a symbol associated with the Ku Klux Klan, warned the crowd to be wary.

"We all know what Pantifa likes to do, right?" he said, using a disparaging term for the left-wing group Antifa. "Run amok in our streets, right?"

"Yeah!"

"Do we do that here?"

"NO!"

"Do we do that on the right side?"

"NO!"

"All right, 'cause they are out there. They are out here! Tonight. They are out here. So make sure you guys are aware of that."

Trickovic said, "I talk to Tucker's publicist tonight," referring to Fox pundit Tucker Carlson. "We'll see. We'll see."

An older man in a red-and-gray cap read an excerpt from Lincoln's Gettysburg Address, ". . . and that government of the people, by the people, for the people, shall not perish from the Earth."

Megaphone man said, "You guys heard that, right? That's important. That's why we're here tonight. We're not just here because some people were forced to use a Sharpie, or some people received fraudulent ballots. . . . We're here because under the Constitution, WE THE PEOPLE have a voice."

A chant caught on:

"Shame on Fox!"

"Shame on Fox!"

"Shame on Fox!"

Another young man with a megaphone implored every Trump voter within earshot to get their friends to come back the next day and the next.

"I just want an answer! I wanna know what the deal is because I wanna know why you're saying that Arizona is blue when it's been red for as long as I can remember," he said. "President Trump won four years ago, and more people told me that they're voting Trump this year than four years ago. So something's off!"

"Right!"

Trickovic introduced himself to another man standing beside him.

"Apparently my video went viral," he said.

"That's cool." The man appeared only marginally interested.

"I'm just glad that it was able to bring attention to what was going on."

Easily disproved, the mini-tempest over Sharpies would wane fast, but in the coming weeks Trickovic would move on to promote a variety of other theories for how the election was stolen, ultimately condemning the state's Republican governor and legislators, Fox News, county officials, and anyone else who claimed that Biden had won the election. They were all in on The Steal.

He considered starting his own political party, "The Patriot Party of Arizona," which would make America safe through what he called "constitutional conservative leadership."

Meanwhile, despite being debunked, the Sharpie myth lived on. A state senator from Mesa, Kelly Townsend, prepared a bill to discourage their use.

The line of armed sheriffs outside the election center was Rey Valenzuela's idea. He coped with the nightly protests as best he could. When a few of the protesters tried to enter the counting center under false pretenses, he had the building locked down. A temporary fence went up to block entrance to the building and to keep the protesters cordoned in one half of the front parking lot. He tripled the protective force around the building and provided escorts to workers returning to their cars.

Those working to get the count right heard themselves denounced as "criminals" and worse.

"You're going to burn in hell," one protester screamed. "You deserve to die!"

One of Valenzuela's district chairmen pleaded with the crowd.

"Hey, I'm one of you!" he shouted. He explained that he was a Republican representing the fourth district. "Why are you yelling? I'm in there!"

The crowd just got more fired up.

Notable among the protesters was regular Jacob Chansley, the tall, balding, bearded conspiracy theorist who would become notorious on January 6, 2021, as the QAnon shaman, strutting through the US Senate chamber shirtless, showing off his heavily tattooed torso, face painted red, white, and blue, carrying a spear, crowned with a flowing fur cap with horns, howling.

GEORGIA

Lawrence Sloan ran with no plan beyond escape. From the parking deck of the State Farm Arena he burst into the crisp sunshine of Atlanta in autumn. His heart felt like it would pound out of his chest.

His feet took him east. Half of the political world had bent itself against him, it seemed, pleased to destroy him for the sake of the US presidency. Where could he hide?

Maybe the old pizza place.

He ducked here and there as he ran east through Five Points and the heart of downtown Atlanta. Off his right shoulder loomed the great golden dome of the Georgia state capitol, symbol of a state that had grown from the southernmost of the original thirteen colonies to become an economic powerhouse, home to more than ten million people, and now the focus of an aspiring American potentate.

Along the way he stopped a moment, and an older white couple recognized him. They had seen something about election workers on Facebook but didn't realize events had taken a turn that morning.

"What are you doing out here?" one of them said. "Are you going to work today?" Sloan wanted to keep moving. "Yo, I just left work," he said.

He ran on for a mile and a half, past the children's hospital, under the towering I-85 overpass, until he got to the neighborhood where he grew up, the Old Fourth Ward. It's best known as the site of Martin Luther King Jr.'s boyhood home on Auburn Avenue, which in the 1950s *Fortune* magazine called "the richest Negro street in the world." After decades of decline, the area has reemerged as an eclectic scene of black-owned businesses.

That included Edgewood Pizza, a central neighborhood spot. It features exposed brick walls and a tin ceiling and a painting of Martin Luther King Jr. hanging behind the bar. The owner, Bob Costanza—that's how friends and customers know him, at least—saw Sloan slip in and take a seat in a corner. He hadn't seen Sloan since the pandemic started, so he walked over.

"One of my favorite customers, man," he said.

Sloan seemed distracted. He pointed to the big television suspended over the bar. "That's me," he said.

Costanza looked up and saw the local news being broadcast.

He laughed. "Shut up, bruh," he said. But then he looked closer. Sure enough, the footage showed Sloan happily sorting ballot envelopes the night before. Sloan said things had gotten twisted in the meantime, and he felt frightened; someone had already posted his private information online, including his car's license plate.

"Bob, I can't go back to my house."

Another laugh. "Get the fuck out of here. You're not that important."

Friends had started to gather around and didn't immediately grasp Sloan's predicament. They started taking photos with him and streaming live on social media, which of course defeated his purpose. "I am on the *run*," he told them. "You cannot go live with me."

All of it contributed to a sense, in Sloan's mind, that he couldn't escape the country's unblinking gaze. He thought of Ahmaud Arbery, a black jogger whose killers followed him and shot him to death in south Georgia months earlier.

Okay, this is messed-up, he thought.

A few minutes later, two men walked in. "These guys were in suits, nice suits," Costanza said. They crossed the restaurant, moving toward Sloan. Suddenly Costanza realized maybe Sloan wasn't joking about the danger. "I thought they had come to kidnap him," he said. So he moved to intercept them.

"What the fuck is going on here?"

One of the men turned in his direction.

"Mr. Deglel?"

Costanza recoiled. *My real name*, he thought. Adonay Deglel. *Nobody knows that name.*

The man showed him identification. Some sort of badge Costanza couldn't focus on, with everything happening so fast. The men took Sloan, and together they left the restaurant, disappearing into a car. Costanza and Sloan's other friends were left to stand and stare at the door. *What just happened here?*

Sloan is cagey in describing exactly what happened next. But he went into hiding and stayed with friends no one else knew—a white couple, he said—and back at their place, he shaved his beard in a bathroom mirror. Then he sat in a chair while the female friend, a hairdresser, dyed his hair.

He felt disconnected from reality for days, hiding out and isolated. Terrified. His mother called and asked him to tell her where he was. "I can't," he said.

For weeks, he moved from place to place, staying a night with friends here or there. Gradually, he ventured back to his regular life.

When, in the months after, did he start feeling safe again?

"I don't," he said.

PENNSYLVANIA

As his loss grew ever more apparent to nearly everyone else, Trump tweeted on Friday:

I easily WIN the Presidency of the United States with LEGAL VOTES CAST. The OBSERVERS were not allowed, in any way, shape, or form, to do their job and therefore, votes accepted during this period must be determined to be ILLEGAL VOTES. U.S. Supreme Court should decide!

So far, only one legal challenge to reach the highest court, one from Pennsylvania, had gone—slightly—his way. Justice Samuel Alito had ordered that mail votes in that state received after Election Day (but mailed before) be counted but kept separate in the event of discovered irregularities.

For Trump's campaign, stopping Pennsylvania's count, or reversing its conclusion, was critical. At that point, without the state's twenty Electoral College votes, he could not win.

It was in this context that Rudy Giuliani stepped up to lead Trump's legal team. For a fee of something like $20,000 per day, the president had hired the former New York City mayor and his longtime confidant to coordinate a nationwide legal assault. Trump's campaign began raising money for this months earlier, warning on its website of "FRAUD like you've never seen." The site, using the fundraising platform WinRed, opted in donors with prechecked boxes that, unless spotted and unchecked, committed donors to weekly donations, a notoriously deceptive tactic that resulted, many months later, in forced repayments from Trump's campaign, the Republican National Committee, and related GOP accounts totaling in excess of $138 million. For the time being, however, during these critical days after Election Day, the president had a heavy war chest and, in Giuliani, a fighter with eye-grabbing credentials.

Ever a seeker of the spotlight and once a presidential aspirant himself, Giuliani had been trying for years to translate his post-9/11 popularity in New York into a national movement of some kind, first as a Green Party candidate, then as a civil rights and gun control advocate, and more lately, as a promoter of right-wing conspiracy theories about murders supposedly committed by Hillary and Bill Clinton and a purported chilling rise of pedophilia. He had represented the president several times. It had been a long fall for Giuliani from his days as a respected federal prosecutor pursuing mob bosses in New York. His legal reputation had plummeted so far that his selection alone reflected on the merits of the election challenge. The Trump team no longer featured the A-list of Republican Party attorneys who had contested procedural challenges to the vote prior to Election Day. Reputable lawyers had fled in droves. Now the legal fight would be led by a man who had no compunctions about telling lies in the context of a political campaign. In a deposition two years earlier concerning false claims he had made on Trump's behalf in 2016, Giuliani had characterized mendacity as "throwing a fake," which he regarded as a legitimate tactic in the political realm. This year, he was going to take *throwing a fake* to a new level.

With his arrival, the Trumpist legal resistance had degenerated into an amateurish, disorganized crusade, sometimes comically so. This was amply illustrated by Giuliani's kickoff press conference that Saturday. Trump promoted it that morning to his enormous Twitter following: "Lawyers Press Conference at Four Seasons, Philadelphia, 11:00 A.M."

A few minutes later, he, or someone, deleted it and tweeted a similar announcement with a curious change: "Big press conference today in Philadelphia at Four Seasons Total Landscaping—11:30am!"

Local reporters scratched their heads. "Four Seasons *Landscaping*?"

Surrounded by his entourage, the former New York City mayor shuffled across the gravel parking lot to a podium before a small, nondescript landscaping business on a busy stretch of road in an industrial area near the Delaware River—just down the road from a prison and a few doors down from the Fantasy Island Adult Book Store. The optics were absurd. Apparently, someone on Giuliani's staff had booked hastily, mistaking the spot for the luxury Four Seasons Hotel in Center City.

Pausing now and then to contend with roaring truck traffic and low-flying planes, Giuliani introduced himself as the president's lawyer and pledged a blizzard of lawsuits all over the country. He listed some of the much-voiced complaints: Observers were prevented from inspecting mail ballots, which were "innately prone" to fraud; that it was "almost mathematically impossible" for Biden to have overtaken Trump's early lead; the wholesale introduction of preprinted Biden ballots (à la Greg Stenstrom); the practice of allowing Democrats, but not Republicans, the opportunity to correct damaged ballots; and so on. Giuliani said he saw an overall pattern. The same fraudulent practices had been employed all over Pennsylvania and the nation. He added, perhaps as a comical aside, or "throwing a fake," that the late boxing champion Joe Frazier and the late father of actor Will Smith, both Philadelphians, had both voted in 2020. City election officials would later deny this; there was no evidence for it, and none would surface. Giuliani's blast included, he said, fifty affidavits "so far," alleging electoral malpractice. The situation, he said, was "extremely troubling."

Trump tweeted that afternoon:

THE OBSERVERS WERE NOT ALLOWED INTO THE COUNTING ROOMS. I WON THE ELECTION, GOT 71,000,000 LEGAL VOTES. BAD THINGS HAPPENED WHICH OUR OBSERVERS WERE NOT ALLOWED TO SEE. NEVER HAPPENED BEFORE. MILLIONS OF MAIL-IN BALLOTS WERE SENT TO PEOPLE WHO NEVER ASKED FOR THEM!

These charges, Giuliani's, and others echoed on defiant social media platforms like Parler and Discord. With no convincing evidence or coherent theory, Giuliani employed what might be called a Blunderbuss Strategy. It welcomed all theories. The strategy embraced every accusation or complaint, conflating the ridiculous with the true but minor, the partly true with the wholly concocted, the possibly significant with the wildly paranoid. It mattered little whether any of it were true or could be proved. What mattered was *how many* claims there were. The idea was to keep them coming, on Twitter and Facebook, in court, at public hearings, on friendly media. If you blasted enough shot, *anybody* might believe you had found a worthy target.

Blunderbuss ammunition comprised the dead people voting theories, the insertion of fake Biden ballots theories, including one that suggested tens of thousands had been flown from China to Arizona. There were multiple theories about voters casting more than one ballot. There were the US Postal Service's backdating ballot schemes. Marko Trickovic's Sharpie theory appeared, along with others that involved fixing machines to not register Trump votes, or election workers who simply did not scan Trump-marked ballots (à la Lynie Stone). There were a variety of schemes that involved either hacking into voting systems (which were not connected to the internet), inserting extra Biden votes into them via thumb drives, or the manipulation of software to switch votes from Trump to Biden. The last involved linking vote-switching ruses to billionaire George Soros, the US embassy in Rome, the late Venezuelan dictator Hugo Chavez, Mark Zuckerberg, Google, and Dominion. There were new ones every day. When lawyer Sidney Powell appeared on Fox TV's *Lou Dobbs Tonight*, attracting Trump's approving notice, she trotted out a theory that had bubbled up from the online cauldron of doubt three days before the election. It held that a supercomputer called the Hammer, running a CIA program called Scorecard, was being used nationwide to switch ballots from Trump to Biden. The charge had been dismissed as a hoax by the director of the US Cybersecurity and Infrastructure Security Agency, and there was no evidence of it, but Americans had been primed by years of Hollywood movies to believe the CIA was capable of anything. Powell, who entered imaginatively into the spirit of the Blunderbuss Strategy, would shortly appear at Giuliani's side.

Despite this onslaught, one by one, major media outlets, including Fox News, joined on Saturday in naming Biden the next president of the United States, winner of both the popular vote and in the Electoral College. The numbers were not close. Chris Wallace, commenting on the development on Fox, pointed out that the wide margin of victory made any chance of overturning it very unlikely. "We're not talking about five hundred votes as we were in Florida in 2000, we're talking about tens of thousands of votes in Pennsylvania," he said. Biden's margin in the state, while narrow in terms of percentage—just 1 percent of more than seven million votes cast—totaled 80,555 ballots.

The results grew certain enough for Biden to declare victory in a speech on national TV that evening.

"Folks, the people of this nation have spoken," he said. "They've delivered us a clear victory, a convincing victory, a victory for we, the people. We've won with the most votes ever cast for a presidential ticket in the history of the nation. *Seventy-four million* [this was a preliminary figure; eventually, his total would top eighty-one million]. Well, I must admit, it surprised me. Tonight, we're seeing all over this nation, all cities and all parts of the country, indeed across the world, an outpouring of joy, of hope, renewed faith in tomorrow to bring a better day. And I'm humbled by the trust and confidence you placed in me. I pledge to be a president who seeks not to divide but unify, who doesn't see red states and blue states, only sees the United States."

Still the concerted effort to stir confusion continued. How could it be over with no traditional congratulatory message from top congressional Republicans? While Trump refused to concede? When so many people in so many states and in so many ways cried fraud?

3

The Blunderbuss Strategy

PENNSYLVANIA

The battle had started to feel lonely and uphill for Delco's Leah Hoopes. The rebuffs and laughter she and Greg Stenstrom had endured at the counting center rankled.

When all the Delco ballots were counted by Sunday evening, the 8th, Biden's winning margin stood pretty much the same as Clinton's had, 63 percent to 36 percent. All the efforts of Valerie Biancaniello, the Trump Lady, had not moved the needle. In Bethel Township, where Hoopes was committeewoman (and, as Biancaniello saw it, had done little), Biden had reversed the 5 percent margin Trump had enjoyed four years earlier, winning by 3 percent, 3,276 votes to 3,127.

To her small Facebook following, Hoopes urged disbelief in these reported results, noting how wrong early results had been in past elections. In a flurry of postings on November 7, she showed images of TV screens projecting Al Gore as the winner in Florida in 2000 and Hillary Clinton on the cover of *Newsweek* under the title, "Madame President." She wrote, "Simmer down peeps this will be a long ride! Exposing mass fraud takes time" and "Stop telling The President to concede. The election is rigged!" She shared some of the rapidly emerging theories of electoral theft. As with most circulating these claims, she wasn't in a position to actually know if they were valid, but they furthered the narrative she preferred. They *sounded* right. They at least deserved to be looked into, right? Their sheer number and variety begged that. Here in her little corner of the internet the Blunderbuss Strategy *worked*.

To Hoopes, it made more sense to doubt the election than to trust it. On Sunday the 8th she posted, "So people commit tax fraud, insurance fraud, mail fraud, check fraud, Medicare fraud, Medicaid fraud, Welfare fraud. . . . But not Election fraud. Please take your blinders off and smack yourself in the face for being blissfully ignorant" (64 likes, 8 shares).

Trump pressed his case on three levels: popular, hammering away in interviews and press conferences and on his social media platforms; legal, the lawsuit blizzard; and political, leaning on elected and appointed officials in key states who might be persuaded to override the numbers and block certification of the vote.

On the popular front, he found enormous success. Trump had tapped into and cultivated a fervent and loyal following, collectively hostile to just about every institution in American life, and no one could kill it. Like Antaeus, it gained strength by being knocked down. Correcting or debunking it seemed to just steel its resolve: *[I] don't need another fact-checker.*

On the legal front, Trump was failing bigly. Judges weren't buying any of it. The cause drew local lawyers from all over the country, whether motivated by a paycheck, faith in Trump, or by a chance at the limelight— *filing a lawsuit on behalf of the president of the United States!* Self-promotion had always been central in Trump's creed. But few were great legal minds, and it showed. Their filings arrived hasty and incomplete, often rife with misspellings and simple grammatical gaffes. Judges decried, often sharply, the lack of evidence to support claims, the substitution of speculation for evidence, and clear errors of both legal interpretation and methodology. The lawyers filed more than a score of suits in the six swing states in the weeks after the vote. Within a few weeks, all had been dismissed as meritless, in some cases withdrawn by the plaintiffs themselves after preliminary hearings disclosed crippling errors. On the internet or in front of the press you could say anything, but lawyers who wasted judges' time risked legal jeopardy.

Yet every time Giuliani or his hirelings asked for an injunction to stop certification of the results, no matter how doomed the legal argument, it generated useful headlines and spurred the hopes of Trumpists. Likewise, when William Barr, the US attorney general, on November 9 authorized federal prosecutors to look into claims of voter fraud, violating the long-standing practice of keeping the Justice Department out of electoral politics, and prompting the chief of his elections crimes division to resign, still more hopeful headlines resulted.

Media Trumpists also went to work, diving uncritically into the myriad claims of the Blunderbuss Strategy, broadcasting every allegation of fraud no matter how minor, mundane, or implausible. Like Giuliani and Trump, they showed no interest in making any of the claims cohere into a coordinated plot, which, given the scale of the crime alleged, would have been indispensable. They used the very confusion created by this onslaught to further it.

"In case you haven't noticed, it's hard to trust anything you hear right now," said Tucker Carlson, kicking off his Monday night program, which reached an audience of more than four million. "We've heard you. We're grateful that you trust us and we will try to be worthy of your trust. We want to begin tonight by assessing some of the things no doubt you have heard about last week's presidential election. There are conflicting versions of virtually every part of that story."

He scorned Biden for setting up an "Office of the President-Elect," pointing out that media declarations of his victory were not the final word.

"If after all the questions have been answered it becomes clear that Joe Biden is the legitimate winner . . . we will accept that and will encourage others to accept it, too. We're Americans first; we want what is best for this country. . . . As of tonight, tens of millions of Americans suspect that this election was stolen from them. . . . In a democracy you cannot ignore honest questions from citizens; you're not allowed. You can't dismiss them out of hand, as crazy or immoral for asking. . . . We need to find out exactly what happened in this election."

He cited all the affidavits being collected by the Trump camp alleging malfeasance and listed the most egregious, including the introduction of fake ballots, votes cast by dead people, and on and on. Carlson said, "All of that is real. We spent all weekend checking it." This was rhetorical legerdemain. Although it was "real" that such claims had been made, it was not true that any of them had been substantiated. Following Carlson's logic, it is certainly true, or "real," that some people still claim the earth is flat, never mind those pictures from space.

Carlson warmed up. He showed a clip from a press conference in which Gabriel Sterling denounced claims of fraud in Georgia. Only, the thrust of his remarks did not interest the pundit. At the beginning of Sterling's talk, he had allowed the inevitability of *minor* instances of fraud.

"We are going to find that people did illegally vote," he had said. "That's going to happen. There are going to be double voters, there are going to be people who shouldn't, did not have the qualifications for a registered voter to vote in this state. That will be found." He added that these were common in every election and that the chances of finding enough to change the results were "unlikely."

From this passage, Carlson chose to repeat emphatically for his millions of viewers, *We are going to find that people did illegally vote. That's going to happen.* Then he leaned on it hard. "That is the official account, before even counting the vote, from a key swing state in the middle of a contested election," Carlson said, as if this made his larger point. "And of course you can believe it because we've already found illegal voting"—no, they had found *claims* of illegal voting—"So much for those claims that *voter fraud never happens!* Of course it happens. They knew it happened when they told us it would never happen because they're liars. So we know that for sure."

Then he admitted Sterling's point that the instances of fraud were, "so far," not enough to overturn the election, but added, hopefully, "of course that could change."

And thus were the hopes of millions stirred. Hoopes, for one, counted on it.

"This is all a show . . . by the Media," Hoopes posted on November 7. "I am on the phone with Trump lawyers," she posted earlier that day. "There are lawsuits everywhere. NO PRESIDENT HAS BEEN DETERMINED." So many lawsuits. So much smoke. Surely, there was fire. She received 174 likes, and 29 shares.

Trump filed yet another lawsuit in federal court in the Middle District of Pennsylvania to stop certification of the vote. This was two days after Giuliani's strange kickoff press conference. It again argued the inherent deficiency of mail ballots and also essentially adopted the complaints of Hoopes, Stenstrom, and other Trump observers that they had not been allowed to observe the counting process closely enough. It also claimed that state and county officials had created a "two-tiered" voting system, allowing only Democratic mail voters the opportunity prior to Election Day to correct mistakenly filled-out ballots. Pennsylvania's attorney general, Josh Shapiro, called it "meritless," a word echoed in the judge's dismissal on November 21, which characterized it as "strained legal arguments without merit and speculative accusations."

Bob Bauer, legal advisor for the Biden campaign, saw the torrent of legal challenges nationwide as a purely extralegal strategy. It was about spreading misinformation.

"[This] is noise, not really law," he said in a briefing issued by the Biden-Harris campaign. "Theatrics, not really lawsuits." Such statements were to be expected from the Biden campaign, of course, but failure after failure in court lent them credence.

"It's independent judges who are doing the fact-checking," said Ari Melber of MSNBC, "and it ain't pretty. . . . It's harder to lie in court than at, say, a White House briefing. . . . Repeating things that other people say that aren't true, maybe that gets you a retweet, [but] it doesn't go far in court."

Something rarely noted: Fraud on the scale alleged would have been glaringly apparent. America has held elections for more than two hundred years. There are detailed records, particularly for voting from the mid-twentieth century onward, when computers began enabling fast, precise analysis. These data show well-defined patterns right down to individual precincts, information that pollsters and campaign strategists plumb to plan campaigns. Such data are not proprietary; they are public, and remarkably specific. Commercially available software can pair prior vote totals with ethnic makeup, party registration, census data, property tax records, and so on to enable extraordinarily precise analysis. This has long been a familiar part of the election year experience. It is why, for instance, election night calls from major news outlets are nearly always early and accurate—we remember the times when they are wrong precisely because they are so often right. State legislators employ such analyses to gerrymander districts, right down to individual census blocks of anywhere from a dozen people to a thousand—how else to draw such crazy maps? Although no one could call the winner of a very close election, the data did define clear parameters, within which results tended to stay. Significant fraud, even in a single district, would jump out of the norm. It would show dramatically, a red flag signaling the need for a recount or an investigation.

For instance, if a precinct in Philadelphia, Trump's favorite punching bag, had ten thousand more Biden votes than registered voters, those numbers would stand out and could be checked. If a precinct in Arizona, say, 80 percent Republican, had suddenly cast 80 percent Democratic votes, this, too, would stand out. If, as Stenstrom believed, hundreds of thousands of Biden votes had been falsely inserted in Delco's count, it would have significantly spiked the data—there were only about three hundred thousand votes to be had in the county. In fact, Trump had received 1 percent *more* of the county's vote in 2020 than he had in 2016. Biden just got more. And his victory margin was not a sudden leap. It was just a 3 percent improvement over Clinton's and was hardly surprising. Not only was it well within the expected parameters, but it was precisely the change projected in a district that had been turning blue for almost twenty years. In Maricopa County, Arizona, the same thing happened. Biden finished with a victory margin of 3 percent even though Trump bettered his 2016 performance. This was in perfect keeping with a voting trend that had long attracted nationwide attention. Traditionally red Arizonians had two years earlier elected both a Republican governor and a new Democratic US senator. Democrats were gaining. Although historic, Biden's 2020 win there was neither shocking nor suspect. Here and there around the country, there had been shifts, some surprising but nothing that cried out for investigation. Nothing that could not be explained by demographic changes that cut both ways, in Trump's favor here and in Biden's there. Data crunching was imperfect, and pollsters sometimes failed to get an accurate read, but the twenty-first-century election results could no longer stray far from the patterns without attracting notice. By the second week of November, the count was almost completely in, and apart from little Antrim County in Michigan, there were no red flags. Anywhere.

On November 10, the *New York Times* published the results of a survey it conducted of election officials in every state, asking them all, Republicans and Democrats, whether they had seen evidence of fraud capable of overturning the election outcome. These were the people most familiar with voting patterns in their states, the very people who would notice red flags first. None had.

"Top election officials across the country said . . . that the process had been a remarkable success despite record turnout and the complications of a dangerous pandemic," wrote *Times* reporters Nick Corasaniti, Reid J. Epstein, and Jim Rutenberg.

They quoted Ohio's Republican secretary of state: "There's a great human capacity for inventing things that aren't true about elections. . . . The conspiracy theories and rumors and all those things run rampant. For some reason, elections breed that type of mythology."

Hoopes and millions like her still believed what they chose to believe. That day, she posted, "This is about transparency, integrity and really seeing the true numbers. Because I know for damn sure these Republican candidates won by a shit ton!" (45 likes, 1 share). She knew.

Myth or no, the president pressed on. Trump had given up governing. He no longer received daily intelligence briefings, and he spent no time on pandemic issues, national security matters, or clearly, on the pending transition. His efforts to overturn the election consumed him. He raged about it publicly and privately and increasingly inserted himself directly into the fading effort, trying to badger state and local officials to accept his version of events.

Some began to fear he'd stop at nothing to stay in office, including using military force. On the 10th, he fired his defense secretary, Mark Esper, and replaced several other senior Pentagon officials with his own loyalists. Esper had previously angered the president by publicly disagreeing with his call for troops to put down unrest in American cities— protests and riots had flared the previous summer after a video showed a Minneapolis police officer calmly suffocating a prostrate George Floyd with his knee pressed against the base of his neck. Officers had arrested Floyd for trying to use a counterfeit twenty-dollar bill. Now, with the president's loyalists in place at the Pentagon, some people worried he might deploy troops to prevent the transition.

"This is scary," one unnamed Pentagon official said. "It's very unsettling. . . . These are dictator moves."

Few were ready to believe that Trump would go that far, but his own behavior and wild rhetoric hardly helped calm the waters.

"People will not accept this rigged election!" he tweeted on November 10, pointing his followers to a post from the creator of the comic *Dilbert*, Scott Adams, who had written, "You are being brainwashed to accept the results of the election as fair." Adams had earlier drawn links between Biden and Satan and then fallen back on the excuse that he'd just been joking. He was, after all, a cartoonist.

The next evening, Stephen Colbert, host of *The Late Show*, comically framed what had become, for many, a real possibility. He characterized Trump as "a toddler too hopped up on sugar to go to bed. There's no reasoning with him at this point. You just have to let him tire himself out and wait until he falls asleep on the kitchen floor and hope he hasn't conspired with the dog to stage a coup. . . . Buckle up, buddy boys, because getting this guy out of office is going to be a bumpy ride."

A possible justification for summoning troops would be evidence of foreign interference in the election. Trump was all in for that. On November 12, he plugged a report from One America News Network, which promoted the Chavez/Iran/China/Germany theory: "REPORT: DOMINION DELETED 2.7 MILLION TRUMP VOTES NATIONWIDE."

That same day, Chris Krebs, head of the US Cybersecurity and Infrastructure Security Agency, established by Trump himself two years earlier to contend with internet-launched threats, directly contradicted him. Krebs's statement was brief: "There is no evidence that any voting system deleted or lost votes, changed votes, or was in any way compromised."

Trump would fire Krebs but could not resist twisting the statement to his benefit.

"For years the Dems have been preaching how unsafe and rigged our elections have been. Now they are saying what a wonderful job the Trump Administration did in making 2020 the most secure election ever. Actually, this is true," Trump said, "except for what the Democrats did. Rigged Election!" Somehow, this was supposed to make sense.

Anyone who denied the reality of The Steal swiftly joined all the other suspects in The Swamp. This wasn't just about Donald Trump versus Joe Biden. You either stood for Trump, or against America.

"This is a spiritual War . . . period," Hoopes posted on November 12 (101 likes, 1 share).

Trump urged his supporters to protest in person, and eleven days after the election, thousands did. Hoopes was among them in Washington, DC, as they marched and chanted, "Four more years!" and "Stop The Steal!" She posted lots of happy pictures. The old campaign juices still flowed. This thing was not over.

On November 9, US Postal Service special agents Russ Strasser and Chris Klein entered a room at the Erie post office and found mail carrier Richard Hopkins sitting in a chair, shaking.

As they sat down, Strasser reviewed Hopkins's rights, reassuring him he could leave anytime or just sit silent. And he looked for soothing personal connections from the moment Hopkins signed the rights form.

"Your signature, dude," Strasser said, laughing.

"I have the worst handwriting ever."

"I would say I want to give you a run for your money, but you win. Sorry, you win."

Hopkins laughed.

Strasser turned to the carrier's background. "I understand you were a marine," he said.

"Yes."

"Thank you, thank you for your service."

"Yes, sir."

"I was air force. So, so, I got to fly over you."

"Oh, you were a pilot?"

"I was not a pilot."

"Air crew?"

"I did intel. Forward intel."

"Yeah, I was a 5952 navigational aids technician."

Strasser asked whether in the swirl of lawyers now surrounding Hopkins—Trump lawyers, Project Veritas lawyers—Hopkins had anyone representing him personally. "Because if you did, I would make whatever efforts possible to have that person here," he said.

No lawyer, Hopkins said. So Strasser continued, "Boy, enough legalese, right?"

"I actually enjoy learning about legal stuff," Hopkins said. He had studied criminal justice in college and once applied to become a police officer. "It's the reason why I went into criminal law. I actually took a lot of psych, because I wanted to be, like . . . ."

"A lot of it *is* psych," Strasser said.

He asked if Hopkins felt comfortable.

"I'm still shaky, so that's why I'm like, 'Oh!,'" he said.

"Nerves don't bother me one bit," Strasser said. Calm. Friendly. "I think that I would be more concerned if you weren't nervous. So don't feel like you have to put up any front with me."

With the slenderest threads of a relationship established—two military vets with messy handwriting and an interest in criminal psychology—Strasser began to gently coax from Hopkins his story, which turned out to be very different from what the public had heard.

"I think you and I are going to find out that we are pretty similar on some things," Strasser said. "But beyond the core—I don't want to say this because I don't want to insult you, but I'm just going to insult you, and then we'll deal with it later, okay?"

"All right."

"Beyond the core, there may have been a little embellishment. And I just want to make sure that there hasn't been, and I just want to make sure if there is, we get rid of that right now so that anything that goes on after this, like I said, you're standing on solid ground. Fair? You understand where I'm coming from?"

"Yes," Hopkins said.

Strasser came to the heart of it: Hopkins's allegation that his postmaster, Rob Weisenbach, had committed voter fraud. "Right now, at the starting point, tell me exactly, not interpretation, exactly what you heard and if you heard some words clearly and some words not, that's fine with me. But right now, let's get exactly what you heard."

"All right, the one I know for sure, like I said, I just happened to peek out at the end of it. They saw me, so they walked away afterwards—"

Strasser stopped him. "So we're gonna rewind thirty or ninety seconds before that."

Hopkins began again. "I'm sitting there casing, and I overhear something about the fourth ballots that were picked up on the fourth."

"So you heard the words 'fourth ballots'?"

"The ballots picked up on the fourth."

"'Ballots picked up on the fourth.' That's what you heard?"

"Yes."

"Okay. And then?"

The interview continued this way, in general, with Hopkins wandering through vague or confusing statements, and Strasser drawing him back toward specifics.

Eventually Strasser announced he'd like to walk with Hopkins to another part of the post office. "Okay," he said, "tell me if this will make you uncomfortable. I want to do a field trip real quick. Do you mind if I walk with you to your casing station? Do you mind if we do that?"

"Sure."

At one point as they moved through the facility, Hopkins seemed perplexed by the agents' authority to come and go. "You don't have to buzz out?"

In the casing area, the men split up. Strasser positioned himself where Weisenbach and a supervisor had stood during their supposed illicit discussion, and Hopkins entered his casing bay. In a conversational tone, Strasser said, "Can you hear me?"

Hopkins didn't respond. Strasser raised his voice. "Can you hear me now?"

"Yeah," Hopkins said.

Strasser joined him. "How loudly would you say they were talking?"

"Like an average conversation like you and me. Yeah."

"What we just did there—and I spoke like this—the first time I said anything you could not hear me."

Back in the interview room, Strasser asked what bothered Hopkins most. The conversation he had overheard or something else?

"I would say the conversation," Hopkins said. "The fact that I heard that, based on my assumption on what I could hear, was that they were postmarking them the third that were picked up on the fourth."

Hopkins rambled a while about how he had voted for Trump but otherwise had libertarian leanings, and Strasser listened a long time. Hopkins had already betrayed himself and didn't realize it. Finally, Strasser spoke.

"So I'm going to drill down a little."

"Okay."

"Because you said something very significant, you may not have realized it," Strasser said. "You said, 'what I assumed I overheard.'"

"Yeah. Because I didn't specifically hear the whole story. I just heard a part of it and I could have missed a lot of it."

"I'm shaving away everything down to the narrowest truth," Strasser said. "The reality is—and please don't let me put words in your mouth—the reality is, you heard words and you assumed what they were saying."

"My mind probably added the rest. I understand that, I understand how hearsay and listening . . ."

"It seems so basic, but that's how important it is."

"And that's why I was really mad when I heard that people were giving Rob death threats because that's fucked."

Hopkins's story had crumbled. He hadn't overheard anything about backdating ballots. The conspiracy existed only in his head. In his head and in Project Veritas's video.

"I wanna talk Project Veritas for a second," Strasser said.

Hopkins said he had not actually written the affidavit he signed about Weisenbach committing fraud—Project Veritas had. They had warned him, too, not to speak with anyone else about what he had seen. If any journalists came asking, they said, Hopkins should let Project Veritas "vet" them first. Then they showed him how to set up a GoFundMe account, he said. Later, GoFundMe closed Hopkins's account and refunded donors' money, so he created a similar page with the crowdfunding site GiveSendGo. It quickly shot to more than $236,000, which Hopkins withdrew.

The entire exercise was a well-paid charade, from the first allegation to Project Veritas's exposé, to Lindsey Graham's call to the Department of Justice and the president's lawsuit citing Erie in federal court. The fraud alleged not only didn't happen, it could not have happened. Among almost 50,000 mail-in ballots counted in Erie, only 129 arrived late. Of those, only two came through the Erie post office. Postmaster Rob Weisenbach could not have defrauded anyone if he had wanted to.

Toward the end of Hopkins's interview with the agents, he revealed—it's unclear whether by accident or on purpose—that he was recording them with his phone. He did it at Project Veritas's behest, he said, and "I'm sorry I'm letting you know now." Project Veritas later released the audio, characterizing it as evidence the agents coerced Hopkins into recanting his story.

Looking at his phone, Hopkins seemed to notice how much time had passed during the interview. "Holy shit!" he said. "I'm never going to get that route started."

"No," Strasser said. "You're not."

GEORGIA

Atlanta attorney Lin Wood, who had earlier labeled Jordan Fuchs a "Wicken," filed suit in federal court to stop the certification of Trump's loss. During a three-hour virtual hearing on November 19, Judge Steven Grimberg—a Trump appointee—rejected Wood's argument with velocity: "The fact that his candidate didn't win doesn't rise to the level of harm."

The judge said Wood's request "would require halting the certification of results in a state election in which millions of people have voted."

Moreover, the judge said, "It harms the public interest in countless ways, particularly in the environment in which this election occurred. . . . To halt the certification at literally the 11th hour would breed confusion and potentially disenfranchisement that I find has no basis in fact or in law."

At that point, with 99 percent of the state's votes counted, Biden had been declared winner by the media but was ahead by only 10,353 votes in Georgia, or two-tenths of a percentage point. It was a margin that Trump and his supporters considered erasable. The president had named former Georgia congressman Doug Collins, who had stepped down in a failed attempt at the US Senate, to lead the push for a recount. The state's two Republican US senators, Kelly Loeffler and David Perdue, both faced a runoff election in January and had bound their fates to Trump.

Secretary of State Brad Raffensperger had promptly refused their demand that he step down.

"The voters of Georgia hired me, and the voters will be the one to fire me," he said. "Politics are involved in everything right now. If I was Senator Perdue, I'd be irritated I was in a runoff. And both Senators and I are all unhappy with the potential outcome for our President. But I am the duly elected Secretary of State. One of my duties involves helping to run elections for all Georgia voters. I have taken that oath, and I will execute that duty and follow Georgia law."

Raffensperger found support from Lieutenant Governor Geoff Duncan that was at first timid. Duncan had always enjoyed Trump's favor, mostly based on appearances; before running for office, Duncan had played professional baseball, and the forty-five-year-old had the hewn waist and jaw that Trump felt befitted a rising political star. The thought of speaking against the president at first nauseated Duncan, and he joined his boss, Governor Brian Kemp, in issuing a mush-mouthed statement about Raffensperger. It started with a soaring line: "Free and fair elections are the foundation of our American government" but landed on a vague insinuation: "We trust that our Secretary of State will ensure that the law is followed as written and that Georgia's election result includes all legally-cast ballots—and only legally-cast ballots."

Duncan knew the insinuation of *illegal* ballots was a spell Trump hoped to cast. A hoodwink. So a couple of days later when a CNN host asked Duncan about voter fraud, he offered a firm declaration: "We've not seen any sort of credible examples."

John Porter, Duncan's top adviser, saw trouble ahead. With his sandy hair swept to the side, framing pinkish cheeks, he looked younger than his thirty-seven years; but looks were deceiving. He was considered one of Georgia's shrewdest political operators.

He cautioned his boss that the thing wasn't over yet in Georgia. From his office, he could see into the capitol's great central atrium, where Raffensperger held regular press conferences to fight back against the tide of disinformation, and he had already announced that the state would conduct a recount of every vote by hand.

Trump tweeted, "Georgia will be a big presidential win, as it was the night of the Election!"

Porter noticed that the crowd at Raffensperger's press conferences kept growing. Right or wrong, it looked like the secretary of state was beginning to flail. Porter warned Duncan that Trump had set himself against Raffensperger and that Duncan didn't want to be "tied to that whale. The sinking whale."

But Duncan, to Porter's chagrin, continued lashing himself to the whale at every opportunity. He trusted Raffensperger, he trusted the electoral process, and he defended both against President Trump's claims.

Scrutiny of elections is high, even in the best of times. But now in Georgia, it had reached an absurd intensity. Things had gotten weird. Even the most innocent occurrence—a misstep, a gesture, an unexpected turn—found a global audience of critics, conspiracy theorists, and bad actors.

Take the leaky urinal, for instance, that had temporarily flooded the counting center at the State Farm Arena early on Election Day. To Rick Barron, director of elections there, it had seemed just a plumbing mishap, no big deal. But in the digital ether, a theory had taken shape that Barron and his workers—remember Ruby Freeman and her daughter Shaye Moss?—had *staged the leak* to create cover while they wheeled out cases of Trump ballots and wheeled in Biden ones. If you could imagine it, it might be true!

The president thought so. He tweeted, "Why did the Swing States stop counting in the middle of the night? . . . Because they waited to find out how many ballots they had to produce in order to steal the Rigged Election. They were so far behind that they needed time, & a fake 'water main break', to recover!"

Just before ten-thirty on election night, Barron had told his workers at the State Farm Arena to go home. They packed up tubs of uncounted ballots for the night. Journalists and observers left.

But then Secretary Raffensperger sent word: "Hey, guys, why are you quitting so early? You need to continue."

So the workers had hauled the tubs back and resumed counting into the wee hours. This packing-up and restarting had nothing to do with the morning's urinal leak, but amateur cyber sleuths reworked and conflated the incidents. They analyzed the architecture of the arena, pored over security video the county posted online to ensure transparency, compared time stamps—and all of it, they claimed, coincided with an uptick in votes for Biden. They began harassing Barron, his staff, and their extended relatives for answers. A Facebook investigation by a group called Patriots for America 1776 offered "evidence," a still from security video of Ruby Freeman, with her big Afro, and her daughter, with her long blond braids, doing their job, which involved carrying trays of envelopes.

"For everyone out there still claiming that there is 'no evidence' of election fraud, what do you call this?" the group asked its thousands of followers. "Why would Freeman and the other ballot counters who were present sneak out suitcases full of ballots after everyone who was there to monitor them had just been told to go home because of a pipe burst?"

The leaky toilet had become a skeleton key to a palace of conspiracy. And the hand holding that key belonged to Freeman, grandmotherly proprietor of Lady Ruby's Unique Treasures, and now lead villain. Later a "confession" attributed to her rocketed around social media, describing crimes she masterminded with her daughter: "I posted this on my Facebook page and wanted to share it with the instagram community," Freeman purportedly wrote. "I am so proud of my baby because today we did something that change history and we decided we will not be silent and allow evil to control this country. I was shocked, hurt, and deeply upset to see how many people support evil, racism, and ignorance while counting many ballots for Donald Trump. I was almost in tears seeing how very few people wanted to support a black women become the first female Vice President or a excellent man named Joe Biden while counting the ballots."

"Freeman" expresses dismay at the landslide of votes for Trump. Then: "My baby knew how racist Georgia was and we knew how the vote was gonna go so we resorted to plan B and now you see the results of my brilliant baby. Joe Biden is now the winner and I'm looking at all of Georgia with a side eye because I know for a fact that Georgia voted for Trump by the largest numbers and if we didn't do what we did he would have won Georgia."

It didn't matter that the confession was cartoonish or the evidence clearly concocted. Or even that the accompanying mug shot featured a different woman altogether. It confirmed the preferred reality for many Trumpists, and they passed it along. Lin Wood, the inventive Georgia lawyer, tweeted an image of the fake confession and tagged some of the most influential people in Georgia and the country, urging others to target all of the state's top officials. He later deleted the post, saying, "It is very difficult to know who can be trusted" and that the confession had "not been authenticated." But more shot had been loaded into the blunderbuss.

There was a sense in Georgia's halls of power that the scrutiny had turned predatory. Everyone felt jumpy. When Gabe Sterling gave the press some mistaken information, then corrected it three hours later, Porter lost his cool. He pulled the lieutenant governor aside, warning him again to keep his distance.

"This is about to become a huge mess," he warned.

He contacted Fuchs, the deputy secretary of state, with a fiery message. Referring to Sterling's misstep, he said he wanted advance notice next time there was a hiccup. He reminded her, "my boss is out there vouching for your boss."

Increasingly, that risk felt more than political. It felt personal. Physical. Thanksgiving came and went, and Porter noticed the police presence grow at the capitol. Key figures moved through the offices with larger and larger security details. The lieutenant governor had long ago stopped parking in his spot on the open Liberty Plaza side of the building, using instead a more secure entrance to the capitol. Porter had inherited his boss's old parking spot, the first one outside the capitol's east entrance. It suited him and his white Ford fine, until he noticed a growing number of people watching him as he got in and out of his truck.

As days passed, the onlookers grew more aggressive, confronting him.

"What are you doing?" someone shouted, repeating Trump's demands that the Georgia state government illegally overturn the election. One day, a group of four or five men approached as he got out of his truck. They weren't dressed for legislative business. And they looked angry.

"Are you going to have a special session?" one man asked.

It was a case of mistaken identity, Porter realized. The parking spot was still marked "Lt. Gov," and people didn't know what Duncan looked like. Porter was taking abuse meant for his boss. He dodged the group of men and hustled up the stairs, ducking into the capitol building. *This isn't going to stop*, he thought.

After that he started parking in a public lot a few blocks away and walking to the capitol through the mix of commuters and protesters on the street.

MICHIGAN

Trump developed a curiosity about some of Michigan's more obscure public servants.

In mid-November, for instance, the Wayne County Board of Canvassers met to decide whether to certify the vote there, including Detroit. Other boards in counties across the state did the same, after which a state-level board would certify the Michigan election as a whole. All the boards included two Republicans and two Democrats, and in Wayne after a first vote, the decision stood at 2–2. The Republicans voted against certification and the Democrats for it. By the end of the meeting, though, after hearing from outraged members of the public and discussion among board members, they updated their vote—they certified the election unanimously.

In the midst of the waffling, though, Trump campaign attorney Jenna Ellis posted a tweet that illustrated the political front of Trump's strategy in Michigan and elsewhere:

BREAKING: This evening, the county board of canvassers in Wayne County, MI refused to certify the election results. If the state board follows suit, the Republican state legislator will select the electors. Huge win for @realDonaldTrump.

It wasn't true, and nothing in Michigan law provides for its legislature to make such a decision. But legislatures in Michigan and other battleground states were predominantly Republican; and here, Trump saw a path to retaining power, if he could just get state and local officials to see it his way. He caused an uproar in Michigan by inviting its two most powerful members, Senate Majority Leader Mike Shirkey and Speaker of the House Lee Chatfield, to Washington, DC. There, at the Trump International Hotel, Chatfield and friends enjoyed at least one $500 bottle of Dom Pérignon champagne.

Minutes after the board of canvassers voted in Wayne County, its Republican members, Monica Palmer and William Hartmann, walked out to her SUV. The meeting had lasted well after nightfall and had stirred up anger from every direction. Now in the cold and dark, they walked quickly into the night. Palmer's phone rang. A call from Washington, DC. Strange.

"Hello?"

It was Ronna Romney McDaniel, she said, chair of the Republican National Committee: "I'm here with the president."

Palmer stepped into the driver's seat of her SUV. Hartmann climbed into the passenger's seat. Palmer put the call on speaker so Trump could talk to them both.

Trump asked if they had a safe ride home, she said.

"It was very, very touching," she said later. "I'm in Michigan, and the president would call me to make sure I'm okay? That was very touching."

Did it strike her as unusual that a president of the United States might phone a minor functionary in Wayne County, Michigan, simply to make sure she had a safe ride home? "No, no," she said.

Did they discuss the vote?

"Um, I—we didn't have a conversation about the vote at all," she said.

No discussion at all?

"We didn't talk about the details of the canvass."

But somehow, Trump had worked magic. The morning after the call, both Republicans signed affidavits saying they wanted to rescind certification of the vote.

The affidavits carried no legal weight. But Trump's strategy pivoted on a fulcrum in the middle of his lawyer Ellis's tweet: "If the state board follows suit. . . ."

All eyes, then, turned to two previously unnoticed members of the Michigan state board of canvassers: Norm Shinkle and Aaron Van Langevelde, the board's Republicans. The parlors and halls of power in Lansing echoed with speculation about how the two men might vote. They presented two very different profiles. Shinkle, seventy, was near the end of his career as a steadfast Republican. But Van Langevelde was forty and presented more mystery. He tended to keep his opinions to himself, which was disconcerting. But he also had much of his career before him as a Republican; surely, he wouldn't throw it away by going against Trump.

On November 23 in Lansing, the state board met in a gray-carpeted room. A few photos of beach scenes hung on the walls but only drew attention to the otherwise white, windowless expanse.

Shinkle seemed to signal a secret solidarity with Van Langevelde with an early remark: "I don't know about my Democrat colleagues, but I know Aaron and I have received quite a few comments, outright threats, nasty emails telling me my family is at risk," he said. "I had one person even suggest, 'Shinkle, you've got to vote yes to certify for the safety of your family.' So we've been through that."

Van Langevelde remained unreadable behind his mask. Near the end of the meeting, after hours of public comment, he lowered the mask; with his slender build and stubbled jaw, he could have passed for a law student in class. But he spoke with professorial authority.

His first words gave hope to his fellow Republicans:

"I want to be clear about one thing. I think any allegation of voter fraud should be taken seriously and investigated. I believe in this case a post-election audit should be conducted. And I believe complaints of election fraud need to be investigated and if found must be prosecuted under the law."

He paused, looking briefly at papers before him. "State law is clear that we do not have that authority, and other entities do," he said. "And I encourage those state officials to act and do what they can to preserve election integrity. But this board must respect the authority entrusted to it and follow the law as written. We must not attempt to exercise power we simply don't have. In this case, the law is absolutely clear. We have a clear legal duty to certify the results of the election as shown by the returns that were given to us. We cannot and should not go beyond that."

He had offered no rhetorical flourishes. No references to the welfare of his family or his career. But in conclusion he did appeal to the history of democracy. "John Adams once said, 'We are a government of laws, not men.' This board needs to adhere to that principle here today," he said.

A clerk called roll, and the board members voted on whether to certify the vote.

Jeannette Bradshaw? "Yes."

Aaron Van Langevelde? "Yes."

Julie Matuzak? "Yes."

Norm Shinkle?

Shinkle leaned back in his chair and rubbed a hand across his chin. "Abstain."

The vote sealed a victory for Biden in Michigan. Reflecting on it later, Shinkle seemed baffled by his younger colleague's defiance in the face of enormous, splintering adversity from his own party. He insinuated that Van Langevelde had buckled under threats from the left, not the right.

"I mean, he's got kids in elementary school," he said later. "They walk outside their house and his wife was in fear of her life and their lives. I mean, it was as bad as it gets, and I don't care who you are, that affects you."

In his telling, Van Langevelde, not he, had made the craven choice.

"He said he voted yes because he had to, he was bound to," Shinkle said. "I think the wife told him, 'You vote yes or I'm leaving.'"

ARIZONA

Clint Hickman continued to hear howls of fraud from protesters in Maricopa County, and he continued to push back. Instead of just feeling insulted by Trump's accusations and those of his hordes of followers, the old egg-industry spokesman put his professional public relations skills to work. He listened. He nodded empathetically. Lots of the criticism came from fellow Republicans, his friends, and colleagues. Maybe there was something to one or more of the complaints leveled at his supervision of the election. Until he'd had a chance to hear all the evidence, he made it clear he was keeping an open mind.

But after nearly two weeks of this, after carefully considering every accusation, after questioning his staff, and after a laborious hand count of the ballots, Hickman was convinced. The count was accurate. A statistical analysis of the county's voting results, which looked at predictable patterns based on standard deviations and historical ones and which would flag things like ballot stuffing or machine rigging, showed it well within the anticipated range. There were no anomalous events. The outcry over fraud was nothing more than an expression of disappointment. Most charges revealed no more than ignorance of the process. He knew these people didn't want to hear it, but he planned to do his job. His own integrity was on the line.

The president wasn't making it any easier. On the 15th, Trump tweeted another sweeping indictment of the election, embracing several of the primary threads in The Steal's argument. He began by seemingly acknowledging Biden's victory:

"He won because the Election was Rigged. NO VOTE WATCHERS OR OBSERVERS allowed, vote tabulated by a Radical Left privately owned company, Dominion, with a bad reputation & bum equipment that couldn't even qualify for Texas (which I won by a lot!), the Fake & Silent Media, & more!" But later he clarified, "He only won in the eyes of the FAKE NEWS MEDIA. I concede NOTHING! We have a long way to go. This was a RIGGED ELECTION!"

In an effort to turn down the volume, Hickman drafted a second letter on the 17th and linked to a "Fact Page" to back up his assertions in detail:

> Members of the Board of Supervisors continue to hear from government leaders and the public about the integrity of Maricopa County elections. We want to assure you that proper steps have been taken to ensure a full and accurate count of all votes.
>
> Here are the facts:
>
> - The evidence overwhelmingly shows the system used in Maricopa County is accurate and provided voters with a reliable election. On Election Day, fewer than 200 ballots had an over vote [a ballot in which a voter made more than the allowable choices] on the presidential race out of more than 167,000 ballots cast.
> - The Dominion tabulation equipment was vetted by a bipartisan, "Equipment Certification Advisory Committee" before the contract was finalized. As required by law (A.R.S 16-442), the committee tested the functionality and accuracy of tabulation equipment before it was used in any Arizona elections.
> - The Dominion tabulation equipment met mandatory requirements during logic and accuracy testing before the Presidential Preference Election, the Primary Election and the General Election. And after each of these 2020 elections, the hand count audit showed the machines generated an accurate count. (See Fact Page)

- Last week, the Elections Department conducted the mandatory hand count of Election Day ballots from two percent of vote centers and 1 percent of Early Ballots as required by Arizona law and it yielded a 100 percent match to the results produced by the tabulation equipment. All three political parties participated in the hand count audit. This is a statistically significant sample of thousands of votes, which would have caught irregularities.
- There are triggers in Arizona law to require another hand count or even a recount in the case of a close contest. None of those thresholds have been met during the 2020 General Election.

More than 2 million ballots were cast in Maricopa County and there is no evidence of fraud or misconduct or malfunction. Board members listened to and considered many theories about the election results. We asked, and continue to ask critical questions of County staff and none of these theories have proven true or raised the possibility the outcome of the election would be different.

The Board is required to canvass the election by November 23, 2020 (A.R.S 16-642). It is time to dial back the rhetoric, rumors, and false claims. I appreciate the efforts of our elections staff who worked tirelessly to run this election during a pandemic. No matter how you voted, this election was administered with integrity, transparency and in accordance with state laws.

Thank you,

Clint Hickman
Chairman, Maricopa County Board of Supervisors

Hickman wanted his letter to demonstrate how seriously the board took allegations of fraud. *This is your government at work. Just give it time.* In retrospect, it all seemed incredibly naive.

The board convened the next morning to conduct its usual business, nothing to do with the election. Because of COVID health rules, only three of the supervisors were present, and the session was not open to the public. Nevertheless, an angry crowd assembled outside the locked doors, shouting, banging on drums, chanting the usual things, hurling insults, and making threats. Hickman could hardly hear himself talk as the meeting got under way. They whipped through their agenda quickly.

They saved the big issues for Friday evening, when the board would meet to officially "canvass" the county's vote, to assure themselves that the election results were accurate, and then to vote whether to certify them.

The allegations were getting wilder. A federal judge would dismiss the last of the lawsuits filed in Arizona seeking to reverse the election results in a few weeks. One had come from eleven prospective Republican electors, joined by Kelli Ward, the state's Republican Party leader and an ardent Trumpist. They had alleged a plot, popularized by Sidney Powell, that had been hatched in Venezuela more than a decade ago by that country's late dictator Hugo Chavez. The upshot was that software used by Dominion's machines had been altered to switch votes cast for Trump to Biden. This fantasy persisted despite being debunked by Trump's own campaign staff. Over county attorney Tom Liddy's repeated objections, the judge had decided to allow the plaintiffs to present it. The story rested on the claim that Dominion had worked as a consultant to Chavez. This turned out to be false. The company had not done any business there, consulting or otherwise. Chavez's regime had, in fact, worked with one of Dominion's competitors. The plaintiffs also made much of the fact that Texas had opted out of using Dominion software for the 2020 vote, calling it inefficient and error-prone. Liddy showed that the software in question was three generations older than the one Arizona employed and had been designed specifically to correct the earlier problems. These and other arguments raised by the lawsuit were so rooted in what Liddy had called "dystopian fiction" and error that they were laughable.

US District Court judge Diane Humetawa was not amused. She had given the plaintiffs their day in court and seemed to regret it.

"Allegations that find favor in the public sphere of gossip and innuendo cannot be a substitute for earnest pleadings and procedure in federal court," she wrote. "They most certainly cannot be the basis for upending Arizona's 2020 election."

Judicial censure had no effect on The Steal movement. The usual crowd of loud dissenters was present outside the county supervisors' auditorium in Phoenix when the canvass meeting convened that evening. It would be televised and offer a chance to address all of the accusations being thrown around.

It was a big moment. Maricopa County was arguably the pivotal district in the 2020 presidential sweepstakes. It had significantly tipped the outcome for Biden, which put the board of supervisors at the center of more than just a local storm.

Hickman and the other supervisors were conscious of the broader audience and planned to use the occasion to publicly grill the county election's codirectors, Rey Valenzuela and Scott Jarrett, and county lawyer, Liddy. And Hickman, even after his letter, was prepared to delay certification of the results if the answers they gave fell short.

Bill Gates was one of the Republican supervisors. Short and square and resolutely uncontroversial, a man more immersed in the currents of state water policy than national politics, he was accustomed to being mistaken, online, for the *other* Bill Gates, the one with a multibillion-dollar software empire. Just recently, anti-vaxxers had targeted his Twitter feed, angry over the worldwide philanthropic campaign to combat the pandemic with vaccines, the one led by the other Bill Gates. Maricopa County's Bill Gates had grown up in Glendale and graduated from Harvard Law School. A lifelong Republican at age fifty, he had a long record of public service, on the Phoenix city council and as vice mayor of the city. His day job was general counsel for a local company that manufactured golf equipment. He was acutely conscious of that night's remote audience and had come with lawyerly intent. He had been peppered all week with texts from Kelli Ward. She had apparently zeroed in on him as the board's weak link, one possibly willing to toss a wrench into the pending certification.

"Sounds like your fellow Republicans are throwing in the towel," she wrote him and then added the very Trumpian trope, "Very sad and un-American."

Then, "Why can't we wait a few days? What's the harm?"

She wanted all the conspiracy theories followed up, which would take some time, particularly because more were added every day.

For Gates, this meeting was a chance to elicit answers and to deliver his own ringing response to the pressure campaign. He was convinced that each delay just produced new reasons for further delay. And with the literal drumbeat of The Steal outside their door, delay was clearly a tactic. Anything that slowed the normal process sped the notion that something wasn't right. One way to convince the public that things were right was to faithfully adhere to correct procedure. He felt manipulated and bristled at being called, along with his colleagues, "un-American." This was not a charge he had ever expected to face. Nevertheless, if only to satisfy Ward and her ilk, he would put his courtroom skills to work on Valenzuela and Jarrett. He wanted to raise all the questions election critics were asking. The cameras would record their answers for all to see. If it took all night, they'd stay there all night.

The small auditorium was an eerie calm at the center of the storm. With only a handful of observers in attendance, all of them masked and well-spaced according to the COVID guidelines, voices faintly echoed. Blond Clint Hickman in his blue suit and blue tie sat at the center of the dais backed by a dark blue curtain and the flags of the United States, Arizona, and Maricopa County. He called the meeting to order and invited Valenzuela and Jarrett to give a presentation.

Jarrett began, somewhat nervously, thanking the board for having appointed him eighteen months earlier and "asking me to work in collaboration with Mr. Rey Valenzuela, to establish a best-in-class election department for Maricopa County." Jarrett was a pale, slender young man with a broad forehead topped by a crisp line of thick, short brown hair, dressed in a plain gray suit, the very picture of an earnest functionary, a man happily engaged in the actual machinery of government and quietly proud of his own unheralded importance and competence. It wasn't often that he got a chance to show off his expertise before a large audience, and he came ready. Boring logistics were his métier.

"And I am absolutely confident that we have been able to do that, and this election is an example of that," he said. "I would not bring forward to you a canvass that wasn't done for an election without great integrity, great transparency, great efficiency over the process. I assure you that this election was done with accuracy, and as we go through this presentation, I'm confident that you will feel the same way."

He reviewed the major hurdles they had overcome, notably the pandemic, which had required them to completely redesign the process to both speed the voting and to allow voters to cast ballots safely. He pointed with pride to the fact that despite these challenges, the 2.1 million county voters who cast ballots were 400,000 more than had voted in 2016. The total turnout had been 80 percent, the highest since Ronald Reagan had ridden an enormous conservative wave into the White House in 1980. He parsed in tedious detail the process they had followed, the rigorous bipartisan testing of the process, and the steps to ensure the computers counting these millions of votes were isolated from the myriad cyberthreats—including glass-encased servers with visible wires stretching directly from servers to the tabulating computers, none plugged into a wall that might lead to an outside connection. For the better part of an hour, he broke the system down. Valenzuela, seated behind him wearing a gray mask, frequently nodded agreement. In time, Jarrett's voice registered the weariness of wading through minutiae, the nearly absurd lengths meant to ensure even to the most skeptical observer that the count not only *had not* been counterfeited but *could not be*. Backing up all the digital layers were, after all, the physical ballots and a live video feed that recorded every step from beginning to end.

Looking for a possible avenue of contamination, board vice chairman Steve Chucri asked about the process by which results from various polling centers were transported, on memory cards, to the main counting center. Jarrett explained the procedure and noted that only one of the two encrypted memory cards (both with tamper-proof evidence seals) was transported, so that the results on one card could be double-checked against the other as well as the precinct ballot report they had generated. Backing up that memory were, of course, the actual ballots that had been run through the machine. These records, the memory cards and the ballots, were sealed and delivered by "two members of different parties," Jarrett said, escorted by county sheriffs, and then stored in a cage that was monitored by cameras continually.

When Jarrett finished, Hickman asked to make a brief statement. He spoke in his high-pitched, boyish voice to everyone watching the session from home.

"If people who are watching this right now, if their eyes are glazing over—this is so important," he said, calmly pleading. "It's so important, because some of these processes were given to us by the state legislature, [unintelligible] 24-7, some of it was processes developed over twenty years of experience, some of it was developed over mistakes. . . . So I just want people that are watching this and hearing this . . . We don't glaze over. We don't glaze over as a board."

Interjected Chucri, "Nobody's eyes should ever glaze over. With all [that people] have said about democracy and fair elections, they ought to be paying attention and watching this meeting. So you've got to put your money where your mouth is."

Hickman and Chucri were touching here on a fundamental feature of The Steal, and of conspiracy theories in general. Ignorance. Few who are not directly engaged in running a complex system understand how it works, and fewer still have the patience to acquire understanding—their eyes "glaze." Conspiracy theorists play on this. They begin with distrust: Only a sucker believes the official story. They then replace the often tedious, mundane details of an intricate process—the ever-evolving preferences of Arizona voters, the details of collecting and tallying their ballots—with a simpler narrative, theft. They invent colorful stories that nonexperts can readily grasp—a deal struck with a late Venezuelan dictator to deliver tainted election machines, or a plot to preprint fake ballots in the dead of the night—to fashion an alternate narrative with its own logic and arcane archive. Around it forms what cognitive scientists have termed "a community of knowledge," a process greatly assisted by the internet. Within this community, believers are impervious to argument, expert opinion, and even hard facts. There was no way that those beating drums outside the county government center would be swayed by experts like Jarrett and Gonzales, or by any analysis of shifting demographics.

Hickman soldiered on. He still believed in his system and those who worked for him. He was determined to counter every crazy allegation. He asked his election directors about something else that had surfaced on social media, another Marko Trickovic production. The activist hadn't fully discarded his false claims about Sharpies and three days after the polls closed had posted another scoop. With his sculpted beard, his sunglasses perched over the beak of his gray cap, he had stood before the windows of a defunct polling place. Inside what appeared to be an empty store were several voting machines, off in a corner.

"Those are actual voting machines," he said with alarm, "where they actually scan ballots into. They are left completely unattended. . . . We don't know if those machines have actual ballots inside of them. But this is just to show you whether or not, if anything, it's sheer, utter incompetence from the Maricopa County Elections Board. Because this is unacceptable. It doesn't make any sense. I don't know why they would leave these things here."

He plugged his earlier video, "that broke the whole thing with the Sharpies bleeding through and messing people's ballots up"—here, he had changed his original claim that machines could not read Sharpie-marked ballots. "This is absolutely ridiculous, we need to get to the bottom of it, but stay tuned, we're going to try to document everything, we're not touching anything, we're not doing anything, but we need to get to the bottom of it."

Either Trickovic never did get to the bottom of it or was disappointed by what he learned, because he didn't post about it again.

But given the circumstances, Hickman was not going to leave it hanging.

"Look, here is election equipment sitting here overnight in this empty storefront," he told Jarrett, referring to the image in Trickovic's post. "Is this where they are transmitting the votes? . . . So tell me about that."

Jarrett gave a little smile, a cat presented with a trapped, wriggling mouse.

"First, I'd like to say, the details are incredibly important about how we process—all of our processes. . . . We have 175 vote centers. . . . The equipment is able to stay there because we have the ballots. We have the memory cards back." In other words, the machines at that point were empty shells. They had done their work, their vote counts "secured in our ballot tabulation center, in our vault, or in that cage that is under a camera with the original hard copy ballots," Jarrett explained. "The equipment is not vulnerable at that point in time. And not needed for us to tabulate ballots. [With] 175 vote centers, it is common to take us a week to pick up that equipment."

The meeting plodded on and on, a live dissection of the process, its rules and redundancies, the subtleties of certification, of adjudicating overvotes and undervotes.

"So, in that case, if someone voted for Joe Biden and Donald Trump, then it just doesn't get counted?" Chucri asked.

Jarrett explained that the vote would not be counted for either candidate but would be noted and recorded as an overvote.

"When you go back to the ink," Chucri asked, "you know, the Sharpie versus the ballpoint, is it, do you think it's better that we just don't use the ballpoint?" He referenced the tendency of ballpoint ink to gum up the machines. "Would you think it's better just to use Sharpies going forward?"

"Yes. Absolutely." He advocated ultrafine tip Sharpies, which create less bleed-through. "It doesn't impact tabulation, but it does impact in the voter's experience."

There was a lot more. At the end of Jarrett's presentation, Hickman, a disappointed Trump voter himself, had another prepared statement to make.

"I continue to hear from government leaders and the public about the integrity of Maricopa County elections," he read. "My own office has received 180 handwritten letters and over 4,000 emails and nearly 3,000 voice mails. I listened to and considered all theories about what might have happened, but let me be clear. There is no evidence of fraud or misconduct or malfunction in Maricopa County. And that is with a big zero."

He said all of the lawsuits filed over the election had "fallen flat" when asked to produce facts. After seeing the evidence, the Trump campaign and the Arizona Republican Party stated for the record in court that there was no allegation of fraud or cheating and that there was no mathematical way that the outcome could be affected.

Liddy, who had been defending the county in court, rose several times to summarize the Dominion voting machine case and others. One of the suits, filed by the Trump campaign alleging that the county had mishandled ballots, had been dropped when its lead lawyer, after reviewing the evidence, had gone to the trial judge to ask that it be dismissed. Liddy, who had been handling election law for the county for twenty years, said that this election had been the best he had ever seen.

Then Bill Gates had his chance. He had prepared for the session like an attorney prepping for a deposition.

"Mr. Chair, like you said, I've had a lot of the same volume that you have in phone calls and emails. . . . One of the other issues that people have brought up, and I hate to bring this up, I'm getting allegations of dead people voting. . . . Can you please assure the voters of Maricopa County that dead people did not vote in this election?"

Valenzuela said that the county had a "robust system" of checks on voter registration. They work off a statewide voter registration database that is shared by other government departments, such as vital statistics (with morbidity records), vehicle registrations, the court, so that it tracks not only deaths but felony convictions in real time.

"Could they cast a ballot before they pass?" Valenzuela asked. "Absolutely. And we do have that. So we do have some folks who say, we know this individual is deceased on November 3 but cast a ballot on October 7.

Arizona law allows for that. But somebody who's deceased on October 7 who cast a ballot on November 3. We don't have any evidence of that occurring. We hear that as folklore . . . so when we usually say, 'please, please, give me a voter ID,' because we have yet to get a voter ID of somebody who has."

Gates then asked, "First of all, were there Dominion personnel who were at the elections department able to move about freely? Can you speak to that? Because that's another thing that I've heard about."

Jarrett took Valenzuela's place at the podium and said that yes, there were Dominion employees working in the tabulation center. His confirmation all but clinched the deal for those convinced that the company had devious ends, so perhaps his explanation of *why* they were there registered little.

"They are the subject matter experts," he said. He described it as a private-public partnership, the kind of thing that had been encouraged, particularly by Republicans, for decades and cited examples of it throughout Arizona, for instance the Phoenix airport: "We don't have city of Phoenix employees flying planes," he said. "We have these private companies that bring in their planes, they hire the pilots. . . . We as passengers trust that these experts are going to get us to our destination safely. And that is the case with Dominion. These individuals know the software better than us. . . . We rely on their expertise in order to ensure that we have a—we can provide an accurate, reliable election for Maricopa County voters."

Liddy got up to reiterate that the claims leveled at Dominion software by Trump campaign lawyers had targeted outdated software. About the updated version, "No evidence of any legitimate criticism at all," he said. Valenzuela then stood to explain that the ballots used had not been provided by Dominion but had been designed by and for Maricopa County. The company experts were there not to conduct the election, he said, but to service balky machines.

Gates and the other supervisors continued to patiently review all the questions they had heard in the previous weeks. "I can go all night," Hickman said again. To address theories about changes in Dominion software, they traced the history of the machines, noting that changes were, in general, necessitated by human errors that had caused prior miscounts. It was not a conspiracy, said Hickman, but an evolving process.

Hickman began to wrap up the hearing by giving, in essence, a valedictory to his difficult year as chairman, which he said he was eager to give up in just forty days. He said he had been disappointed by some of his fellow citizens, "but I am not going to violate the law or deviate from my own moral compass that some have pushed me to do." He thanked Jarrett, Valenzuela, and his staff for their loyalty and help.

Gates then offered an impassioned statement, which would go viral on the internet. He praised the election officials and noted that he had asked all the "tough questions" he had gotten from his constituents, "and I am satisfied by the answers."

"The reason that I am here is because I was inspired by my grandfather, who was a World War II vet. He went to Europe to fight for democracy." Gates admired his grandfather, who with only a high school diploma, became a learned man, who would ask him, as a boy, if he had read the day's newspaper and, if the answer was yes, would engage him in discussions about world events and often enough change his mind. Shortly before his death at age ninety-six, Gates's grandfather and he had taken a trip together to the newly unveiled World War II Memorial in Washington, DC.

Gates continued, "And Mr. Hickman referenced the fact that I am a lawyer, and when I became a lawyer, I took an oath to support the Constitution and the laws of the United States and the state of Arizona, and then, when I was fortunate enough to become a member of this board, I again took an oath to support the Constitution, and the laws of the United States, and of Arizona. And we may all be disappointed by what happened in this election, but that's not what we are supposed to be focused on here as a board of supervisors. We are to be focused on whether or not this count was done properly. And whether it was done with integrity.... This group of individuals [referring to Jarrett, Valenzuela, and their staff] has gone beyond what has ever been done before in the state of Arizona, with two full logic and accuracy tests ... the hand count has been done, a statistically significant hand count, tens of thousands of [ballots] that have been checked, and there's no errors. And finally we have heard about the Dominion software. We have heard that this was done in an accurate way, and frankly, those people who have problems with this software have had multiple opportunities to go to court to present evidence. And the courts have found that there are not any issues that should keep this body from deciding today. So based upon everything that I've heard today, I believe that there is no reason that we should refuse to fulfill our statutory duties and certify this election today."

At the end, all five supervisors voted to approve. Within months, Trump supporters would erect a guillotine outside the Arizona state-house, calling for their execution.

When the meeting concluded, Gates overheard sheriff's deputies offering to escort Jarrett and Valenzuela to their cars. The protesters were still raising Cain outside and were sure to be fired up by the vote. Gates's own car was in a garage that he could reach indoors, and he felt relief. He was struck by this. Here were public servants who needed a security escort on a Friday night in Phoenix, Arizona, just to cross a parking lot to their cars. For doing their job.

It didn't feel like America.

And that ought to have been the end of it for Maricopa County. All the questions had been asked and answered. The votes had been counted and recounted. Every procedure had been followed to the letter. It was over.

A few nights later as Gates walked his corgi, Steve, about a mile from his home in Phoenix, he received a call from Karen Fann, president of the Arizona state senate. Gates respected her as a hardworking lawmaker. She was about sixteen years his senior and owned a construction company. He considered her solid, a woman who had her feet in both government and commerce.

"Hey, Bill," she said. "We know there's nothing to this, but we need to do something. Could you guys do an audit? If you could do that, that would be great. That would really help us. Are you open to that?"

PENNSYLVANIA

On November 17, Pennsylvania's supreme court knocked down one pillar of The Steal's argument. Like Hoopes and Stenstrom in Delco, observers in Philadelphia had objected to being corralled too far from the vote-counting process to actually inspect individual ballots. They wanted to be close enough to inspect each mail ballot for themselves, which they defined as *meaningful* access.

The ruling had a direct impact only in Pennsylvania, but leveled an indirect blow to the same argument being raised in other states. Election officials dealing with high volumes of mail ballots had automated the process and set what they considered suitable distances between observers and counters—human and machine. There were concerns about social distancing because of the pandemic and also concerns about maintaining the secrecy of the ballot: the problem of watchers being close enough to see how individuals had voted. There were also safety concerns about getting too close to the machines, which had fast-moving parts, some of which were sharp.

A Philadelphia judge had upheld these precautions on Election Day, when Trump lawyers had sued to get closer, noting, "Watchers are not directed to audit ballots or to verify signatures, to verify voter addresses, or to do anything else that would require a watcher to see the writing or markings on the outside of either envelope, including challenging the ballots or ballot signatures."

Trump's legal team had appealed to the next judicial level, and two days later, that became the latest of the legal challenges to be swatted away. Pennsylvania Commonwealth Court judge Christine Fizzano Cannon did, however, offer Trump a fillip. She ordered that observers could move to within six feet of the counting. That order was immediately appealed by the city, setting the stage for the state supreme court to define "meaningful."

It did so days later, essentially affirming the first ruling and overturning even the small concession granted by Fizzano Cannon. "Meaningful" access did not mean inspecting every ballot. Under governing law, it ruled, poll watchers were "permitted to *remain in the room* in which the absentee ballots and mail-in ballots are pre-canvassed. . . . While this language contemplates an opportunity to broadly observe the mechanics of the canvassing process, we note that these provisions do not set a minimum distance. . . . The General Assembly, had it so desired, could have easily established such parameters; however, it did not."

So monitoring the count did not require the level of inspection sought by Hoopes, Stenstrom, and others, who wanted the same proximity as the old precinct-level hand counts. Election officials were within their rights to cordon poll watchers off in a corner of the room away from the machines.

That same day, November 17, Giuliani appeared in federal court in Williamsport to repeat his claims of nationwide fraud and to ask that Pennsylvania's election results be scuttled. His case had been severely weakened before the hearing even started. Despite the wild allegations being made everywhere else, all fraud claims in this lawsuit had been dropped by Trump's lawyers at the last moment. It was becoming apparent that the crusade was on legal footing so flimsy that it could damage an attorney's reputation. Just days earlier, Porter Wright Morris & Arthur, a respected Washington, DC, law firm that had prepared the case, had backed out. It was one of several such big-salaried law firms to withdraw from further representation of the president. The heat was being felt even within Trump's inner circle. Matt Morgan, general counsel for the campaign, had cut the fraud claims from Giuliani's case after Porter Wright had withdrawn, telling his White House colleagues, "I am not going to lose my fucking law license because of these idiots." Giuliani evinced little such concern for his own standing, and even though he had not argued a case in court for years, he stood up before Judge Matthew W. Brann himself.

His lawsuit now rested entirely on the stories of two GOP voters who claimed they had not been afforded the opportunity to make corrections to their mail ballots. This complaint, like most of those among Giuliani's mountain of affidavits, amounted to little more than a precinct-level squabble. Brann seemed bewildered by the magnitude of the celebrated lawyer's ask.

"You're alleging that the two individual plaintiffs were denied the right to vote," said Brann, "but, at bottom, you're asking this court to invalidate more than 6.8 million votes, thereby disenfranchising every single voter in the Commonwealth. Can you tell me how this result can possibly be justified?"

Giuliani narrowed his target, saying he was asking that only 680,000 votes be thrown out, and then shifted the focus of his complaint. He said Republican poll watchers had not been allowed to meaningfully observe the counting—the argument just rejected by the state supreme court. Pressed by Brann to justify his sweeping claims of fraud, Giuliani did an about-face. "Tossing a fake" before a federal judge had serious repercussions.

"This is not a fraud case," Giuliani said.

Mark Aronchick, an attorney representing several Pennsylvania counties, accused Giuliani of living in "some fantasy world" and of pushing allegations that were "disgraceful in an American courtroom."

The judge booted the case. He characterized it as a "Frankenstein's Monster . . . haphazardly stitched together" and the remedy it proposed, "unhinged."

Such legal pratfalls were increasingly embarrassing. Former New Jersey governor Chris Christie, a Trump ally and longtime Giuliani friend, called their legal crusade "a national embarrassment."

Giuliani phoned him to complain, but Christie was not apologetic.

"Rudy, this is ridiculous; you need to stop," he told him. "What are you waiting for, man? If there's all this evidence, what are you waiting for? Christmas? Don't wait. Time to put it out there."

Whatever the merits, the state was obliged to take seriously all formal accusations of election fraud. In response to a criminal affidavit filed by Leah Hoopes, recounting the "criminal" activity she believed she had witnessed at The Wharf, two state agents stopped by her house to follow up. Hoopes was not at home, so the agents spoke to her teenage son and then phoned her. She referred them to her lawyer. Even though she described them as "polite" and she had instigated the investigation, she interpreted it as harassment:

"If this is an attempt to silence law abiding, honest citizens, this mission has failed considerably," she posted (228 likes, 207 shares).

Two days later, Giuliani appeared at the Republican National Committee headquarters on Capitol Hill, unabashed, accompanied by Sidney Powell. Billing themselves as "an elite strike force team," they held a bombastic press conference. Away from the courtroom, they were back to arguing that yes, the central issue was fraud. Powell reiterated the debunked theory that election results had been manipulated by the Dominion Voting Systems. Then Giuliani called the Biden team "crooks" and saluted the "patriotic and brave American citizens that have come forward" to reveal "mass cheating," a pattern of fraud that had taken place in states around the country. With brown hair dye running down both cheeks under TV lights, he claimed to have assembled enough evidence to "fill a library" and accused the "censored press" of covering it up—although his press conference, like his previous one, was being broadcast live. His evidence showed a nationwide conspiracy, he said, because the same complaints were being raised in all of the key states.

"Almost *exactly* the same pattern," he said. "Which to any experienced investigator [or] prosecutor would suggest that there was a plan from a centralized place to execute these various acts of voter fraud, specifically focused on big cities . . . controlled by Democrats." Citing mail ballots, "particularly prone to fraud," Giuliani talked about ballots being entered without inspection, again repeating the claim rejected by the state supreme court two days earlier. He decried the separation of outer envelopes, with voter identification, from the secret inner ballot, claiming that the outer envelopes were not inspected (which is false; each had a barcode with voter information, which was scanned, and the voter's signature) and then thrown away "for eternity" (also false; the envelopes were kept). Hammering back on the meaningful observation claim, he said that poll watchers had been "pushed" out (again, false).

Hoopes basked in it. She was in the front row. Music to her ears. Speaking truth to power. She wrote, "Past 2 days have been incredible."

She had been pounding away on Facebook, but despite the persistence of Trump's lawyers and his own unflagging tweets, the cause seemed to be losing traction. She felt herself in the political wilderness besieged.

"I have to say that 18 months ago I would never have seen my life this way. My intent was to get involved in my community, and advocate for those who feel they are unheard. . . . I believe that people in my circle or that surround me have the same heart and intentions that I do, but in the end, they prove themselves to not have my heart at all. What I truly have witnessed is the lack of loyalty, integrity, and the valuing of human life. This truly breaks my soul. . . . What we are witnessing and are unfortunately a part of, is a spiritual War. A fight between good and evil. As of right now, I have a human being and a few others who literally use their time to try and destroy my name and make false accusations. . . . Why all this effort when all I am asking is for the truth and transparency?"

Her Republican neighbors and the local party leaders were moving on. As the lawsuits crashed and burned and as Biden assembled his cabinet and prepared for the changing of the guard, complaints that the election had been stolen were sounding increasingly crank. Some of her fellow local Republicans asked her to step down from her position as committee woman. "Look at that bipartisanship happening here in Delco," she posted. "Republicans and Democrats both want me to resign as a Republican committee woman. Looks like I am a diplomat after all." People acted like she was loony. She posted a video from her car explaining that she had *not* been forced to resign and would not.

Hoopes wrote, "In need of some prayers. Guidance, safety, and strength! Faith has led me here and no turning back!"

It looked bleak.

Then—*mirabile dictu!*—validation. It was like a scene from a movie. On the 25th, the day before Thanksgiving and the day after Pennsylvania certified its election results, a hearing before Pennsylvania's Republican

Senate Majority Policy Committee, spurred on by the colorful and ambitious Trumpist state senator Doug Mastriano, commanded the national stage. It was more of a rally than a hearing. The committee had no role in election oversight and could not even introduce legislation. The purpose was clearly to drum up support among state lawmakers for some undefined move to upend the election, to further belief that the election had been stolen, and in no small part, to promote Mastriano's fledgling campaign for the governorship. Whatever its purpose, the hearing afforded Rudy Giuliani a quasi-official platform for his Blunderbuss Strategy. He was going to, at last, as Christie had implored him to, *put it all out there.*

Spotlights! Cameras! An array of beaming lawmakers! An enthusiastically supportive Gettysburg crowd. Apart from the few rather sour-looking faces of the lying press in the front row, there was electricity in the room. Biden had picked Pennsylvania's electoral pocket! The truth was finally going to come out! Trump had promised to attend in person!

The event was televised live nationally on a number of platforms.

State senator David Argall, the committee chairman, kicked off with a veiled swipe at Democratic governor Tom Wolf, whose aggressive public health efforts during the pandemic had branded him a tyrant among the stubbornly maskless. Argall emphasized that he and the others arrayed around him were, unlike Wolf, servants of the people, "agents of public opinion." He noted the "massive numbers" of phone calls and emails he said his office had received complaining about the election, thus framing the hearing as a popular revolt against a tyrannical effort to suppress the popular will. Mastriano, a big, bald, jovial man wearing a fat silver paisley tie, went further. The session was "historic," one that would amount to "a turning of the tide." He said that in the balance hung nothing less than the very idea of America, articulated so brilliantly by Abraham Lincoln at that very place: a "government of the people, by the people, for the people." Everything was at stake. Sustained applause and cheering.

The senators had invited Giuliani and his team to show their hand. He launched into his now practiced litany of imputation. He assured the friendly row of lawmakers that he was at long last going to lay it all out. The disgraceful tactics in Pennsylvania that his witnesses would describe were identical to those in six other swing states. He damned mail ballots again specifically, on principle. He said they had enabled "a party that had become pretty expert at voter fraud to really go wild." He was fed up with mainstream media stories that said he had presented no evidence of fraud. He had affidavits by the hundreds. Today, his army of brave whistleblowers would step out of the shadows.

And what expert had Giuliani chosen to kick off his examination of the election in Delco? Not elected county councilwoman Christine Reuther, who had taken up the burden of managing it and labored for many months; not Howard Lazarus, who had taken down the outer wall of The Wharf to winch the giant new sorting machines into place and found the workers to man them; not Gerry Lawrence of the board of elections, who had been overseeing votes there for more than fifteen years; not Tom McGarrigle, the county's Republican leader; nor John McBlain, the former council president and attorney for the Republican Party who had obtained a court order to gain observers greater access to the counting center; nor Val Biancaniello, the Trump Lady.

Mastriano intoned, with biblical grandiloquence:

"Leah, please come forth."

And there she was, Leah Hoopes, patriot, warrior, at center stage, heavily made up, straight blond hair framing her big-eyed slender face. She stepped from the shadows of dismissal and disdain, calm and focused as she leaned into the mic to speak her truth.

"My name is Leah Hoopes. I'm from Delaware County, Pennsylvania. I was a poll watcher on the day of election, and I was also present at the counting center in Chester, Pennsylvania. So, first and foremost, thank you to this committee and all those involved, and especially Senator Mastriano and former mayor Rudy Giuliani. To our fearless and brave president, thank you for being our shield and putting us first, and I am forever grateful."

She said it was an "absolute honor" to "finally have an opportunity to speak about what took place. . . . I feel as an American that it is my duty to help protect the integrity of our elections, not just for me but for every American."

She talked about how she had become involved, from Donald Trump's fateful escalator descent and promise to "take back our country." Her rhetoric was forceful; she was about to reveal shocking truths. What she offered was this: The county council and election board in Delco were both majority Democrat. Grant money to purchase new voting machines had come from the civic philanthropy of "Google and Mark Zuckerberg." More pop-up polling places and ballot collection boxes had been placed in the county's urban areas where there were more people than in rural townships, where there were fewer voters. The county's election machine supervisor was a "Bernie Sanders delegate." The old counting center had been moved from the Media courthouse to The Wharf, which was surrounded by "a huge parking lot." She named the corporate owners of the property ominously. Assigned viewing positions at the counting center were inadequate, and election officials were uncooperative when asked to change them in mid-counting. It had taken a court order to grant them access to the "back room," where they found what one might arguably expect to find at a vote-counting center, boxes of ballots.

All of these things were true and not especially surprising, but viewed through Hoopes's lens and Giuliani's, they were "evidence." The Democratic majority on the council and election board meant that "lying hacks" were in charge. The "Google and Zuckerberg" grant money to purchase sorting machines hinted at big-money liberals providing rigged devices. Placing more ballot boxes where more people lived amounted to delivering more Democratic votes. A "Bernie Sanders delegate" was perforce corrupt. Moving the counting center to a large, isolated building gave fraudsters privacy to commit their crime. The assigned viewing positions prohibited observers from spotting false ballots. The closet contained, at least according to Stenstrom, Delco's *real* votes, while the great show of sorting, opening, and scanning the fake ones was taking place to fool observers out front.

Hoopes was just getting warmed up. Her facts may not have been explosive, *sans* lens, but her tone was hot.

"We have stuck our necks out, have been intimidated, threatened, bullied, have spent countless hours away from our families, friends, and jobs. . . . I'm here for one thing only and that is to speak the truth. This is not about party; this is about my country. Every American deserves transparency, truth, and to be able to question those in power without fear of intimidation, bullying, or backlash. I hope this committee takes action if needed, and justice will be swift to anyone involved in fraudulent activity. The Republic is angry, disgruntled, tired, beaten-up, and ready to defend this country."

Murmurs of "Yep" and "Yes" and then applause.

"Thank you," she said, acknowledging the approval. "Without election integrity, we are just another Banana Republic."

More applause.

Then big, square-jawed, broad-faced Greg Stenstrom took over. Speaking with impressive exactitude and clarity, he led the lawmakers through his litany of Election Day duplicity, the separation of envelopes from ballots, the lack of closer access to pre-canvassing workers, the introduction of USB V cards outside the approved chain of custody, the mass of unopened ballots in the "back room"—citing his count of 60,000–70,000. For this event he added the claim, denied by the county board of election and baseless—although curiously exact—that forty-seven USB V cards "are missing." Stenstrom summed up his turn by saying that no one in good conscience could certify the numbers reported out of Delco.

That was just the start. One after another, Giuliani's eighteen witnesses presented "evidence" that amounted to little more than comments about difficulties encountered on or around Election Day. Most of the complaints were about access. Like Hoopes, other Trump poll watchers still felt they should have been closer to those handling ballots, close enough to actually check each of the hundreds of thousands of them for themselves. There were several who, like Stenstrom, believed the things they observed *might have been* evidence of deep fraud. Some brought sophisticated hypotheses, like Phil Waldron, who with formidable technical proficiency, testified that the voting machines used in Pennsylvania "were built to be manipulated."

He had scant evidence that this had actually happened, however, beyond pointing out curious "spikes" in readouts of the vote count that indicated they were operating beyond their capabilities. It might have been that they had been pushed to do more faster.

Gary Phelman, the man who had sought to be Trump's "eyes and ears" in Philadelphia on Election Day with his golden pass, told of being disrespected at the polling place in South Philly. Barbara Sulitka described her confusion over the printout she received after casting her ballot in Erie County for the president. Olivia Jane Winters described her rude encounter with a Philadelphia poll worker. A few complained about long waits and noted confusion over new rules governing mail ballots. Viewed objectively, nothing of importance emerged. Not a single witness revealed a thing to prompt a story or headline. Yet Argall, the state senator, enthused that it had been "the most important public hearing ever held by this senate committee."

No one questioned any of the witnesses searchingly. No one tried to determine where Phelman's golden pass had come from or if it in fact did entitle him to observe at the polling place that evicted him. He offered to pass it around, but there were no takers. No one attempted to find out if Sulitka's ballot had actually been scanned. No one bothered to note that even if Stenstrom's claim about the missing forty-seven USB drives were true, it would not compromise the vote count since the machines—the primary counting method—had recorded the image of every ballot scanned. In other words, no one scratched the surface of any witnesses' story. Why? The most obvious answer is that none of it was significant enough to bother.

Minus the indignation and histrionics, the entire exercise was more like a complaints bureau session than Giuliani's promised sweeping indictment. It was a fair assumption that no one beside those participating would ever sit through all three hours of it. But exhausting viewers was the point. It wasn't what the witnesses said so much as how many of them there were. Despite his assertion that the same tactics had been coordinated nationwide, Giuliani made no effort to mold any of them into an intelligible plot. How, for instance, did Waldron's suspicion that the voting machines had been hacked square with Stenstrom's belief that the Democrats had preprinted a hundred thousand or so Biden ballots in advance? Why jigger with the machines if you already had counterfeit ballots?

The epoch-making importance of the session was sealed by a phone call from Trump himself. He had backed out of attending personally, but he wanted to salute the witnesses, one and all, as "fantastic people . . . great patriots." He assured those present and listening that "we won it by a lot" and then offered his own scattershot testimony.

"We have many, many cases of people walking in, looking forward to voting," only to be told, "'I'm sorry, but you've already voted.' In all cases for Biden, by the way. It's a disgrace . . . people were getting two and three and four ballots in their home, people that were dead were signing up for ballots. . . . The whole world is watching us. We can't let them get away with it. And we have judges that are afraid to make a decision. We have hundreds and hundreds of affidavits . . . more votes than you have voters. But that was the least of it. . . . This was going on all over. . . . It's a very sad thing for our country to have this. This election was lost by the Democrats; they cheated."

There was loud applause, but Trump apparently couldn't hear it on the telephone connection because he plowed straight ahead.

"You're doing a tremendous service. This is a very important moment in the history of our country. Bad people, they're horrible people, people that don't love our country. . . . We're talking about numbers far in excess—they went absolutely wild and they just stepped on the gas and they got caught. We have to turn the election over. All we need is to have some judge to listen to it properly."

He thanked Giuliani for "having the courage to do this. . . . This is going to be your crowning achievement because you are saving our country."

Nothing resulted. The Pennsylvania contest was over. But it served the larger purpose of blowing wind into the sails of The Steal—a state legislative hearing! Real witnesses! Testimony, albeit by phone, from the president of the United States! Every little bit helped.

It felt monumental to Hoopes. She posted exuberantly on her Face-book page, "Today was worth all its weight in gold. Never give in to the hate, intimidation or anyone telling you to stay in your lane. Thank you to all the supporters . . . for having my back. Thank you to Greg Stenstrom for believing in me and standing by me! To my husband and son you are my rock! All you Americans. This isn't over."

In the wilderness no more, Hoopes's star turn brought her interviews and speaking invitations. She appeared on Newsmax's *Wake Up America* with Rob Schmitt—"Poll Watcher from PA Speaks Out"—and Steve Bannon interviewed her and then saluted her on his broadcast *The War Room*.

"I'll take a Leah Hoopes every day of the week over some elite from Davos [a reference to a recent world economic forum in Davos, Switzerland]. This is the difference, and I say this all the time. Would you rather be governed by the first hundred people that showed up to a Trump rally with red ball caps on, or the top hundred partners at Goldman Sachs, or McKinsey, or the first hundred people that walked in, the badge-holders at the world economic forum in Davos? Who would you rather be governed by? Who would you rather be governed by? To me it's pretty straightforward. Leah Hoopes. More common sense, more grit, more patriotism than all of the elites in the United States of America."

Hoopes posted a video of her testimony on her Facebook page, along with a shot of her posing with Giuliani, his arm around her shoulders. For his part, the emphatic Stenstrom would briefly become a star in the Trumpist-sphere, appearing on Fox TV's *Lou Dobbs Tonight* and on *Hannity* as one of several guests Sean Hannity promised would at last provide evidence of The Steal. Stenstrom's statement would later be part of the big Supreme Court filing being prepared by the state of Texas to overturn the whole thing.

GEORGIA

Secretary of State Brad Raffensperger felt danger.

A state trooper guarded him at all times, but he worried about his family. One evening in late November, he and his trooper had just left his house to pick up dinner when his phone rang.

His wife, Tricia, sounded upset: Someone had just broken into their daughter-in-law's house while she was out. The Raffenspergers' son had died a couple of years earlier, and they felt protective of his widowed wife and their grandchildren.

Raffensperger blurted out, "Someone broke in the house?"

The trooper, thinking Raffensperger meant his own home, whipped the car around and gunned it back. Living with fear had made the secretary of state hyperalert so that as the vehicle wheeled around, he took note of the out-of-state plate on a truck that flew past them, and then spotted a car that also had out-of-state plates.

Back at the house the family regrouped. The break-in might have been random or might have been a message. The front door and garage doors had been left open. Objects in the house had been rearranged.

Another trooper left to follow up on Raffensperger's tip about the two vehicles. He found them parked together and approached the drivers.

What are you doing here?

"We heard that the BLM [Black Lives Matter] might be coming by your place," one of them told the trooper, referring to the secretary of state's home. "So we just wanted to see if you needed any help."

They said they were Oath Keepers, members of a far-right, pro-Trump militia that would soon play a role in the January 6 attack on the US Capitol.

"No, we've got it under control," the trooper told them. "You can move on now."

After that, the Raffenspergers vacated their house for a few days.

Radical Trump supporters also harassed ground-level election workers, none of whom enjoyed police protection. Ruby Freeman was in hiding, for instance. Ralph Jones, who helped oversee voter registration, had endured vile online messages, slurs, and threats. Then one night a group of men knocked on his door, claiming to be his new neighbors. They were white. Jones, who is black, had never seen them before. No one new had moved into the neighborhood. He refused to open his door and told them to come back in daylight. He never saw them again.

4

Pressure

Trump celebrated Thanksgiving at the White House, nervily calling it the first of his "second term." On the second to last day of November, he tweeted, "NO WAY WE LOST THIS ELECTION!"

In his first lengthy interview since losing, Trump telephoned Fox News anchor Maria Bartiromo. It was a chummy conversation. Bartiromo was less a journalist than a coconspirator. Clearly excited to have him on her show, she allowed the president to ramble through nearly all the contentions in his Blunderbuss Strategy, interrupting frequently, not to question him but to voice agreement.

"The whole world is watching, and nobody can believe what they're seeing," Trump said. "You start with these machines that have been suspect—not allowed to be used in Texas. The Dominion machines, where tremendous reports have been put out. We have affidavits from many people.... They had 'glitches.' A glitch is supposed to be when a machine breaks down. Well, no, we had 'glitches' where they moved thousands of votes from my account to Biden's account. And these are 'glitches.' So they're not glitches. They're theft. They're fraud, absolute fraud."

He once more lamented the evaporation of his election night lead as mail ballots were counted, blaming "These massive dumps of votes" for Biden in the swing states.

As for Philadelphia, "They cheat and they cheat like crazy." Dead people voting. People casting multiple mail votes. He suggested that the FBI and Department of Justice might have been "involved." He then smeared Hunter Biden, the president-elect's son. He said the press was suppressing facts. He claimed there were fraudulent ballots with Biden votes. "Tremendous numbers of ballots like that." Backdated ballots. He had tons of proof: "Hundreds and hundreds of affidavits," he said and referred to the Gettysburg hearing he had phoned in to the previous week. Stuffed ballot boxes. COVID was used as an excuse to stuff the boxes. "Everybody knows that."

Bartiromo added her own, referring to "impossible statistics."

"Biden magic," she called it, echoing the president's disdain. She raised the question of whether computers like Dominion's were capable of circumventing election controls. (Months later, she would be named with a swarm of other air talent at Fox in a $1.6 billion lawsuit by Dominion for spreading demonstrably false claims about the company. Dominion also filed suits against Newsmax, and other Trumpist platforms.)

"This country cannot have fake elections like we have fake news," Trump said.

Neither he nor Bartiromo paused to actually drill down on a specific claim. Nor did Giuliani or other high-profile Trumpists. Proof was of secondary importance. It was quantity that mattered. So many. It was why they seized on every pretense, no matter how minor, speculative, contradictory, or preposterous. If you strongly believed the election had been stolen, then it mattered little whether you could prove this one or that one. They had cumulative force. The idea was to buttress a preformed conviction, which is why Trump so often repeated, everybody knows.

Despite its failures in court, where evidence actually mattered, The Steal movement gathered steam through the holidays. Many of Trump's faithful chorus of TV boosters clung to a safer ledge, insisting not that his claims were true, only that they deserved to be investigated. But there was no such hedging in street protests and on the internet. Here, the self-styled patriots wanted election officials locked up or summarily executed. They were traitors. It wasn't just Trump whom they had betrayed; it was America.

GEORGIA

On December 1, state election officials Jordan Fuchs and Gabriel Sterling ate lunch at Manny's, a spot in downtown Atlanta. As Sterling worked his way through a hamburger, tater tots, and Coke Zero, someone forwarded him a tweet that ruined his appetite. A Trumpist had named a twenty-something-year-old Dominion counting machine technician, claiming he had been "caught committing treason" by doing his job.

He showed the post to Fuchs, who pushed aside her falafel. The tweet included a short video of a noose slowly swinging in the wind.

Fuchs had expected something like this and viewed it with detachment. But her lunch partner was less stoic. She looked up to find the skin on Sterling's neck had turned red, then his face.

"I've got to do something," he said. "I've *got* to do something."

They called Raffensperger and told him Sterling wanted to speak out against conspiracy theories and violent threats, and their boss gave his blessing.

So they summoned the press corps and made their way to the capitol steps. Sterling strode purposefully up to the lectern, whipped off his mask, and sighed. Fuchs watched from the wings.

"I am going to do my best to keep it together," he said and took a long pause, then drew out each word slowly, "because—it—has—all—gone—too—far. All of it!"

Trembling with anger, he cited Joe diGenova, a former federal prosecutor and a member of Giuliani's legal team, who had just called for the torture and execution of Chris Krebs, the recently fired cybersecurity czar. DiGenova wanted Krebs, who had been fired by Trump after saying there had been no widespread fraud in the election, "drawn and quartered, taken out in the morning and shot." The violence of the rhetoric appalled Sterling. He called Krebs "a patriot." He spoke about the young election worker who had just been accused of treason and threatened with a noose and whose family had also been threatened.

Then he addressed Trump directly.

"Mr. President," said Sterling, "you have not condemned these actions or this language."

His voice shook.

"Senators, you have not condemned this language or these actions. THIS—HAS—TO—STOP! We need you to step up and if you're going to take a position of leadership, *show some!*

"My boss, Secretary Raffensperger, his address is out there. They have people doing caravans in front of their house. They've had people come onto their property. Tricia, his wife of forty years, is getting sexualized threats through her cell phone. IT—HAS—TO—STOP!

"This is elections. This is the backbone of democracy. And all of you who have not said a DAMN WORD are"—Fuchs had advised him to use a word, and now he did—"*complicit* in this. It's too much. Yes, fight for every legal vote, go through your due process. We encourage you. Use your First Amendment. That's fine. Death threats, physical threats, intimidation, it's too much. It's not right. . . ."

"I don't have all the best words to do this," he said, although his rang in the capitol atrium. Then he addressed the president again directly, in words that would prove prophetic.

"Mr. President, it looks like you likely lost the state of Georgia. We're investigating. There's always a possibility, I get it, and you have the rights to go through the courts. What you don't have the ability to do, and you need to step up and say this, is stop inspiring people to commit potential acts of violence. Someone is going to get hurt, someone is going to get shot, someone is going to get killed. And it's not right. . . . If you want to run for reelection in four years, fine. Do it. But everything we're seeing right now, there's not a path. Be the bigger man here. . . . Step in. Tell your supporters, don't be violent. Don't intimidate. All that is wrong. It's un-American."

After the press conference, Raffensperger called.

"Well, you didn't tell me you were going to say *that*."

Trump came down to Georgia.

He came not to heed Sterling's plea but to double down on the dangerous rhetoric; he came to boost the two senators the angry election official had called out. Kelly Loeffler's and David Perdue's runoff election against Democratic challengers would be held January 5, 2021. Hoping to rally Trump voters, both had joined the president in denigrating their own state's electoral process. Now, at a December 5 rally in Valdosta, the defeated president was going to repay the favor.

That evening, one of the best-connected political operatives in Georgia, Brian Robinson, settled in after dinner to watch the rally on television. His wife and daughter had had enough politics, so he watched alone from the recliner in his living room, where his TV hangs above the fireplace.

Robinson contracts as a crisis consultant, and for weeks he had advised Republicans to stop vilifying election officials. "If we tell our voters their votes don't count, that's a terrible turnout strategy," he said.

With Trump's presidential loss increasingly apparent, the close Senate contests offered, as Robinson saw it, a "perfect message for the middle." The two Republican senators were the last chance for conservative Americans to prevent total Democratic control in Washington. With Biden in the White House and Democrats in the saddle in Congress, who was going to stop the left's progressive socialist agenda? Here was a message tailored for centrist voters, ambivalent about party. And in a pair of races with razor blade margins, those voters would be key.

Robinson watched with rising dismay as Trump, on stage in Valdosta, did the opposite. Instead of lifting the senators, commending the electoral process, and embracing the middle, he spewed his usual list of grievances, trashed valuable Republican election officials, and reiterated—over and over and over—that the vote had been a sham.

Then at last, in the rally's second hour, the two senators stood to speak for just a few seconds each. They were the rally's ostensible honorees, but instead, the crowd *jeered* them.

They're getting booed, Robinson thought, startled. *There's something going on here.*

It felt like a political, and maybe historical, inflection point. This audience had no affection for either candidate or the Republican Party. They tended to one man alone.

As Loeffler spoke, a chant arose.

"Stop. The. Steal!"

"Stop. The. Steal!"

Loeffler quickly handed off the mic to Perdue, and the chanting swelled until it drowned him out. He realized his only hope was to shame the chanters for disrespecting Trump, so the longtime business titan and current US senator, made a savvy—if pitiful—move to cloak himself with Trump.

"Hey, guys, I want to take literally just one second. I want to say something personal to President Trump."

He was drowned out.

"Fight. For. Trump!"

"Fight. For. Trump!"

But he kept at it.

"Hey, guys, I want to say something for President Trump, personally," fighting against the chant. "I want to say something personal for President Trump."

As Perdue struggled, Trump beamed. He couldn't have cared less about the candidates' humiliation. He pumped a fist and pointed at the crowd.

"Fight. For. Trump!"

"Fight. For. Trump!"

Surrendering, Perdue blurted, "God bless you. We love you, Mr. President."

He handed over the mic, defeated. The chant grew louder still, and Trump let it carry on for a half minute, an eternity of adulation at a public podium. During the chant, he turned toward Perdue and Loeffler, grinned and pointed. The message was clear. *This is not about you. It's about me.*

Watching at home, Robinson felt sorry for them. They had done everything Trump had asked, had even echoed his ugliest talking points. But the crowd wasn't interested in electing them; it was only interested in overturning the election for its hero.

As the senators ducked off the stage, Trump made things still worse. He turned to the real subject of his rally: his grievance against the state of Georgia, the futility of voting, and the specific criminality of certain election workers at the State Farm Arena. Sterling's sharp message about danger for election workers had clearly missed its mark.

"We're all deeply disturbed and upset by the lying, cheating, robbing, stealing that's gone on with our elections," Trump said. "We know the Democrats will have dead people voting and you gotta watch it, dead people. You wouldn't believe how many illegal aliens from out of the state and they'll be filing out and filling out ballots for people who don't even exist. They put up names, they have people signing their own name over and over. They have people signing names with the same pen, with the same signature. They don't even change because they know once they get it in it'll never be looked at, it'll never be looked at again because of people like your secretary of state and your governor."

Then Trump did something remarkable. After giving just over a minute and a half of stage time to Senators Loeffler and Perdue, he directed the audience's attention to a "very, very powerful and very expensive screen" and stood aside for six and a half minutes for a video that centered on Rick Barron, the leaky urinal, and the "crime" that had been committed by Georgia's election workers like Shaye Moss and Ruby Freeman.

After the Valdosta rally, still more threats rained down on these state employees like verbal munitions. The messages and voice mails for Barron himself came in so thick that he eventually stopped listening.

The mildest of them said, "When I'm done with you, you'll be in prison."

Others called for Barron's execution in a variety of styles. One predicted, "There will be a riot, I think."

MICHIGAN

In December, an unfamiliar feeling bloomed in Michigan state senator Ed McBroom: doubt.

McBroom lived by faith. He was a thirty-nine-year-old dairy farmer, church music leader, and Republican state senator from the rural Upper Peninsula. When he first heard allegations of fraud in his state, he took them as questions in good faith: *Were* computers flipping votes from red to blue? *Were* there more ballots coming in than were mailed out? And why *did* election workers cover up the windows in Detroit?

People in the Upper Peninsula regarded McBroom as a man who kept his word. Years ago, he and his brother had married two sisters, and they lived in two homes on the family farm. When McBroom's brother, Carl, died in a terrible auto accident in 2018, McBroom could have cashed out the farm and cast himself into his promising political career full-time. But he didn't. He kept the farm and cared for his brother's family, which meant raising a combined thirteen children. He stayed faithful. And to McBroom's thinking, faith—whether in family, an ideology, or God— required a "strong commitment to what's true, no matter what."

So he resolved to find the truth about the election. The best way to check his dairy herd for disease was to roll up the sleeves on his arms and investigate their mouths, their eyes, their udders. And as chair of the senate oversight committee, he resolved to do the same for election fraud.

But during hearings on December 1, as McBroom listened to hours of testimony from witnesses, doubt began to spread in his mind. His fellow Republicans could have brought proof of wrongdoing but instead described contradictory conspiracy theories or insignificant slights by harried election workers. Some did bring pieces of information worth more investigation, but others were plain silly. A temporary local contractor for Dominion, Mellissa Carone, described her particular indignation. "They told me that I would be parking in a parking lot, and I would be shuttled in? Through a shuttle?" Carone told the senators. "I called my mother, and I told my mother about this, and my mom said, 'No, absolutely not. You're not doing that.'"

McBroom drew Trump's ire by not allowing Rudy Giuliani to testify. He was not interested in another reiteration of every cockamamie claim. The hearing was for "folks with first-hand knowledge," he said. So during the proceedings, Trump tweeted to his eighty-eight million followers, "Michigan voter fraud hearing going on now!"

Those supporters, in turn, gathered outside the hearing room's windows and chanted "Four more years" and "Do your job" so loudly that McBroom stopped the proceedings.

He kept his voice level but leaned toward a mic to speak through his mask. "If there is somebody here who has some credibility with the crowd and has the opportunity to share with them that their disorder is only disrupting what they're trying to accomplish, I'd appreciate you taking time to do that," he said. "Otherwise, I'll have to be forced to adjourn the meeting."

Several voices in the hearing room shouted in response. McBroom hammered with his gavel. "If the audience inside also needs that same assistance, we can adjourn the meeting for that reason, too. I have worked hard to put this together, and I would appreciate the opportunity to continue the work and listen."

The crowd, inside and outside, quieted.

The day after the senate's hearing, the house oversight committee held one of its own and did not show the restraint that McBroom had. The committee chair not only allowed Giuliani to testify but ceded the floor to him, allowing Trump's legal champion to question witnesses instead of congress members. Mellissa Carone, who had complained about the shuttle to McBroom, now returned as a star witness. Giuliani positioned her as a Dominion company insider, with technical insight. But in reality she was, according to Dominion attorneys, "hired through a staffing agency for one day to clean glass on machines and complete other menial tasks."

Carone slurred as she spoke to the house committee, berating even Republican representatives. Her testimony drew laughter from the audience, to the degree that Giuliani reached to touch her arm and shushed her.

"Melissa is great!" Trump tweeted, misspelling her name.

To McBroom, it sounded like what he calls "blatherskite," an old Scottish word for nonsense.

He planned to get to the bottom of it.

The call came December 4, a Friday evening. The weekend had started, but Sheryl Guy answered her phone anyway.

On the other end of the line she found sixty-year-old Bill Bailey, an Antrim County real estate agent and fellow Republican.

"We've got an order from the judge, Sheryl," he told her. "We need access to the machines."

What? she thought.

She knew Bailey had sued the county after Election Day but never expected anything to come of it. Now, sure enough, he had a decision from Circuit Court judge Kevin Elsenheimer that Bailey faced "irreparable harm" as a voter.

"Specifically, in the recent election, the Village of Central Lake included a proposed initiated ordinance to authorize one marihuana retailer establishment within the village," the judge wrote, using the spelling for marijuana common in Michigan officialdom.

On Election Day, residents in small Central Lake village had voted for both president of the United States and whether to let a pot shop open downtown, across from the post office. The marijuana vote tied at 262–262, which meant it didn't pass. After the election, during the rescan of Antrim County's ballots, the Dominion machines wouldn't accept three ballots, like a vending machine rejecting a crinkled dollar bill. So two election workers, one Republican and one Democrat, transferred the marks on two of them to fresh ballots. They scanned fine. But the third unscannable ballot was peculiar—it didn't show any mark for or against the marijuana shop and shouldn't have been counted in the first place. It was the statistical oddball inevitable in any election. So the two workers didn't count it as a vote for or against the pot store.

The new total, 262–261, meant that the proposal passed.

The judge wrote, "Plaintiff argues that failure to include the damaged ballots in the retabulation resulted in the marihuana proposal passing and violated his constitutional right to have his vote counted. The temporary, let alone total, loss of a constitutional right constitutes irreparable harm which cannot be adequately remedied by an action at law."

So Bailey and his lawyer, the judge ordered, could access and photograph the county's central computer, Dominion machines, thumb drives, memory cards. And they needed access right away, Bailey said. A team was coming in . . . get this . . . *by private jet.*

"Sheryl, this isn't about you, ya know," he told her. The private jet was a clue that it wasn't really about the pot shop either.

Two hours later, Rudy Giuliani tweeted:

BIG WIN FOR HONEST ELECTIONS.
Antrim County Judge in Michigan orders forensic examination of 22 Dominion voting machines.
This is where the untrustworthy Dominion machine flipped 6000 votes from Trump to Biden.
Spiking of votes by Dominion happenned (sic) all over the state.

Some powerful people had been snooping around on Bailey's behalf. For instance, the lawyer Katherine Friess, a member of Trump's legal team, had called Guy at her office.

"We want to clear your name," Friess told her, according to Guy. She wanted access to Antrim County's equipment. "You want to show that this isn't you."

But Guy knew it *was* her. Her mistake.

"I think she tried to woo me," Guy said. Friess contacted election workers in the townships, too, Guy said, and tried to impress them with tales of recent dinners with Trump and Giuliani.

On Sunday, December 6, Trump's attorney Jenna Ellis removed any doubt about who was behind the push in Antrim. She told Fox News, "Our team is going to be able to go in there this morning and we'll be there for about eight hours to conduct that forensic examination."

Within hours, the team—ostensibly working to bring down a local pot shop—arrived at Sheryl Guy's office from all over the country, led by Dallas-based Allied Security Operations Group, or ASOG. Its operatives arrived and took pictures of the machines, the memory cards, the red canvas zipper pouches in which election workers carried them. Sheryl Guy stood watching from a corner as they moved through her office.

This was a pivotal moment, not just in Antrim County but across Michigan and perhaps the country. If the pro-Trump team could show Dominion machines were vulnerable in some way, they could cast doubt on the election as a whole. Biden won Michigan by an untouchable margin of 154,000-plus votes. But the Trump team planned to stir up enough doubt about the votes that the Republican-led state legislature could step in and simply hand the victory to Trump.

A week after its visit to Guy's office, ASOG released a report about Antrim County that might have had a profound influence elsewhere in the country. More than any other document, it outlined the narrative of a stolen election and, ultimately, undermined Americans' faith in the vote.

It began by succinctly stating the conspiracy theory that would grip Trump and his supporters: "We conclude that the Dominion Voting System is intentionally and purposefully designed with inherent errors to create systemic fraud and influence election results."

The report warned of potential "advanced persistent threats and outside attacks" from hackers and denied Sheryl Guy's admission of her own mistake: "The statement attributing these issues to human error is not consistent with the forensic evaluation, which points more correctly to systemic machine and/or software errors."

Then the report delivered the sentence the Trump campaign hoped for most: "Because the same machines and software are used in 48 other counties in Michigan, this casts doubt on the integrity of the entire election in the state of Michigan."

Shortly after the report's release, Trump tweeted, "WOW. This report shows massive fraud. Election changing result!"

Immediately after that, Trump directed aide Molly Michael to email the report to the Department of Justice with the subject line, "From POTUS." It included a set of "Antrim County Talking Points" for Jeff Rosen, soon to be acting attorney general.

The talking points were breathtaking and included "This is the evidence that Dominion Voting machines can and are being manipulated."

And "This is not human error as we have proven."

And "This is a Cover-up of voting crimes."

This strategy required that Sheryl Guy not be a mildly bumbling county clerk but a techno-criminal mastermind. People believed it. She received a deluge of voice mail, letters, and sideways glances on the street from neighbors she'd known her whole life. They took the word of interstate political operatives motivated by enormous power and wealth, rather than her, the local clerk who had certified their births and marriages. People called her a liar, a fake Republican, and a whole dictionary of vulgar names. She was "stupid" and "should be put in front of a military firing squad." They called her, in the only way she could bear to tell it, "an f'ing c." They called for her death and for her disgrace, not because she had draped herself in glory but because she had admitted her own mistake—because she had told the truth.

Bill Bailey disagreed, of course. But did he truly believe Sheryl Guy, the Republican grandmother who struggles with her smartphone, perpetrated a sophisticated digital crime?

"I got a different view of Sheryl that I didn't have at the beginning because I've always thought she's just a sweet woman," he said. "She's very emboldened now. A different girl than I knew, I can tell you that."

But did she pull off an electoral heist?

He hesitated. "I got a feeling that there was some pretty nefarious stuff that happened across the country, including here in Antrim County," he said. Then he added, "I personally don't think the clerks know about it."

After Bailey's team descended on Guy's office but before their inflammatory report, the local newspaper, the *Record-Eagle*, found a scoop. The judge had made a mistake: Bailey didn't actually live in Central Lake Village, site of the proposed marijuana shop. The "marihuana" question had not been on his ballot, so he couldn't have voted for or against it. He suffered no "irreparable harm."

The partisan ASOG report would face its own reckoning, soon. But the damage to Sheryl Guy had been done.

For a long time afterward, she cried often at home. Her husband, Alan, encouraged her to resign. Four decades of public service was enough. And Antrim County was changing underneath her anyway. Even the farm stands were polarized now; Republicans bought their cherries from Friske's, not King's, because Friske's defied the pandemic mask mandate. And there were the right-wing militias. Just weeks before Election Day, the FBI arrested fourteen men for allegedly plotting to kidnap the governor at her house in Antrim County.

At first, Antrim County had seemed so unlikely as the setting of a major attack on an American election. But the qualities that made it seem that way—its rural remove, its small population, its Luddite clerk and drowsy judge—in reality made it *ideal* as a political target.

Guy retreated from society. "You feel like you can't get air, you're just . . ." her voice faded. "I drank a little more, I ate a little more."

Drank?

"I drank a lot of Mike's Hard Lemonade," she said. "I was drinking the Mike's Hard and then I started diluting it with Crystal Light and ice, so I wasn't drinking as much."

As she talked, a couple walked into the clerk's office and approached the counter. They were both twenty-four years old and nervous. They needed a marriage license, please.

"That'll be $20," Guy said. They seemed so young. Babies to her. She pulled out her old mechanical embossing stamp and made it official. They beamed, then exited, leaving her alone in the office once more.

She doesn't plan on running for county clerk again.

WISCONSIN

Dean Knudson's moment of truth came on December 11. The former chairman of the state's elections commission, he had angered Trumpists leading up to Election Day by failing to condemn voting by mail.

Now he had been asked to testify before a joint legislative commit-tee at a hearing that afternoon in Madison to "examine" the election. The political front of Trump's strategy hoped to convince legislators in Republican-controlled swing states to refuse the election results. Unable to get anyone to hold official hearings on the matter, Giuliani had pre-vailed on pliable state legislators to convene unofficial ones like the show in Gettysburg. As with that one, this was billed as an inquiry into charges of election irregularities but was in fact an effort to drum up enthusiasm for The Steal, to make the case plausible enough to move forward.

With only a fig leaf of bipartisanship—a few Democratic lawmak-ers would have their say—the bulk of the proceedings, the whole point, was not to examine the election but to vilify it. Knudson, until recently chairman of the state's elections commission and a loyal Republican, was on the agenda, and he knew exactly what the committee wanted to hear.

The cause was losing ground. Nine days earlier, the president had filed a lawsuit in federal court—*Donald J. Trump v. the Wisconsin Elections Commission*—arguing that the influx of absentee ballots in the state had "cast doubt" on its outcome and asking the court to allow the state's largely Republican state legislature, not its voters, to appoint presidential electors. The judge promptly rejected it with what appeared to be mea-sured shock and historical alarm.

"This is an *extraordinary* case," wrote US District Court judge Brett H. Ludwig, who had been appointed by Trump. "Plaintiff Donald J. Trump is the current president of the United States, having narrowly won the state of Wisconsin's electoral votes four years ago . . . with a margin of just over 22,700 votes. In this lawsuit, he seeks to set aside the results of the November 3, 2020, popular vote in Wisconsin, an election in which the recently certified results show he was defeated by a similarly narrow margin of just over 20,600 votes." Ludwig explained that Trump was "hoping to secure federal court help in undoing his defeat," because the state elections commission issued three pieces of guidance—all related to the pandemic and mail voting—which, the judge noted, "it is specifi-cally authorized to do. . . . A sitting president who did not prevail in his bid for reelection has asked the federal court for help in setting aside the popular vote based on disputed issues of election administration."

Ludwig wrote that the claims "fail as a matter of law and fact." With magisterial scorn, Ludwig concluded, "Plaintiff 'asks that the Rule of Law be followed.' It has been." An appeal to the 7th US Circuit Court of Appeals and the US Supreme Court were summarily denied.

Having whiffed in court, Trumpists in Madison were now bent on ginning up public support for what amounted to a legislative coup d'état. Republican officials statewide were feeling pressure to get on board.

The show started with a skeptical statement by Campaigns and Elections Committee cochair Ron Tusler, a Republican assemblyman from Appleton, who proclaimed the state deserved "a 100 percent transparent election system where no one is asked to trust without the ability to verify" but then concluded, "Sadly, many in Wisconsin may have reasonable doubts." There was artful fuzziness here, focused not on evidence but "doubts," which voters did not necessarily have but "may have." Without any real evidence of fraud, Tusler was trying to keep up momentum for The Steal. He pointed to a thick stack of complaints his office had received and estimated that the legislature as a whole had received "over a half million contacts from voters who do not trust the outcome of this election." Again, quantity, not content, was the argument.

He then turned the mic over to Dan O'Donnell, a cocky, conservative talk show host. There would be no fuzziness in his remarks. A pale man with thick black hair, speaking with stentorian umbrage, jerking his head emphatically, he was a compelling speaker. He was even dressed dramatically, in a dark suit with a gray shirt and black tie. He aimed scarcely contained outrage at the elections commission, which had decided months earlier, because so many were self-isolating due to COVID, to ease the rules for declaring "indefinite confinement status," which entitled people to vote by mail. In this seemingly benign act, which the judge had noted the commission was authorized to make, O'Donnell saw "the systematic erosion of the rule of law." The rule change, like those in so many states, had prompted a flood of mail ballots. O'Donnell saw it as nothing less than an existential crisis. The "disturbing truth" he had come to deliver was that Wisconsin's election had thereby been "perverted by fraud allowed to run so rampant by the very people we trust to administer our elections that the most vulnerable among us are having their most sacred right, the right to vote, stolen from them."

Livestreamed from a finance committee hearing room, this fiery speech was a performance few of the lawmakers present could hope to match. Certainly not Knudson. He was a bland, if respected, fixture at hearings like these. He knew well the faces around the room, even though many were masked, from his years as an assemblyman. A former mayor of Hudson with years of experience on the elections commission—he had stepped down as chairman shortly before the 2020 vote but was still on it—he bore responsibility for the rule change O'Donnell had attacked.

Studiously noncontroversial, Knudson had nevertheless annoyed Trumpists before Election Day by urging all voters who applied for mail ballots to send them in early. And even though he had promoted in-person voting as perfectly safe, he hadn't expressed antipathy for mail voting. He had treated the two voting methods as equivalent.

A storm of criticism had followed. Today's hearing, in the eyes of some, offered Knudson, an otherwise obscure regional official, a highly visible platform for redemption.

Many of those testifying would do so remotely, but Knudson had come in person. He knew O'Donnell's rhetoric was just wind. He wasn't going to debate the man. In his own temperate way, he planned to tell the panel and the home audience what they *needed* to hear, not what they *wanted* to hear.

Knudson was a veterinarian. He had grown up on a farm in North Dakota with horses, cows, sheep, pigs, and poultry and had been inspired by watching a horse vet at work. There was no way to console or reason with an ailing animal. You could only assess the problem carefully and apply what you knew. He'd founded his own practice and with his wife, Joy, had raised two children. Knudson was a strict conservative. He admired the articles he read in the right-wing *National Review* and considered editorials in the *Wall Street Journal*, regarded by many as strident, as wishy-washy. Conservative convictions had motivated him to get into politics and guided him still.

His elections commission work capped almost three decades of involvement in the electoral process. He had seen it from every angle, as a volunteer, a candidate, and a supervisor. The commission was annoyingly bipartisan (three Republicans, three Democrats). On matters of controversy, neither side could win, so compromise was obligatory. But the work was rarely controversial and made headlines even more rarely. It usually concerned picayune matters like whether mail ballots arriving via FedEx or UPS and not the authorized envelopes could be counted, or how to handle ballots with mistakes. Tinkering with the mechanics of voting appealed to Knudson's pragmatism and appetite for detail. He was not a man to be swept up by the passions of the moment. His expertise outweighed that of anyone in the Madison hearing room, or watching, for that matter. No one was going to challenge him.

On the YouTube livestream of the hearing, remote viewers left comments to the side of the screen as the hearing progressed: "leaders of Wisconsin, America is watching you" read one. Another from a user with the handle Hex Scoop wrote, "And my dead grandmother voted from Mars."

After a brief scrap over rules, Tusler said, "All right, moving on, let's hear from Dean Knudson."

Knudson took a deep breath and removed his mask. He was a few sentences into his remarks when he noticed a murmur in the room. He'd forgotten to turn on his mic. He flipped the switch and started over.

Firm but nervous, the picture of conventional conservatism—glasses, charcoal suit, short gray hair, powder-blue shirt, red tie—he began by explaining that Wisconsin, of all states, was one of the least likely, if not *the least*, to be victimized by fraud. With a voting system so decentralized—there were 1,850 local election clerks—it would be virtually impossible to coordinate malfeasance on a large scale. He acknowledged that "voter fraud happens in elections despite all our safeguards," but, he explained, "the fraudulent ballots we discover are typically numbered in the dozens to the hundreds," far fewer than enough to sway a statewide canvass. "These tend to be scattered and unorganized violations most often committed by individuals who fraudulently double vote, [or] illegally vote despite a felony conviction." An audit of Dominion voting machines under the commission's purview had found just one problem with folds in ballots and no evidence of the trickery widely alleged. The number of ballots cast matched the number in the voter rolls. Without the slightest modulation of voice, Knudson said, "I have not seen credible evidence of large-scale voter fraud in Wisconsin during the November election."

On-screen, it was clear some in the audience felt this fellow Knudson had not gotten the memo. He was grossly out of tune, quite literally *beside the point*. The comments on the screen sped up:

"THE TRUMP TRAIN IS BEING DERAILED BY FRAUDULENT DEMS"

"TRUMP TRUMP TRUMP TRUMP"

"FAKE HEARING"

"Rigged election Money talks . . . 3rd world country."

To Knudson directly:

"YOU ARE TALKING TOO MUCH, YOU ARE LYING. I smell China."

And then the occasional startled Democrat:

"WHY IS HE TELLING THE TRUTH? HE IS SUPPOSED TO PRETEND THERE IS FRAUD!"

Knudson droned on. "I speak to you today sincerely and directly about Wisconsin only; in Wisconsin there were no dumps of ballots during the night. None. There is no evidence of any fraud related to Dominion voting machines in Wisconsin. None." Knudson acknowledged that he found certain of the changes prior to the election troubling and agreed that looser rules for claiming to be "indefinitely confined," O'Donnell's bugaboo, ought to be carefully considered, but these were not things that meaningfully altered the count.

"I'D LOVE TO PLAY POKER WITH THIS GUY! ANYBODY CAN TELL HE IS LYING!"

"LISTEN TO THE QUIVER IN HIS VOICE. LIAR"

"So scared."

"FRAUD APOLOGIZER"

"Jail these crooks."

"Send this liar a Facebook message."

"Get him tf outta here"

"Liar"

"Fake News"

Knudson was wrapping up now, outlining technical voting reforms that he would support, not to address fraud, which had not been a problem, but to address a crisis in "voter confidence." Tusler stopped him when his twenty minutes of allotted time were up. Knudson puckered his lips, frowned, took a sip of water, packed up his notes, and left.

One of the few supportive comments on screen popped up at the end.

"Republicans are running a Tokyo Rose propaganda campaign. Mr. Knudson is making sense."

Another wrote, simply, "Sure pal."

Nevada

The coordinated assault on Clark County had three prongs. On the popular front, activists sent protesters daily to Joe Gloria's offices in North Las Vegas, beefing up the ranks with recruitment in hopes of sparking genuine grassroots support. The political front lobbied friendly state lawmakers to help thwart the popular vote. The legal front looked to short-circuit the whole process in court, trying to stop the count, discredit it, and ultimately upend it completely.

Commanding the legal front in Nevada was an Alexandria, Virginia, lawyer named Jesse Binnall, a curious, jug-eared, often disheveled fellow who had an odd way of over-enunciating that lent emphasis to his every remark. He had entered Trump's orbit four years earlier in the lead-up to the Cleveland convention. He worked then to ensure that GOP convention delegates from around the country were Trump supporters, a key job. That work had netted him an invitation to an inaugural ball and a White House tour but not an appointment in Trump's administration.

Binnall was a lifelong contrarian, which is what you had to be back in 1996 to work as a youth organizer for Bob Dole. It was a time when relatively few teens identified as conservative Republicans or with the former Republican majority leader. Binnall had gone on to work on the Arizona staff of former vice president Dan Quayle in 2000 in his memorably unsuccessful run for president. Quayle, too, was an odd choice for a budding political activist. As George H. W. Bush's running mate, he was known more for bloopers than anything else. Binnall next emerged as a libertarian, a critic of big government, and a campaign staffer for Senator Rand Paul's failed 2016 presidential run. When Paul's campaign faltered, Binnall climbed on the Trump train, at a time when very few people gave the Manhattan real estate heir a breath of a chance at the White House. After Trump was surprisingly swept into office, Binnall landed in a small law firm in northern Virginia. He had no government job, but now he did have high connections. During Trump's tenure, he was appointed to the legal team headed by Sidney Powell representing Michael Flynn, the former general and national security adviser who pleaded guilty to lying to the FBI in the Robert Mueller probe.

On his active Facebook account, Binnall steered clear of politics generally, presenting himself as a single man, Dodger fan, dog owner, Anglophile, legal nerd, pilot, and avid scuba diver, posting videos shot on boats and underwater in sunny resort destinations worldwide. But on his Twitter feed, he was an unabashed "MAGA lawyer," warning (using the acronym for Republicans in Name Only) "RINOs beware!"

In the months leading up to the election, Binnall had filed a lawsuit in Nevada on behalf of the Trump campaign, alleging that the machines used to scan mail ballots inadequately verified the signatures of registered voters and that the use of these machines and pandemic precautions meant that election watchers would not be close enough to allow "meaningful observation." Both arguments failed.

These two strikes hadn't dampened Binnall's enthusiasm or resolve, nor did they dissuade Mike Roman, director of Trump's election day ops, from tapping him to lead the assault on Nevada's election. On the Friday before Election Day, he took a call from Roman in his Alexandria office early in the evening.

"Can you go to Nevada for me?" Roman asked.

"Yes, sir," said Binnall. "I'll go wherever you need me. When do you need me there?"

"I was thinking tomorrow morning," said Roman. "Don't worry. You'll only be out there for five days."

Binnall left with clothing for just a few days and wound up spending eight weeks in Las Vegas, living out of a succession of casino hotels and looking increasingly rumpled and helpless. The look was particularly noticeable working alongside his very put-together media director, Amanda Milius, and equally glam lawyer Heather Flick. They worked out of office space borrowed from Trump backers—there were plenty of empty ones available during the pandemic.

A big part of their task was herding all the complaints being solicited by campaign workers, collecting statements from those who claimed to have seen or experienced fraud firsthand. They had phone banks of women handling these calls—one of them was Binnall's mother. In the midst of assembling this wall of evidence into a convincing case, they were dismayed when Judge James T. Russell refused to cooperate. He intended to spare himself the Blunderbuss Strategy. Talking to Binnall on speakerphone early in the week after Election Day, with Flick and others listening in, scribbling on legal pads, Russell said he would allow the team only fifteen of their hundreds of witnesses and gave them a strict filing deadline. He also insisted that the fifteen testify by deposition, not live. Binnall, who believed the large number of the stories they were collecting added up to proof of substantial fraud and that it was important that the judge meet witnesses in person to gauge their credibility, did his best to wheedle for more without success. He thought Russell had made up his mind against their case already.

Flick scanned those around the room listening to the call and saw looks of incredulity. It felt like state and county officials were treating

Binnall's crew as carpetbaggers out to usurp Nevada's sovereign authority to conduct elections. Servers delivering summons to official witnesses were being turned away from government buildings. The clock was ticking on the team's effort, so when Joe Gloria himself managed to dodge service for a full weekend, it was maddening. Their hands were tied behind their backs!

Milius led a contingent to the North Las Vegas elections center to demand "forensic access" to the counting machines. Gloria and his staff would allow them only to observe the machines from a distance—per the ruling in Binnall's early lawsuit over access. Also, any access to the county's voting machines by a partisan group would taint them for future use; it was precisely the scenario that allowed for tampering. The refusal was taken by Binnall's team as further evidence of conspiracy.

Binnall had clashed with Gloria during his earlier failed lawsuit and found the burly elections director defensive and uncooperative. He had questioned him under oath and believed Gloria had not just avoided telling the truth but had lied. To the Trump lawyer, it seemed as though Gloria was more interested in finding an answer that would keep him out of trouble than in testifying forthrightly. Gloria told him, for instance, that he had no reason to think that any election watchers had seen any irregularities in the primary earlier that year because none had filed a complaint. Binnall pointed out that observers had been forced to agree beforehand that they would not challenge any votes. The question Gloria had answered concerned "complaints," not voting challenges, but Binnall felt he'd caught him in a lie. Gloria was not charged with lying under oath, but Binnall remained convinced he had. In his eyes, this was just one more instance of official resistance to transparency and the truth.

On November 17, ten days after the count in Clark County gave Biden a commanding lead in Nevada, Binnall was part of the team that filed a lawsuit seeking to annul the results, claiming it had assembled enough evidence of equipment malfunction, improprieties, outright fraud, and "questionable votes" to "bridge" Biden's winning 33,596-vote margin. One of its more striking claims was that more than forty-two thousand people voted twice. That alone gave them enough votes to overtake Biden's lead. The number came from a statistical analysis of voters by Jesse Kamzol, a Republican campaign worker. Overall, the lawsuit zeroed in on changes Clark County had adopted to account for the huge influx of mail ballots, an argument resting again on the baseless assumption that mail ballots were inherently vulnerable to fraud.

The boyish Binnall proudly announced his filing at a press conference before the courthouse.

"Donald Trump won the state of Nevada, after you account for the fraud and irregularities that occurred in the election."

Ten days later, just before presenting his case, Binnall brimmed with confidence. Interviewed on Newsmax, the Trump-friendly network, he said, "I never know exactly what a court is going to do. . . . I can only say what evidence that we are going to present, and the evidence we are going to present will be compelling. Will be extremely strong, showing that the result of Nevada was wrong . . . because, in fact, Donald Trump is the one who won Nevada. And so that is what we can do. We can go in and put that evidence forward, and we are very confident that it will be very compelling for any court that hears this evidence."

Trump tweeted a link to the interview on his account, a special thrill for his admirers. Milius, no doubt alarmed by how shabby her boss was beginning to look, took him shopping that day. The two spent some of their rare downtime losing money together at Caesars Palace and together took a few roulette and craps lessons—Binnall won $100. The shopping trip took a while. Back at the office, Flick kept calling to ask them to return, but Milius was a serious shopper and Binnall was distracted by his phone, which blew up with congratulatory texts and calls from friends after Trump's tweet. It was a heady day.

Binnall's confidence in Nevada must have come as a balm to Trump in a losing season.

One of his first thoughts, after the election results showed Biden winning, was that the US Supreme Court would set things right for him.

"U.S. Supreme Court should decide!" he had tweeted on November 6, the day before the networks called the race for Biden. After all, he had appointed three of the nine justices, giving the court a clear conservative majority. The way he saw it, the court *owed* him.

The first of his appeals reached the justices in early December, a case that concerned Pennsylvania's 2019 law allowing universal mail voting. It had been enacted with strong Republican backing. Several of the claimants in this federal appeal, state lawmakers, had themselves urged for mail ballots. Their about-face had been rejected by the Pennsylvania Supreme Court.

"Now, let's see whether or not somebody has the courage . . . whether it's a justice of the Supreme Court, or a number of justices of the Supreme Court—let's see if they have the courage to do what everybody in this country knows is right," Trump told reporters on December 8.

That same day, the court denied the appeal in a one-sentence statement.

"The application for injunctive relief presented to Justice Alito and by him referred to the Court is denied."

Days later, the court rejected an ambitious attempt by Texas attorney general Ken Paxton to amalgamate all the claims of fraud into one final Hail Mary. Paxton wanted to nullify the election results in four swing states over allegations of fraud—one of those it featured was Greg Stenstrom's theory of fake Biden ballots in Delaware County, Pennsylvania. The justices, including the three appointed by Trump, declined to hear it, ruling that Texas had no legal standing to contest elections in other states.

Trump vented on Twitter: "The Supreme Court really let us down. No Wisdom, No Courage!"

But perhaps the most stinging blow had been Attorney General Barr's betrayal. Barr had spent years ignoring the traditional wall between his office and the presidency, a division meant to ensure that federal criminal prosecution was free of political influence. Trump thought the nation's top law enforcement officials should act more as his personal lawyer.

Barr had mostly obliged him and had been roundly criticized for it. Weeks earlier, his order for federal prosecutors to look into allegations of voter fraud had generated useful headlines. But a month into Trump's campaign to make people believe he had been robbed, Barr was done pretending. He told a reporter that there was nothing to it. The Justice Department saw no evidence of widespread fraud. The president was furious.

To summarize a scene reported by Carol Leonnig and Phillip Rucker:

"Bill, did you say this?" Trump asked him when they met that same day in the White House.

"Yeah. I said it."

"How could you say that?"

Barr said the reporter had asked, and he had told him the truth.

"Why didn't you just not answer the question?" Trump asked, his voice rising with anger. "There's no reason for you to have said this! You must hate Trump!"

Binnall's sanguine expectations in Nevada were similarly dashed. His "compelling" arguments were heard by Judge Russell, a Republican appointee and son of a former Republican Nevada governor. The judge was not compelled. He crushed every point Binnall raised. He found no evidence of higher rates of fraud in the counting of mail ballots. He affirmed the reliability and integrity of the machines. Of Kamzol, the "expert" who came up with the forty-two-thousand multiple-vote figure, the judge concluded that he "had little to no information about or supervision over the origins of his data, the manner in which it had been matched, and what the rate of false positives would be. Additionally, there was little or no verification of his numbers." The testimony of all of Binnall's experts, Russell wrote, was "of little or no value." He found no evidence that Gloria or his workers had acted improperly.

The ruling was upheld by the Nevada Supreme Court, and the state's electors met over Zoom on December 14 to cast their six votes for Biden.

Binnall and his team packed up and left town. They still had dreams of prevailing but could not find a federal question that would merit consideration by the US Supreme Court. It was humiliating, or ought to have been.

It was strike three for Binnall, but he did not consider himself out.

MICHIGAN

When Ed McBroom began his investigation, he had clashed with Democratic colleagues, who accused him of looking for fraud in the same way Giuliani and company were—hoping to find any means to cast shade on the election. But as it became clear that McBroom sought only the truth, he found himself in conflict with his own party and its leader. Trump began calling him a RINO, and urged the people of Michigan to vote him "the hell out of office!"

"The Senate 'investigation' of the election is a cover up," Trump wrote in a press release.

But McBroom felt determined to do what the president and his supporters would not. He would dig into their claims. Often between chores on his farm, he tackled them one by one. To check out claims of dead people sending in ballots, he and his committee scoured old obituaries. He called citizens, issued subpoenas, listened to hours of testimony. Combed social media posts. Each time McBroom heard a new allegation, he traced it through witnesses to its principal source. And the closer he looked, the more convinced he became that his own party leaders were the ones perpetrating a fraud.

Regarding the allegation of dead voters, for instance, he found two. The first was a man named William Bradley, who shared that name with his dead father; when the son voted, a clerk had accidentally attributed it to the father. In the second case, a ninety-two-year-old woman sent in her vote by mail, then died four days before the election. She was dead, but her vote had been legal. Neither case involved deceit and certainly didn't add up to massive fraud.

In the midst of McBroom's investigation, on December 11, Trump attorney Sidney Powell filed an emergency petition to the Supreme Court of the United States, claiming "Dominion alone is responsible for the injection, or fabrication, of 289,866 illegal votes in Michigan." That margin would give Trump the victory and then some.

So McBroom looked into it.

The number, he said, came from a group called the Voter Integrity Project, who had called fifteen hundred residents to ask whether they had received an unsolicited, illegal absentee ballot. The group then extrapolated the number of "yes" answers to match the entire population of Michigan and arrived at more than a quarter million illegally sent ballots. Even if they were right, McBroom knew, illegally sending ballots to voters does not equal "illegal votes." But beyond that, after McBroom and his committee started calling the voters alleged to have received such ballots, he realized those in question had not grasped the distinction between an application to vote by mail and an actual ballot. Most had received only applications. A couple of others seemed to have forgotten that they had requested absentee ballots.

When ASOG issued its report on Antrim County—the "marihuana" boondoggle that had resulted in a ringing condemnation of Dominion voting machines—McBroom dug into that, too.

The most obvious problem with the ASOG report was that it didn't bother to note that the Dominion tally tapes reflected a correct total and showed Trump winning Antrim County. The only error had been in the way the numbers had originally been reported. That error belonged to county clerk Sheryl Guy, who had admitted and corrected it.

Bailey's team spun a tale of remote hacking, wireless chips, algorithms, and espionage. But that was impossible, McBroom said—the Antrim machines had no modems or wireless chips. They had no internet access whatsoever.

On December 17, the Michigan Bureau of Elections and the Antrim County Clerk's Office, joined by a bipartisan team of clerks from around the state, undertook a hand recount of every presidential vote in Antrim. For six hours, a livestreamed feed showed the workers sorting and counting ballots, and in the end, they confirmed Antrim's certified count. After recounting more than sixteen thousand paper ballots, Trump netted twelve more. The machines had flipped no votes. No hackers had meddled. Sheryl Guy had hidden nothing.

A few days later, McBroom issued a statement. "The simple answer given by the clerk of Antrim County still stands: human error is the factor that contributed to the unofficial vote count errors."

McBroom had come to realize the fraud accusations had *not* all come in good faith. Those making them either did not believe them or had not taken the trouble to ascertain that they were true. Instead, political players were leveraging public credulity to empower and enrich themselves. Trump had lost. His efforts to overturn that truth in Michigan had been stopped by previously anonymous people like Sheryl Guy and Aaron Van Langevelde. But winning or losing was beside the point; a class of political parasites had stirred up outrage to gain populist support and raise cash.

"I've taken more time to evaluate some of these things," McBroom said. "And I recognized several of these big players, nationally, are clearly making a substantial amount of money to litigate these issues."

It's nearly impossible to know exactly how much money Trump and his allies spent in the effort to overturn the 2020 election. Some of it is public and traceable; for instance, Trump's political action committees spent about $8 million on legal fees in the first half of 2021 as they fought the election and his impeachment. But Trump also pays associates through limited liability corporations, which makes those payments impossible to track. To an enormous degree, he has allowed other private interests and allies to foot the bill. Entrepreneur Patrick Byrne, for instance, who stepped down as CEO of the shopping site Overstock.com after admitting a romance with a Russian spy, has poured millions of dollars into Trump's effort to overturn the election. That included funding "a team of hackers and cybersleuths, other people with odd skills" to crack Dominion's voting machines. Meanwhile, Trump's believers across the country donated extraordinary sums to fight voter fraud; in just the eight weeks after the election, followers sent in more than a quarter billion dollars. Instead of spending his new crowdsourced fortune to root out fraud, though, Trump shuffled some around to pay off political debts—including part of the *nine-figure* refund owed donors misled by the WinRed donation platform, for example—and he pocketed the rest, rolling up a war chest of more than $100 million. He can use that money to keep himself relevant by funding—or at least teasing—Republican candidates who support him and possibly funding his own run at reelection.

Bill Bailey, who brought the suit against Antrim County, is quick to note that he made no money from the debacle. As a matter of fact, his real estate business came to an abrupt stop.

Then the question remains, in light of McBroom's epiphany: Who paid for it? Never mind the private jets and teams of analysts—who paid the fees for his lawyer, Matt DePerno?

"We were able to get funding through patriots across the country, that's who's funding this. That's where the money's coming from," Bailey said. "And it's well over—I bet it's getting close to $2 million now."

But, he said of his lawyer, "if I thought he was a conniver, or anything—if I'd have thought he did anything that he shouldn't be doing—I'd call him out on it because that's just the way I am."

As a matter of fact, he said, he supports DePerno's new political career. He's running for attorney general of Michigan.

ARIZONA

On December 15, Trump tweeted:

"Tremendous problems being found with voting machines. They are so far off it is ridiculous. Able to take a landslide victory and reduce it to a tight loss. This is not what the USA is all about. Law enforcement shielding machines. DO NOT TAMPER, a crime. Much more to come!"

That day, Arizona's state senate Republicans, led by Karen Fann, subpoenaed the Maricopa County Board of Supervisors demanding that it share all 2.1 million ballots it had certified and all its election machines. It was the first step on Fann's long march toward a private, notoriously partisan "audit."

Conservative Republicans tend to be in a minority on the local level, so when they do find each other, they bond. Bill Gates, the Maricopa supervisor who had invoked his grandfather's war record on the night he voted to certify the vote, had formed a working friendship with Fann right away. They supported each other's aims and consulted on local issues like fireworks ordinances or those to ban plastic bags. Gates valued Fann's opinions. He thought she was reasonable, had a good understanding of urban issues, which was uncommon in the state legislature, where Phoenix and Tucson representatives often found themselves at odds with those from suburban and rural districts. When Gates had moved from vice mayor of Phoenix to the county board, he and Fann had some overlap. They both represented Prescott, where she was from, in Yavapai County to the north, which bleeds into upper Maricopa County. So their existing friendship became in some instances an official partnership, particularly over water issues, critical in a desert state. Gates considered Fann the expert on such matters.

At sixty-six, Fann had earned a reputation for working hard for her constituents. Her company, DG Fenn Construction, which erected offices, gas stations, restaurants, and industrial buildings, also contracted with Arizona to install highway railings. This lent her gravitas in the eyes of many, a woman with one foot in government and the other planted firmly and successfully in the private sector, or the real world. With her sculpted silver blond hair in a neat bob, glasses, round face, and colorful yet prim attire, she looked more like a college dean than a politician but a dean ready at all times to hop on a horse. In public, she emphasized common sense over expertise and liked to offer crisp Sarah Palin-esque quips. The greater part of Fann's Mohave County constituency resented and was often at odds with what they—and she—sometimes referred to as "The State of Maricopa." From Gates's perspective, her region was home to "off the grid" individualism. Mohave's town of Kingman had nurtured America's most famous right-wing domestic terrorist, Timothy McVeigh.

Fann managed the urban-rural divide with, at least in part, the proven strategy of telling each side, in private, what it wanted to hear. To a woman who wrote condemning the recount as fraudulent, she wrote that she had no intention of trying to overturn the results. "Biden won," she wrote. "45% of all Arizona voters thinks there is a problem with the election system. The audit is to disprove those theories . . . ." When a Trumpist accused her of insufficiently backing the president, she responded, "I have been in numerous conversations with Rudy Giuliani over the past weeks trying to get this done. I have the full support of him and a personal call from President Trump thanking us for pushing to prove any fraud."

Although Fann would insist later that her call for the independent audit, which would ultimately be carried out by a company with Trump ties called Cyber Ninjas, was not motivated by a desire to sway the outcome, her emails from those weeks leaked out and showed she was coordinating her moves with Trump directly and with Giuliani. Her push for the private recount earned her a flurry of attention from Trump's media allies, and the president himself sung her praises. The One America News Network began providing her a platform day after day.

This all surprised and disappointed Bill Gates. After he had looked carefully at the questions raised about the vote, after he had publicly grilled the county's election directors, he had expected friends and fellow conservatives to stand up for him and his fellow board members.

Instead, Fann undermined their work and their reputations. Her demand for the county's records came with the threat of imprisonment if he and the other board members failed to comply. As Gates saw it, her request wasn't just insulting; it was stupid. A Trump-inspired "forensic audit" would just blow more smoke about fraud and would, in the months ahead, turn Arizona into a laughingstock, the last-ditch hope of conspiracy theorists.

WISCONSIN

As the winning Democratic electors met in the governor's office in Madison on December 14 to formally cast their votes for Biden, Bill Feehan joined a group of defeated electors in protest. Instead of stepping aside for the victors, as was the custom, Republican electors met in another room at the capitol to cast their votes for Trump.

They didn't mean it as a symbolic gesture. They insisted Trump had won their state.

For Feehan, it was the final step on a monthlong journey away from pragmatism and the Republican mainstream that had begun with a phone call on November 16 from Sidney Powell. Feehan had been starstruck. Here was a lawyer for the president of the United States, calling him! He had seen Powell's stern visage on TV and read about her in news reports. A national political player! Folks like that rarely appeared, even telephonically, in western Wisconsin, where Feehan was chairman of the Republican Party of the state's Third Congressional District.

The district follows the wide and winding Mississippi River almost the entire length of the state. Names of many of its small cities and towns—Eau Claire, La Crosse, Osceola, Menomonie—reflect the influence of native tribes and the French fur traders who settled among them. Today, the district is overwhelmingly white and still leans Republican, although only moderately so. With the sprawling Wisconsin suburbs of Minneapolis–Saint Paul, and the cities of Eau Claire and La Crosse, its political character had grown less certain. It had sent Democrat Ron Kind to Congress every election year since 1996 and went for Al Gore, John Kerry, and Barack Obama in presidential elections, but in state contests, Feehan's party was competitive. Trump narrowly carried the district in 2016, and when Feehan had gone to bed on election night, he was confident that the president would repeat with a wider margin.

That's what he had told everyone at the party that night at Castaway's, a bar and restaurant with a wide porch that looks out over the Black River. There had been hundreds there, nearly all of whom shared Feehan's outlook.

So the numbers Feehan woke up to on Wednesday morning were dispiriting. It was the same feeling he'd had two years earlier, when Republican governor Scott Walker, campaigning for reelection, had seen his hopes for victory vanish in the late report of more than one hundred thousand votes from Milwaukee. Trump would take Feehan's district again in 2020, and it still looked close statewide. But serious Wisconsin politicos like him knew that Milwaukee and Madison were Democratic, late reporting, and usually decisive. It was a pattern that riled him and many Republicans in his rolling green district, where one could drive for miles without seeing a Biden sign.

Feehan is a beefy man, with short-cropped curly reddish hair gone white, small blue eyes, and a broad, pink face. He and his wife run a business that schools beauticians and operates salons, an industry hit hard by COVID. Both of them spent a lot of time caring for a disabled adult daughter and for parents who need assisted care.

Feehan had been bitten by the political bug in 2008, when Barack Obama was elected president. He saw the country's first black president as a socialist, a threat to his business and family and to what he saw as the proper American way of life, so he looked for a way to enter the arena. Mostly, he'd been disappointed. He ran for the state senate and lost, then for mayor of La Crosse and lost again. His passion for the political game seemed sidelined, except along the way had learned that leadership positions in the state GOP organization went begging. Here was his ticket in. He put up his name and won. The job paid nothing. He even had to foot his own expenses when he attended the state convention. It wasn't all he'd wanted, but at least he was in the game. It was a start.

Feehan saw himself as a realist. When the big-city numbers came in and Biden carried the state, he was disheartened but neither surprised nor outraged. He had no reason to believe the results were untrue. It was personally disappointing. He was a Republican elector, and a Trump victory would have sent him to Madison with nine other electors to cast Wisconsin's ten votes for Trump. For a political junkie, it would have been a memorable moment. But still another Republican win had vanished in the night. It was maddening. At a November 9 meeting of the La Crosse County GOP, Feehan was asked what he was going to do about it.

"I haven't even thought about it," he said. He added that he saw nothing to make him doubt Biden's Wisconsin victory. "I'm a man of reason, so I look to see what evidence is there right now, and essentially, I haven't seen any evidence that proves that there was massive voter fraud, enough to change 20,000 votes in the state of Wisconsin."

But Powell's call started him thinking differently. Here was a lawyer who represented the president himself, the attorney who had defended General Michael Flynn, Trump's former national security adviser convicted of lying to the FBI, and now seen as something of a conservative martyr. When her spotlight and the national stage beckoned, Feehan jumped. He became, overnight, a warrior for the defeated president.

What Feehan did not know was that he was allying himself with someone who was considered, even by Trump's White House staff, as beyond the pale in her embrace of election conspiracy. Her plot-spinning had gone well past the CIA story she had told on TV weeks earlier. It was now so far-fetched that even Rudy Giuliani, who had been bundling every allegation and suspicion he could find into his blunderbuss, had pronounced her "crazy." The two lawyers ended up "sulking" in separate rooms in the White House after Giuliani had challenged her. When Trump insisted he wanted her on the team, key members stepped back. As author Michael Wolff put it in his book *Landslide*:

"She did become the tipping point into utter flapdoodleness. All in Trumpworld with any amount of professional concern and grounding now stepped pointedly aside, became only observers of the circus."

Feehan knew none of this, of course. To him, Powell was a big-time lawyer representing the president of the United States. He allowed himself to become more convinced that something illicit had happened. Those late votes from urban areas were no longer just an annoying reflection of partisan reality; they were an assault on democracy itself. The stakes were huge. Feehan posted on his Facebook page, "May God help our nation."

And so it was that Feehan was thrust from the pay-your-own-expenses obscurity of party politics in western Wisconsin into the national arena. This was big. And Feehan was all in. He became the lead plaintiff on a lawsuit filed by Powell in federal court against the Wisconsin Elections Commission. The lawsuit asked the court to order decertification of the recent vote by state electors for Biden and instead direct the governor to send to Congress the state's ten votes for Trump. The complaint alleged "massive election fraud."

Feehan told anyone who would listen that he believed that a six-thousand-vote Biden bump in La Crosse could not have happened without "absentee voting and ballot harvesting," both of which were legal in Wisconsin but which Trumpists had condemned as Democratic trickery. Picking up on the charges O'Donnell had so vehemently proclaimed at the televised state senate hearing—and ignoring Dean Knudson's measured rebuttal—he characterized the easing of mail vote restrictions as a plot. They had been undertaken in order to secure victory for Joe Biden.

He was not unduly discouraged when US District Court judge Pamela Pepper flatly dismissed the lawsuit, or when his co-plaintiff, losing Republican congressional candidate Derrick Van Orden, bailed, tweeting, "To be clear, I am not involved in the lawsuit seeking to overturn the election in Wisconsin." A somewhat bewildered Judge Pepper wrote:

"Federal judges do not appoint the president in this country. One wonders why the plaintiffs came to federal court and asked a federal judge to do so. After a week of sometimes odd and often harried litigation, the court is no closer to answering the 'why.'"

Nor was Feehan deterred when Powell herself was jettisoned by Trump on November 22. Having estranged all the serious legal talent surrounding him, including his White House counsels and the Department of Justice, the president reluctantly decided that her cheerleading for him was hurting more than helping. In a spirited and ugly verbal brawl a few days earlier in the Oval Office, complete with crude insults, his coterie of family and White House lawyers had pushed back hard when Powell suggested that Trump declare a national emergency, seize voting machines, and put her in charge of investigating them. She waved five affidavits that proved her claim that Dominion voting machines had been rigged. On examination, all came from the same source, a self-styled military intelligence expert who never even completed an entry-level course in the subject. They were, like all of Powell's "evidence," worthless.

Eric Herschmann, Trump's impeachment lawyer and now senior adviser, pointed out the clear conflicts in the fantastic array of charges she and Giuliani had been making. He asked Powell, "Is your theory that the Democrats got together and changed the rules"—which was, in effect, what Giuliani had been arguing all over the country—"or is it that there was foreign interference in our election?" She said it was foreign interference and that Giuliani had failed to grasp it. "All you do is promise, but never deliver," Herschmann told her. When Giuliani arrived late to the meeting, he laid into Powell, too. Scanning her affidavits, he said, "This is gibberish. Nonsense."

Trump did not, however, want Powell to stop. Gibberish has its uses. But the clash with the rest of the team had become untenable. Henceforth, the White House announced, she would be "practicing law on her own," an unofficial combatant.

Such setbacks had the effect in Wisconsin of pushing Feehan to the front. He was now the one carrying the state flag for The Steal.

He appeared on MSNBC as a defeated Trump elector, still defiant. Biden had not yet won the race, he said. "The Electoral College will meet on January 6, a joint session of Congress, and that's where the vote will take place to determine who the president of the United States is. So that hasn't happened yet."

The show's host, Ari Melber, displayed the comment Feehan had made a month earlier, that he was a "realist" and that there was no evidence of widespread fraud.

"Are you of the view that Joe Biden is not the president-elect and didn't win the election?"

"I'm of the view that there's still legal cases that are moving forward, and one of those I am plaintiff in that is being appealed to the Supreme Court—"

Feehan tried to enumerate the questions he and others had raised, but Melber cut him short.

"Are you of the view that Joe Biden is the president-elect or not? That's a yes or no question?"

"No," said Feehan, with a slight smirk on his wide pink face. He knew that his stance would invite public scorn, particularly from viewers of this partisan liberal TV channel. In fact, privately, he had already accepted that Trump's cause was doomed when the US Supreme Court had declined to hear the Texas challenge.

But he wasn't going to admit it, not now that he was a featured player on national TV. He would linger a while longer in the spotlight. He posted on Facebook, "I am fighting to the end. Yes, this election was filled with illegal activities by the Wisconsin Elections Commission. Yes it effected (sic) the outcome." In reply to comments on his post, he wrote: "I urge everyone who loves our country to keep fighting. I am certain that our president will fight to the end. . . . The Democratic party has proven they will lie, cheat and steal their way to power. We can't let them prevail."

GEORGIA

On a cold day in mid-December, John Porter took a stroll in Tumlin Park, near his house. It's a leafy place with a playground, an open field, and a path Porter liked to follow during his regular walks.

The park felt like a respite from political life, which had become treacherous. A few days earlier, Lieutenant Governor Geoff Duncan's teenaged son, Bayler, had tweeted to his handful of followers a sort of family motto— "Doing the right thing will never be the wrong thing!"—and Duncan retweeted it. His wife, Brooke, had been furious, afraid Trump's supporters would come after their son. And they did. "You're a boil on humanity's ass," one responded. Another said, "Scum." And one posted a sinister, threatening photo in response. It showed smooth-faced, twenty-year-old Harrison Deal, the boyfriend of Governor Brian Kemp's daughter, who had died in a car accident a few days earlier. Conspiracy theorists already speculated he had been murdered in a political cover-up. None of it made sense. Politics in Georgia had passed through the looking glass.

Now, as Porter walked through a ring of trees, his phone rang. A call from the lieutenant governor's office.

"The FBI wants to have a briefing with us," the person on the other end said. Could Porter join the call?

"Sure," Porter said, confused. He found a spot to sit down in the park and waited while he was patched into the call. Why would the Feds want to talk with him?

On the call, he found himself with Governor Kemp, his chief of staff, the lieutenant governor, FBI agents, and "some international, foreign affairs guys."

Holy fucking shit, Porter thought.

"We want you to know, the website that you guys are familiar with," one of the agents said, "we have traced that back to the Iranians."

Porter immediately knew which site.

The whole, terrifying thing had started back in November. Ever since Election Day, Trump had offered up wildly untrue, easily disproved theories about voter fraud in Georgia. He had leveled accusations at Secretary of State Raffensperger by name.

The secretary of state had corrected the president's claims patiently, with deference, but not without a sense of personal hurt. In late November, for instance, he had published a letter in *USA Today*, noting that despite howling accusations, Georgia's election had gone smoothly.

"This should be something for Georgians to celebrate, whether their favored presidential candidate won or lost," he wrote. "For those wondering, mine lost—my family voted for him, donated to him and are now being thrown under the bus by him."

A few days later, Trump had responded viciously, calling Raffensperger "an enemy of the people."

The website referenced by the FBI featured a list titled "Enemies of the People."

Among the Georgians on the list were Raffensperger, Fuchs, and Sterling. It showed their photos in crosshairs, as though seen through a rifle scope. And it listed their home addresses. It posted a cheery holiday message for Trumpists:

"A Merry Christmas and Happy New Year to all the Patriots who have supported us! . . . First, we're not Iranian. We are Americans who, for obvious reasons, need to conceal our whereabouts. The FBI is not loyal to Trump and have worked against him from the start."

If Iran was behind it, it was a head-spinning revelation, particularly for public servants who rarely attracted attention from their own constituents, much less hostile foreign powers. If the Iranian connection was true, Trump had handed America's enemies a lever to pry apart the American people. And it was working.

One evening in mid-December, Georgia attorney general Chris Carr came home at dinnertime, bearing a rotisserie chicken he'd picked up at Publix. His wife, Joan Kirchner Carr, was also a powerful figure in Georgia politics—chief of staff to Senator Kelly Loeffler. On this night, though, they planned to set work aside and watch a Christmas movie with Chris's sixteen-year-old daughter.

They had just picked out a favorite, *Elf,* when Chris's phone rang. Senator David Perdue calling.

Trump is mad, Joan remembers Perdue telling Chris. The attorney general in Texas was rallying other Republican attorneys general to join in a lawsuit against several battleground states Trump had lost, including Georgia. Perdue told Carr that the president believed he had been calling fellow Republican AGs and "telling them not to join that lawsuit."

"No, that's not what I'm doing," Chris answered. "Some of them are calling me to find out more information, and I'm answering their questions, but I'm not telling anyone to get on or stay off."

"Will you tell the president that?"

"Yeah, if he wants to talk to me."

An hour and a half later, Chris's phone rang again. A White House scheduler put Trump on. Chris paced the house as he explained his position to Trump: "I'm not trying to encourage people to stay off of the lawsuit, but it's my duty and the oath I took to defend our state from it, and that's what we're doing."

As Joan and her stepdaughter resumed watching *Elf*, they could hear the angry president's voice in the next room.

Wow, she thought, *this is where we're at.*

After the call ended, Chris rejoined the family. Then a few minutes later his phone rang again, Joan said. This time Senator Loeffler relayed the news. The president, she said, was still "mad."

ARIZONA

Lynie Stone, still dubious about the fate of her Trump ballot and spooked by the sinister number "666" she'd found in state spreadsheets, sent letters to congressmen and senators—to everyone.

After doing all she could to cry foul, she had begun to feel ignored. Like dirt swept under the carpet. As far as she was concerned, we the people had been duped. Early voting was all a scam. If only she could get others to pay attention! She felt like she wasn't big enough for people to notice her.

She begged her friends to care. She told them, "Are you telling me out of the hundreds of thousands of people, nobody looked at the Excel sheet, only me? I'm the only one that added the numbers up? Are you kidding?"

They didn't see it. They shrugged off her arguments. They didn't seem to care. She would tell them, "You know, this is *your country*, right?"

Then, at last, a connection. She found the Amistad Project through the only friend she had who shared her passion for the subject. Stone called their hotline—weeks after Fox News had named Biden the winner.

And Amistad took her seriously. It was a national legal effort to block the certification of Biden's victory, launched by the right-wing Chicago antiabortion, antigay marriage organization that had helped Leah Hoopes in Pennsylvania, the Thomas More Society. It was named after the Catholic saint who condemned Protestant heretics to be burned at the stake in the sixteenth century and who was himself executed for refusing to renounce papal authority over the church in England. More had become a symbol of standing alone against the enormous power of the state. Amistad was going to formalize the Blunderbuss Strategy by bundling fraud accusations from all over the country into one big federal lawsuit. Among its dizzying array of claims was that the massive donation by Zuckerberg's charity to buy voting machines and drop boxes had been an effort that "illegally circumvent[s] absentee voting laws to cast tens of thousands of illegal absentee ballots." This particular claim, like many others bundled in the Amistad suit, had gotten no traction in state courts.

Lawyers for the project didn't just hear Stone out; they asked her to join. At first, she was intimidated. Would she be brave enough to put her name on the lawsuit, to say, *I smell fraud and I'm calling you on it?* She sat with the decision for two days, discussing it with her husband. He was wary.

"Do you really want to do that?" he asked. "Do you really want your name on there?"

And finally, she said yes. Because somebody had to; somebody had to say, *I've had enough,* and be brave.

This was how the name Lynie Stone wound up as the first individual plaintiff on the Amistad lawsuit filed in federal court in Washington, DC, on December 22 by attorney Erick G. Kaardal of the Thomas More Society. Leah Hoopes was also on the plaintiff list. Stone felt proud. Even though she had been born a Kozlowski, the suit gave her a feeling of distant kinship to Thomas P. Stone, one of the signers of the Declaration of Independence. She felt connections like that were important. Somehow, through the centuries, the name Stone was again speaking up for liberty.

Kaardal took issue with the election in every swing state, resting his arguments primarily on rule changes regarding mail ballots. There were more specific allegations here and there and some questionable statistical analyses. It would cite Stenstrom's affidavit from Pennsylvania, and claim, "The 2020 General Election results are so severely flawed that it is impossible to certify the accuracy of the purported results."

There had still been no satisfactory explanation, as Stone saw it, for the disparities she had found on the Excel sheets, disparities that hinted darkly at the presence of evil. QAnon briefings linked the forces arrayed against Trump with an international pedophile ring. Any decent person would want to ally herself against that.

Above all, she wanted the light of truth. That's what it was all about to her: truth, love, and light.

These things might have motivated Hoopes, too. Certainly her sense of liberty did. But she and Stenstrom also sought to settle some scores. They had not forgotten the scorn they encountered at The Wharf. On the same day Amistad filed its suit in DC, the two joined with a defeated local candidate to ask Delaware County judge John Capuzzi, the one who had granted the election night request, for access to the "back room." The new petition asked that Delco's election officials be held in contempt for failing to fully comply with his order. Hoopes and Stenstrom objected to having been confined to a "pen" at The Wharf, a restriction their lawyer, in a gust of hyperbolic indignation, called "draconian," a reference to the ancient Greek legal code that decreed death for even minor crimes. Her argument, of course, ignored the state supreme court ruling that had rejected this exact complaint. Hoopes and Stenstrom wanted those who had confined and rebuffed them punished. The lawsuit asked for them to be fined $1,000 and/or imprisoned for up to a year. They also wanted the results of one local congressional election enjoined, demanding, like Karen Fann and the Arizona senate, an "independent forensic examination" of the election results.

The same day both those actions were filed, Clint Hickman, the egg industry scion and chairman of the Maricopa County Board of Supervisors, got a tip. Stop The Steal protesters were coming to his house.

The Hickmans, Clint and his wife, Jennifer, and their three children, lived in a sprawling five-thousand-square-foot, one-story home in Litchfield Park in the far western suburbs of Phoenix. Its short driveway made a U up to the front door and then back out to the cul-de-sac. The door stood behind four white pillars. The house was in a neighborhood crowded with million-dollar homes claimed from the surrounding desert. The land around it stretched flat, brown, and sunbaked, and the community decorated its lawns not with grass but with scattered palm trees, stones, and succulents.

The tip came from someone allied with The Steal movement who still considered Hickman a friend. He and the other county supervisors had been harassed continually since voting to authorize the election results weeks earlier. There had been so much abuse on Hickman's Twitter account, with calls for his arrest and execution, that he had finally closed it and then took criticism for doing so by Kelli Ward, the state Republican chair and an ardent Trumpist. She said Hickman was "slapping millions of Arizonans in the face."

Other political leaders who stood up to the protesters had been "Trump-Trained," with cars driving past blowing their horns. The group heading toward Hickman planned to leave their cars. The tipster forwarded Hickman online instructions for participants to convene at a nearby Lowe's parking lot and then "rally to the traitor's house," giving the address.

"You live here, don't you, Clint?" his friend asked. "Isn't this your house? They are coming tonight."

He called the sheriff's office and was promised help. Two patrol cars would monitor the assembly at Lowe's and then come to his house before the protesters arrived. He contacted his fellow supervisors to warn them that something similar might come their way. Bill Gates had already relocated temporarily with his family, expecting the storm to eventually blow over. The police had suggested that the Hickman family do the same, but they weren't willing. Hickman felt he was a solid citizen seriously engaged in doing his civic duty; he was not about to be run off for it.

"If you're staying, I'm staying," Jennifer told him. They found the whole scenario so outrageous that it was surreal.

Hickman texted his neighbors a heads-up and walked around knocking on doors to make sure everyone got the message. It wasn't the first time protesters had visited. In June, a group had convened to inveigh against the county's pandemic health protections, which required people to wear masks indoors.

"They're coming back," he told neighbors.

One of his friends, angry and more confrontational than most, offered to be out in front of his house to meet them.

"You can't come out," Hickman said. "You can't send your wife out. You can't." He said there would be deputy sheriffs present. "I'm fine," he told his friend. "The family is going to be fine. Don't come out. Don't engage."

He explained that he'd rather not see a brawl livestreamed from his block. He and Jennifer and their teenage boys and daughter planned to ride it out inside. Hickman's mother had dropped off four dozen eggs from the family farm that morning, and his sons suggested that they target the protesters from their walled backyard, lobbing them over the house.

Hickman nixed that idea.

Wouldn't it be fitting to egg them? they pleaded. *It goes with being the egg guy.*

"I don't want to egg them on," deadpanned Hickman.

The protesters showed up at dusk, walking from nearby side streets. Police, with their car lights flashing, blocked the cul-de-sac and turned cars away. Hickman's parents drove in from their farm to be with them but were turned back. The body camera of one deputy captured an encounter with a neighbor, who pulled up to the blockade and lowered the window of her SUV.

"Can we be mean to them?" the woman asked.

"No," he said and laughed.

"Can we throw some Hickman eggs at them?"

"No, no, no, no."

"Really, I can't? Are you sure?"

"We don't want to provoke," the sheriff said. "We just want you guys to live in peace."

"Such bullshit," she said. "I'm glad my twenty-two-year-old is not here. That would be ugly. The Hickmans are really good friends of ours."

"Nice folks," the deputy said.

As she pulled away, she spotted a protester standing in her yard. His face was wrapped in a bandanna decorated with a skeleton face.

"Get off my property!" she shouted at him.

"Where's your property?" he asked.

"Fuck you!" she told him.

The protesters milled in a large group before the house, about a hundred of them, chanting the things Hickman had grown accustomed to hearing.

"Traitor!"

"Lock him up!"

The deputies informed the group that chanting in a private neighborhood was actually against the law in Arizona.

"I'm going to start arresting anyone near me!" one called out.

So the group began singing. It was just days before Christmas.

"You can't stop us from caroling!" one said.

They tried out some yuletide fare without much success. Too few knew the words. They then attempted "God Bless America," which also didn't last. Folks knew only the chorus. When more deputies arrived, the crowd dispersed.

This kind of protest was worrisome but also silly. Hickman had more troubling matters to deal with. He was getting pressure from politicians, colleagues, in his own party, statewide. He stopped picking up calls from state Republican chair Kelli Ward and from any numbers he did not recognize. They could leave voice messages. One of those he got was Rudy Giuliani:

"Hey, call me back," the lawyer said. "I hear that you are interested in doing an audit. We want to help with that. Call me back."

Hickman and his fellow board members were already involved in litigation over Fann's demand for the election material. He could see himself dragged still further into a legal morass. He did not return Giuliani's call.

Shortly before Christmas, he received a voice message from Ward.

"The president wants to speak to you about an audit and the ballots."

He did not return that one either.

"Is there a chance that Kelli Ward is actually talking to the president?" Hickman asked a friend.

"There's no way," his friend said. "Kelli Ward is not that close. He's not going to call you."

But Trump did call. On New Year's Eve. Hickman and his wife were out to dinner with friends when he got a call from the White House switchboard. He didn't pick up. The caller left a message.

"The president is expecting a call back."

Hickman felt torn. He had, in fact, voted for the guy. Trump was still president of the United States. It would be something he could tell his grandkids someday. An honor. The president had called him, and they had spoken. But there was nothing honorable about this.

He did not return the call.

What did Trump expect of him?

What did Trump expect? Time was running out for the president. There only remained a formal, ceremonial acceptance of Electoral College ballots, which was slated to happen on January 6. The votes had been cast, signed by the governors of all fifty states, and stamped with state seals. America waited for the proverbial fat lady to sing.

In the sense that Trump believed true what he *wanted* to be true, there was room to believe he was sincere in using every crumb of conspiracy he found on the internet to press for audits and investigations. Perhaps he really did believe he had been robbed by Ruby Freeman and Clint Hickman and was struggling for America's sake. It was the most charitable interpretation of his motives. But a few days before this effort to reach Hickman, in a conversation with Jeffrey Rosen, the acting attorney general, Trump made clear this was not true.

Rosen was due to assume the job that William Barr had just left, after angering the president by stating publicly that there was no evidence of fraud. Rosen had received several emails from the White House in recent days. He'd gotten the talking points from Trump about the Antrim

County, Michigan, dustup, for instance. The presidential emails pressed claims made in several lawsuits that had been rejected in courts everywhere, including the Dominion voting machine theory and a new wildly speculative one suggesting that an Italian defense contractor had used satellites to hack American voting machines. The president wanted the Justice Department to lend its authority to these conjectures. He called Rosen nearly every day.

Notes of one of these calls show Rosen and his deputy, Richard P. Donoghue, declining to intervene. They told the president that the Justice Department could not and would not "snap its fingers and change the outcome."

Trump said he understood, but he wanted the agency to, according to the notes taken by Rosen's assistant, Donoghue, "just say the election was corrupt + leave the rest to me and the R. congressmen."

Just say the election was corrupt.

The approach was exactly the one taken the year before when Trump's team pressed Ukrainian president Volodymyr Zelensky to investigate Joe Biden and his son Hunter. When Zelensky protested that there was no evidence to warrant investigating them, even asking Trump to provide some, Giuliani told Zelensky's senior adviser, "all we need from the president is to say" that he was investigating.

In politics, just the announcement of an investigation could be damaging. In both cases, the goal was not the truth but to raise doubts, then about the Bidens' integrity and now about the integrity of the 2020 election.

Leave the rest to me and the Republican congressmen.

It was exactly what Bob Bauer, Biden's general counsel, had meant back in November when he said that all the president's bluster and legal challenges were not about the law or the truth; they were about misinformation.

Clint Hickman would have particular reason in a few days to be gratified that he'd dodged the president's call. What did the president expect of him?

Nothing honorable.

NEVADA

Few of those in Trump's orbit still had illusions. They had failed. The clincher came on December 15 when Senate Majority Leader Mitch McConnell publicly congratulated Biden on his victory. McConnell had also begun telling his colleagues that he wanted no dissent in the chamber when the Electoral College results were certified. For anyone with any sense of the law or the realities of political power, it was game over.

Not for Trump and his obliging attorneys. One was MAGA lawyer and RINO scourge Jesse Binnall. After striking out completely in Nevada, he was undaunted. As he saw it, the truth had simply not prevailed. Despite having had the opportunity to present his case in court and having every one of his assertions flatly rejected, Binnall continued to propound them vigorously.

He did so on December 16, testifying before the Senate Homeland Security and Governmental Affairs Committee. He led his presentation with the number of people his statistical expert, Jesse Kamzol, said had voted more than once—over forty-two thousand. It was a great number because it alone, if those voters were disqualified, might erase Biden's winning margin of 33,596.

"Our experts were able to make this determination by reviewing the list of actual voters and comparing it to other voters with the same name, address, and date of birth," Binnall said. The list of "actual voters" he referred to were those who had received ballots in the mail.

And so it was that the Nevada number, forty-two thousand, gathered steam on the internet, lending an air of exactitude and science to the "community of knowledge" about The Steal.

But Judge Russell back in Nevada had been right. The number didn't bear scrutiny. He had rejected Kamzol's argument after a long evidentiary hearing. Trump's team had presented a deposition of Kamzol, during which he had been cross-examined. He was, to begin with, less a scientist than a political activist. He was a nine-year employee of the Republican National Committee with a bachelor of arts degree from the University of Michigan. He had no academic credentials as a statistician nor any professional affiliations.

After the trial, Derek T. Muller, a law professor at the University of Iowa's College of Law, took a hard look at Kamzol's study and his deposition. He noted that unlike Binnall, Kamzol, to his credit, had hedged at the outset, saying that forty-two thousand was the number of voters who "appear to have voted twice." He might more accurately have said, "could have voted twice." As Judge Russell concluded (emphasis added), "The record does not support a finding that *any Nevada voter* voted twice."

How did Kamzol come up with forty-two thousand? He did not have access to actual voting records from 2020, so, as the judge noted, he did not know if anyone voted twice. He had reached his conclusion by comparing voter registration files with data from various sources, including Department of Motor Vehicle (DMV) records and US Postal Service change of address records, noting "multiple data point matches," without saying what they were. Muller pointed out that identifying actual duplicates in state data is an extremely difficult undertaking.

"Kamzol's report offers a beginning for an investigation," Muller wrote. "It is not the end in itself. And when pressed under cross examination, he could not defend even this conclusion."

The data sets Kamzol compared could not yield such a finding. There were many legitimate reasons for names and addresses to show up twice in the voter rolls. For instance, the DMV data he used did not disclose name suffixes or date of birth, according to Muller and contrary to Binnall's assertion. So if ballots had been mailed to John Smith Sr., John Smith Jr., and John Smith III, all at the same address, Kamzol counted all three as one person. By his count, John Smith voted three times. Some duplicate names existed in the various databases because of changes of address. In those cases, ballots may have been mailed to the same person at more than one place. Kamzol counted these as double votes. It was more likely that a ballot mailed to the wrong address was returned as undeliverable or simply failed to reach the recipient. Some women received ballots mailed to both their maiden name and their married name. Kamzol concluded that such women voted twice, although there is no evidence that any of them did. There were people who showed up to vote in person after having already cast their ballot by mail. They were allowed to fill in a new one, and their first was disregarded. The data would show that person voting twice, but only one ballot had been counted. Across the board, Kamzol's study ignored safeguards in place to prevent double voting. Its central flaw was the assumption that because a voter may have had the *opportunity* to vote twice, she had.

Kamzol's report was "minimized and in some cases retracted on cross-examination," Muller wrote. His claims withered when questioned. But Binnall, the MAGA lawyer, hasn't backed down an inch, and he's speaking on stages far more elevated than the deposition room in Nevada. As Muller wrote, "When someone testifies before a committee of Congress about a hard figure like 42,000, that's what gets picked up."

The law professor was, of course, just another fact-checker.

5

The Popular Front

Trump's campaign to overturn the 2020 election had three fronts: legal, political, and popular.

The legal front was an unmitigated disaster. The campaign filed sixty-three lawsuits contesting the 2020 election and lost every one. None of the theories or evidence of fraud presented by his small army of lawyers held up in court, any court. Some were dismissed by judges Trump had appointed himself. Some were appealed, none successfully. The US Supreme Court had refused to hear them.

Failure also marked the political front, even though Trump's claims were endorsed and echoed by many Republican lawmakers at every level. Despite this, every state in the union certified the popular results and delivered its electoral votes in accordance with precedent and the law, giving Biden 306 votes to Trump's 232. The flailing president then adopted a fringe legal view penned by John Eastman, one of his lawyers, that Vice President Mike Pence, acting as president of the Senate, could reject the Electoral College results, override the voice of the people, and simply proclaim Trump the victor.

This is surely the most seditious document to emerge from the White House in American history. Eastman advised that Pence could refuse to count electoral votes from seven states that had, in a spirit of protest, sent an unauthorized slate of Trump electors in addition to those officially certified. If Pence ruled that the outcome in those states was in dispute, which it was not, he could then simply refuse to count them. Subtracting those votes would give Trump a winning margin. Eastman noted that this would likely provoke "howls" from Democrats, at which point Pence could throw the election to the

House of Representatives, where Republicans had enough of a majority—controlling 26 of the state delegations—to accomplish the same thing. It was a prescription for a coup d'état, which the defeated president took seriously. He acted on it, leaning on his vice president. Pence, despite years of loyal servitude, sided with the US Constitution and more than two hundred years of American precedence. He told the president that he did not have the power to do it.

This left Trump only one avenue. He could still lead people into the streets. Demonstrations at election centers throughout the country had gone on for weeks. There had been "Stop The Steal" marches throughout the country. Trump had an "army" of true believers. Within their ranks were militant extremists like the Proud Boys and Three-Percenters, who, recruited by Trump campaign consultants, meant business. They showed up armed, organized, and outfitted for combat. The same arguments that fell flat in court were swallowed and circulated online and reported as legitimate by his media allies. His victory was being stolen . . . unless they stopped it. There was still time. Pence could still halt Congress from certifying the Electoral College results. If the vice president wouldn't do it, maybe Trump's army, "the people," could.

Trump summoned his eighty-nine million Twitter followers to the capital on December 30, tweeting: "JANUARY SIXTH, SEE YOU IN DC!"

GEORGIA

Brian Robinson, the crisis consultant who had been so horrified by Trump's performance at the rally for Senators Kelly Loeffler and David Perdue, was hired by Secretary of State Brad Raffensperger to help deal with the flood of misinformation and abuse directed at him and his staff.

When he arrived at the Atlanta offices, he felt struck by how jumpy the place seemed. It was a building under siege. Staffers kept bulletproof vests within reach. At one point, an alarm sent them all rushing from their offices. Once, as he and the secretary of state prepped for a press conference, Robinson, playing the part of an aggressive reporter, raised his voice. A security team burst into the room. Although there was always a chance things could get worse, so far the only actual attacks were digital or verbal. Those came from everywhere.

Including the White House. On January 2, the president himself called, three days before Georgia's senate runoff election and four days before Biden's victory was scheduled to be certified by Congress. Trump was out of time. He had stirred up a great deal of trouble all over America, a lot of it at Raffensperger's state, but he hadn't stopped the American electoral process yet.

The call lasted an hour. The president—after calling Raffensperger an enemy of the people, leading militants to his door, stirring dissent among his constituents—wanted a favor. It began with introductions by Mark Meadows, the president's chief of staff. Several lawyers joined the call on the White House end. With Raffensperger were Jordan Fuchs, his accused "Wicken" deputy, and Ryan Germany, the office counsel. Trump wanted more votes from Georgia. He claimed he had, in fact, won Georgia by fantastical numbers of votes. Hundreds of thousands were owed him, but he didn't want all of them. Just enough.

He accused one individual in particular of stealing them.

"We had at least eighteen thousand—that's on tape, we had them counted very painstakingly—eighteen thousand voters having to do with Ruby Freeman," Trump said. "She's a vote scammer, a professional vote scammer and hustler, Ruby Freeman. That was the tape that's been shown all over the world that makes everybody look bad, you, me, and everybody else."

Ruby Freeman of the big Afro, purveyor of ladies' accessories at Lady Ruby's Unique Treasures, whose singular act of national betrayal had been taking a part-time gig to help out on Election Day. The same Ruby Freeman whose voice mail tells callers she is "living holy and having fun without backsliding" and reminds them to "remember, in all thy ways, acknowledge God and he shall direct your path."

Ruby Freeman had become a vested item in the Blunderbuss Strategy, right there in the president's spiel with Dominion voting machines, secret CIA software, Joe Frazier and Will Smith's father, Italian satellites, and a leaky urinal. A video circulated online of her working at the election center, where hauling ballots was part of the task, and claimed to show her and her daughter, Shaye Moss, stealing Trump votes. Some people apparently believed it simply because the two women were black. The fake confession—wherein Freeman implausibly admitted swinging the election to Biden—sealed the deal. Giuliani tried to portray them as a pair of thugs. He had named them in testimony before a Georgia house committee, describing the mother and daughter this way:

"They look like they're passing out dope, not just ballots."

They had been, he said, "quite obviously, surreptitiously, passing around USB ports as if they [were] vials of heroin or cocaine."

This had consequences for Freeman. She stayed out of sight. Police records show she received hundreds of messages—too many for police to read—including death threats. Strangers turned up at her home. A group of men came to the home of her elderly mother and told her they planned to make a "citizen's arrest" of her daughter and granddaughter. According to police, someone sent Freeman a message that read simply, "We know where you live, we coming to get you." One of the people who knocked on Freeman's door was Trump supporter Trevian Kutti, who according to police "stated that she was a crisis manager and was sent from a high-profile individual and that she traveled from Chicago, Illinois." Kutti works for Kanye West, the music star and onetime presidential hopeful who had grown chummy with Trump during visits to the White House.

Now, at eight-thirty at night, Kutti said she needed to deliver an urgent message. Freeman called the police, who offered to escort her to the local precinct so she could hear out Kutti's cryptic report. There, as officers stood by, Kutti extended a double-edged dagger of an offer: "I am aware of an indictment that's on the table and ready to be served on you," she told Freeman. "What I would like for you to do is consider talking to a US attorney in the northern district of Georgia who is willing to take a statement from you and your daughter. And who in turn, if you are honest about the course of events that took place at State Farm Arena, will possibly be willing to grant you and your daughter immunity from charges that will imminently be brought." No one paid for her to visit Freeman, she said, but she felt "I have an obligation to the republic." And all this would unfold, Kutti said, within forty-eight hours. After listening to the terrifying message, Freeman told Kutti no—she didn't need her help or immunity. She only needed police to escort her back home.

Now Trump threw the story of Ruby Freeman at Raffensperger. Freeman and the leaky urinal, too. The leak, see, had provided cover for the big ballot switcheroo.

"Number one, they said very clearly and it's been reported that they said there was a major water main break," Trump said. "Everybody fled the area. And then they came back, Ruby Freeman and her daughter and a few people."

Raffensperger bit his tongue as Trump rambled. He cited ballot stuffing, dead voters, shredded ballots and burned ballots, voters who discovered at the polls that they "were already voted for," and more.

Finally, Meadows interrupted. "So, Mr. President, if I might be able to jump in, and I'll give Brad a chance. Mr. Secretary, one of, obviously there is, there are allegations where we believe that not every vote or fair vote and legal vote was counted, and that's at odds with the representation from the secretary of state's office. . . . I was hopeful that, you know, in the spirit of cooperation and compromise, is there something that we can at least have a discussion to look at some of these allegations to find a path forward that's less litigious?"

Raffensperger answered in his flat, firm way, "Well, I listened to what the president has just said. President Trump, we've had several lawsuits, and we've had to respond in court to the lawsuits and the contentions. We don't agree that you have won."

He began a point-by-point response until Trump interrupted.

"The people of Georgia are angry; the people of the country are angry. And there's nothing wrong with saying that, you know, that you've recalculated."

No, Raffensperger told him. He was not making a political calculation. The information Trump had been given was simply wrong.

"We're so far ahead of these numbers," Trump insisted, "even the phony ballots of Ruby Freeman, known scammer. You know the internet? You know what was trending on the internet? 'Where's Ruby?' Because they thought she'd be in jail. 'Where's Ruby?' It's crazy, it's crazy . . . She stuffed the ballot boxes. They were stuffed like nobody has ever seen them stuffed before . . . She's known all over the internet, Brad. She's known all over. I'm telling you, 'Where's Ruby' was one of the hot items. Ruby. They knew her. 'Where's Ruby?'"

He quizzed Raffensperger's lawyer about her:

"Every single ballot that she did through the machines at early, early in the morning went to Biden. Did you know that, Ryan?"

"That's not accurate, Mr. President," Germany said.

"Huh. What is accurate?"

"The numbers that we are showing are accurate."

"No, about Ruby Freeman. About early in the morning, Ryan. Where the woman took, you know, when the whole gang took the stuff out of the—from under the table, right? Do you know, do you know who those ballots, do you know who they were made out to, do you know who they were voting for?"

"No, not specifically."

"Did you ever check?"

"We did what I described to you earlier—"

"No, no, no. Did you ever check the ballots that were scanned by Ruby Freeman, a known political operative, balloteer? Did you ever check who those votes were for?"

"We looked into that situation that you described," said Germany.

"No, they were 100 percent for Biden. One hundred percent. There wasn't a Trump vote in the whole group. Why don't you want to find this, Ryan? What's wrong with you?"

It was an astonishing call, from the President of the United States. At one point Trump made a direct demand: "What I want to do is this," he said. "I just want to find 11,780 votes, which is one more than [the 11,779 vote margin of loss] we have, because we won the state."

Raffensperger finally responded, "We have to stand by our numbers. We believe our numbers are right."

Near the end, Trump came back to Freeman. He wanted something done about her.

"Hey, Brad, why wouldn't you want to check out Ruby Freeman?" he asked. "I mean, I've been watching you, you know, you don't care about anything." He repeated facetiously, *Your numbers are right.* "But your numbers aren't right. They're really wrong, and they're really wrong, Brad. And I know this phone call is going nowhere other than, other than ultimately, you know—look, ultimately, I win, okay?"

The call ended with Trump unsatisfied and with Raffensperger shocked. His election system, like those around the nation, relied on workers like Ruby Freeman and her daughter, who showed up to work long hours for minimal pay. Harassment like this would scare everyone away.

Later, Raffensperger read a book he had not picked up since high school: *The True Believer,* written by the philosopher Eric Hoffer. It describes the cyclical appearance of mass movements, which elevate charismatic leaders capable of sweeping away existing institutions. It had seemed outdated to Raffensperger as a teenager—all that postwar talk about magnetic leaders and fanatical followers—but now it seemed so current.

America had a leader in Hoffer's mold.

ARIZONA

A tape recording of the president's hectoring call to Raffensperger leaked less than a day later. Maricopa County supervisor Clint Hickman, who had, after careful consideration, not returned the president's call on New Year's Eve, listened eagerly to the whole thing. He told his wife, Jennifer, "I'm really glad I didn't take the call now."

But that evening, Sunday, January 3, he got another message from the White House switchboard.

"Please call the president."

He was taken aback. Jennifer asked if he was going to do it this time.

"No," said Hickman. "I don't have my lawyer here. And I'm definitely not going to tape the president."

The White House called again. Same night, same message.

"Please call the president."

Jennifer asked, "What are you going to do?"

"I'm going to call my lawyer. And I am going to ask him what I should do."

After hearing the Raffensperger call, he was afraid that in the pressure of the moment, he might promise something he would regret. He called Tom Liddy, the county attorney.

"I can't tell you what to do," Liddy said. "You're an elected official; he's an elected official. I can only guide you. And my thoughts would be do not call him. But I can't guide you to that. It's hard to turn down a call from the president of the United States. It's up to you."

"Okay, so this is the president," said Hickman. "Am I willing to put him on tape or not? And I need a lawyer. And you can't be here. So I'm not going to answer the call. But do you see what's going on here, how surreal this is for me, Tom?"

"I can," said Liddy.

"Do you grasp the significance of where we are together in history right now?"

Liddy's late father, J. Gordon Liddy, had led the Watergate burglars in 1972, so he had perhaps had a better feel for a historical moment than most.

He said, "It's not lost on me."

WASHINGTON, DC

The op-ed in the *Washington Post* on Sunday morning, January 3, showed that fears of a Trump coup were no longer on the fringe. It was a document unique in American history, in effect an open letter to the leaders of the US military from all ten living former defense secretaries: Ashton

Carter, Dick Cheney, William Cohen, Mark Esper, Robert Gates, Chuck Hagel, James Mattis, Leon Panetta, William Perry, and Donald Rumsfeld.

The men listed made strange bedfellows. They had served in both Democratic and Republican administrations. They had long histories of sharp and public disagreements about defense policy and, if anything, leaned more conservative than liberal. Two of them, Mattis and Esper, had served Trump and had resigned or been fired by him. But on the danger he now posed, with his refusal to accept the nation's verdict, they spoke as one.

It wasn't just Trump's tweets or phone calls or public pronouncements that concerned them. He had made prior efforts to enlist military leaders to promote himself, such as his early desire to preside over a Pyongyang-style military parade in Washington, his use of the military to help clear protesters from Lafayette Park across from the White House so that he could create a photo op, his desire to invoke the Insurrection Act to deploy the military in US cities, his recent replacement of top Pentagon officials—Esper was one—with men known to be loyal to him. Their fear was that the defeated president might try now to enlist the military to keep himself in power.

They wrote:

> Each of us swore an oath to support and defend the Constitution against all enemies, foreign and domestic. We did not swear it to an individual or a party.

Only the secession of southern states after the election of Abraham Lincoln and the ensuing Civil War had presented a crisis like the one Trump was threatening:

> American elections and the peaceful transfers of power that result are hallmarks of our democracy. With one singular and tragic exception that cost the lives of more Americans than all of our other wars combined, the United States has had an unbroken record of such transitions since 1789, including in times of

partisan strife, war, epidemics and economic depression. This year should be no exception.

Our elections have occurred. Recounts and audits have been conducted. Appropriate challenges have been addressed by the courts. Governors have certified the results. And the electoral college has voted. The time for questioning the results has passed; the time for the formal counting of the electoral college votes, as prescribed in the Constitution and statute, has arrived.

As senior Defense Department leaders have noted, "there's no role for the U.S. military in determining the outcome of a U.S. election." Efforts to involve the U.S. armed forces in resolving election disputes would take us into dangerous, unlawful and unconstitutional territory. Civilian and military officials who direct or carry out such measures would be accountable, including potentially facing criminal penalties, for the grave consequences of their actions on our republic.

Transitions, which all of us have experienced, are a crucial part of the successful transfer of power. They often occur at times of international uncertainty about U.S. national security policy and posture. They can be a moment when the nation is vulnerable to actions by adversaries seeking to take advantage of the situation.

Given these factors, particularly at a time when U.S. forces are engaged in active operations around the world, it is all the more imperative that the transition at the Defense Department be carried out fully, cooperatively and transparently. Acting defense secretary Christopher C. Miller and his subordinates— political appointees, officers and civil servants—are each bound by oath, law and precedent to facilitate the entry into office of the incoming administration, and to do so wholeheartedly. They must also refrain from any political actions that undermine the results of the election or hinder the success of the new team.

We call upon them, in the strongest terms, to do as so many generations of Americans have done before them. This final action is in keeping with the highest traditions and professionalism of the U.S. armed forces, and the history of democratic transition in our great country.

The story of January 6, 2021, unfolded before the eyes of the world. Trump's call to action, his pledge to lead the crowd to the US Capitol building, the storming of the building—with Trump safely back at the White House, watching on TV—Congress in hiding, and finally, a late-night vote to certify Joe Biden's Electoral College majority. One hundred and forty-seven Republican legislators, 139 House members and eight senators objected.

Later, even as Trump faced impeachment for instigating all this, his supporters rallied to defend the indefensible. Many argued that those who broke into and sacked the US Capitol had not been real Trump supporters but agents of the omnipresent Antifa disguised. Or, the rioters had not been rioters but ordinary tourists who had grown rambunctious. But no serious person felt the need to rebut such nonsense. The story was told plainly enough in the video recordings, photos, and boasts posted by the rioters themselves. Little wonder fellow Trumpists were trying to disassociate themselves. Many have been charged with crimes, and some already convicted and sentenced to prison.

The man who rallied them and sent them down that path was impeached—for the second time—but acquitted. He continues to insist he won. This is, perhaps, easier for him to believe than to accept that 81,268,924 Americans voted to deny him a second term. Fraud is also, perhaps, easier for his faithful to believe than to accept that so many of their fellow citizens disagreed with them. Biden's was the largest winning total for any president in US history.

When all the counts were finished and all the legal avenues exhausted, Donald Trump left office with a begrudging statement that "Even though I totally disagree with the outcome of the election, and the facts bear me out, nevertheless there will be an orderly transition," but never explicitly conceded Biden's victory. This wasn't just some ceremonial break with a tradition that dates back to John Adams. It was an attack on the integrity of American elections, the cornerstone of its democracy. Since retiring to Florida, he and his allies have kept at it.

In the weeks and months after the January 6 riot, it was labeled an "insurrection." If so, it was a sloppy, ill-planned, and tragic one but also buffoonish, a mob with a horned, spear-carrying faux barbarian chanting gibberish in the US Senate chamber and combat-clad rebels rifling lawmakers' desks at random looking for "evidence." It had no more chance of overthrowing the US government than hippies in 1967 had trying to levitate the Pentagon. The real insurrection had already played out in the months prior, in the courtrooms and streets of the six swing states. Led by Trump and his coterie of sycophants, it was only slightly better organized than the mob but considerably more calculated and dangerous. And it failed.

No investigation, audit, recount, or fact-check will ever sway Trump or his most ardent followers because distrust is their organizing principle. No one in a position to know can be believed. It is what Joe Gloria discovered to his dismay standing behind the podium at his daily press briefings in Las Vegas. If he himself were a tainted source, a man who had administered elections in Clark County for two decades, who knew the process inside out and who had never been accused of dishonesty or partisanship, what could he say that would make a difference?

To believe Trump's claim that there was a nationwide scheme to steal the 2020 vote means believing in a coordinated plot by Erie, Pennsylvania, postmaster Rob Weisenbach, Antrim County, Michigan county clerk Sheryl Guy, and Rohn Bishop, the most authentic Republican in America; in Delco, Pennsylvania, voting machines warehouse supervisor Jim Savage, county solicitor Bill Martin, former county council chairman and Republican attorney John McBlain, councilwoman Christine Reuther, county judge John Capuzzi, and even Valerie Biancaniello, the county's Trump Lady; in Atlanta, elections workers Ruby Freeman, her daughter

Shaye Moss, and envelope-opening machine operator Lawrence Sloan, and . . . oh, the secretary of state Brad Raffensperger and his entire staff; in Arizona, all the Maricopa County supervisors, its election directors Rey Valenzuela and Scott Jarrett; and, oh yes, George Soros, the US embassy in Rome, the founders of Google and Facebook and the Canadian-based voting machine manufacturer Dominion Voting Systems, one of the most successful in the world. The list is much longer just with those presented in this book, people who for the most part have never met each other, and stretches far, far beyond it. Given the decentralized way elections are held in America, it would be nearly endless. Yet, all were somehow in it together—Giuliani repeatedly insisted the same fraudulent patterns were repeated in every swing state. As such, it would be a stunning master-piece of coordination. And cunning, too, as Wisconsin's Dean Knudson likes to point out, because it would include Republican conspirators who somehow managed to throw votes to Biden while also electing their own slate to state and local offices. It is utterly preposterous.

And yet, the belief persists. To question it is heresy. So Trump's loyal attorney general, William Barr, who had initially horrified career prosecu-tors by instructing Justice Department lawyers to look into allegations of fraud, became a "spineless RINO" when, in a position to know, he said publicly that the department had found no significant evidence of it. Vice President Mike Pence was often ridiculed for his abject subservience to Trump through four years. When he stood by his conviction that he could not, as president of the US Senate, use his ceremonial role to overturn the Electoral College vote, Trumpists storming the Capitol erected a scaffold and threatened to hang him. Trumpism demands absolute fealty. "I alone can fix it," he boasted to the GOP convention in 2016. No one else is to be trusted.

Distrust. If there was anything like genius in Donald Trump's meth-ods, this was it. Democracy depends on that modicum of trust it takes to bring competing parties together after an election to govern. Without it, there can be no majority rule. With the vote itself discredited, the will of the people is sacrificed to a mob of self-styled "patriots" who have decided that they and only they speak for everyone—the opposite of democracy. From the day he entered public life, Trump had chipped away at the vote, that cornerstone. He sowed and planted and nurtured widespread distrust of many things, of government, of institutional and academic expertise of any kind, of mainstream media, of judges, of whole industries, but most often and most insistently, he chipped away at trust in elections. And when he lost, he mobilized that distrust to try to stay in power.

This failed, stopped by the integrity of hundreds of obscure Americans from every walk of life, state and local officials, judges, and election workers. Many of them were Republicans, some were Trump supporters. They refused to accept his slander of themselves, their communities, and their workers, and they refused to betray their sworn duty to their office and their country. They were the true patriots.

They saw The Steal for what it was: a fraud on the United States of America.

6

Epilogue

Delco's Leah Hoopes was disturbed by what she saw on TV on the 6th. She had been watching the rally, which was familiar to her. It was beautiful. A peaceful gathering of the faithful, people dancing, singing, talking about being Americans, their love of the republic, Trump's speech. She talked on the phone to people who were there.

Then as the attack on the Capitol unfolded, she was shocked, but she also understood. People like her were angry, tired of the corruption they believed came from that building. At the same time, she was unconvinced that the rioters were people like her. She grew to believe that outsiders in the crowd had instigated the violence, people *planted* there, and she felt skeptical of the way the mainstream press framed events. Some of those arrested in the following weeks and months she now regards as "political prisoners." Months later, she wasn't sure if the storming of the Capitol building was a good thing or a bad thing. It needed, she said, to be "thoroughly investigated, a serious investigation from every angle." It's unclear whose investigation she would trust.

Not the FBI. Agents came to her house in February to follow up on a tip that she had been part of the riot, which she says she was not. As with the visit made by state investigators after filing her formal claim of fraud, she was not at home when the federal agents came, so they left a card. She called them and referred them to her lawyer. Again, she was incensed.

"It was fucking infuriating," she said. "I don't have so much as a parking ticket."

She wondered why they were investigating her instead of the tip itself, although questioning her would seem to be a first step in doing either. Later, she heard that FBI agents asked a friend about her, whether she had played a part in organizing transport to Washington for the protesters. Hoopes laughed at the suggestion, although given her very public activism and the fact that she had helped organize Trump rallies in the past, it was hardly a stretch.

She believes that President Biden, whom she has called a "communist front" on her Facebook page, is turning America into a police state. Posting frequently and derisively, she continues to attack public health measures to curb the pandemic as stupid and oppressive, still claims the 2020 election was fixed, cheers a Trump candidacy in 2024, and berates local political figures—notably Christine Reuther, the councilwoman, and Valerie Biancaniello, the Trump Lady—whom she feels conspired in The Steal. She is thinking about running for office herself.

The lawsuit she and Greg Stenstrom filed in late November boomeranged. They had asked the Delaware County Court of Common Pleas to fine and imprison board of election officials for contempt and to order the county to turn over ballots for an independent audit. Their case was dismissed thumpingly by Judge John Capuzzi on January 12. He wrote that their "claims lack a scintilla of legal merit" and went further. He accused their lawyer, Deborah Silver, of "dereliction of duty" for failing to notice that several of the issues she raised had already been adjudicated in Pennsylvania and recently. He said her failure, which he called "unconscionable and inexcusable," had wasted the court's time.

"While the petitioners [Hoopes, Stenstrom et al.] seek sanctions against the Board of Elections, they come before this court with unclean hands and they themselves are the ones whose conduct is contemptible."

Hoopes and Stenstrom have appealed, and the board of elections has responded by asking the courts to compensate the county for its legal costs. The amount would likely be between $50,000 and $75,000.

State senator Doug Mastriano, the big, bald man with the colorful ties who orchestrated the hearing in Gettysburg on November 25, marched with the Trump rally to the Capitol steps on January 6. Continuing to champion doubts over the 2020 election, he demanded that three Pennsylvania counties—Philadelphia, Tioga, and York—turn over election materials so that he could conduct a "forensic audit" of their certified results. They refused. Then Mastriano secretly arranged for a privately funded audit in Fulton County, which concluded by upholding its vote count. The effort resulted, however, in the county's voting machines being decertified by the state, which, if upheld, will require its taxpayers to fund the purchase of all new machines. And despite his doubts about Pennsylvania's election process, Mastriano is still running for governor. His effort to force an audit of the 2020 vote in Pennsylvania has been endorsed by Jake Corman, the leading Republican in the state senate.

In Erie, after mail carrier Richard Hopkins recanted his story of fraud at the post office, he then *recanted* that recantation in another video for Project Veritas. In it, Hopkins's face was no longer blurred and his voice no longer distorted. He wore a red T-shirt instead of his US Postal Service uniform. He wore his hair slicked back, with a thin moustache.

Of the amiable interview he had with USPS agents Russ Strasser and Chris Klein, he said, "They were grilling the hell out of me."

His interviewer, James O'Keefe, squinted in concern. "How are you feeling right now?"

"I'm kinda pissed. I feel like I just got played."

In thousands of comments, viewers described Hopkins as a patriot, a hero, and a saint. "They didn't crucify Jesus Christ for telling a lie," one wrote. No one had suggested crucifixion.

Postmaster Rob Weisenbach received no such adulation. He filed suit against his accuser Richard Hopkins, James O'Keefe, and his Project Veritas.

Thanks to them, the suit says, Weisenbach "suffered unprecedented and irreparable harm to his reputation in the community. Among other things, he received death threats, was 'doxxed,' and confronted by a stranger at his home, prompting a response by local police with guns drawn. In addition, Mr. Weisenbach and his wife, Carolyn Ann Weisenbach, were forced to temporarily abandon their home and secure alternate housing."

The suit goes on to describe a man completely overwhelmed by his moment in history, when "his alleged criminal conduct became a political talking point for the President of the United States, ranking members of the U.S. Congress, the U.S. Attorney General, and also became fodder for the unrelenting 24-hour news coverage that saturates legacy media platforms. Literally, overnight, the slanderous and defamatory statements by HOPKINS thrust PLAINTIFF into the middle of a post-election frenzy heretofore never before witnessed in modern day America."

It resulted, according to Weisenbach, in "enormous stress, anxiety, sleep deprivation, depression, anger and torment."

Project Veritas's lawyer, Jered Ede, described the suit as "a fantasy land of baseless supposition upon which meritless claims are built," which sounds like a motto for the organization he represents.

Hopkins, according to Weisenbach's attorney, appears to have moved to West Virginia.

ARIZONA

Karen Fann's "independent audit" of the 2020 vote turned Maricopa County into both the last hope for Trump and, as Supervisor Bill Gates had feared, a laughingstock.

Headed by a Florida-based firm called Cyber Ninjas, led by a Steal adherent and funded in part by millions from Trumpists, this "audit" would be the state's third. The first two failed to find fraud. There was widespread anticipation that this private one would do the trick. Chances were good. Cyber Ninja CEO Doug Logan was determined. "I'm tired of hearing people say there was no fraud," read a tweet he retweeted. "It happened, it's real, and people better get wise fast."

Even as the recount inched toward this planned revelation, it was plagued by scandals, errors, reversals, delays, COVID infections, and the scathing denunciations of election experts. Dr. Barry Burden, who heads the Elections Research Center at the University of Wisconsin–Madison, concluded a detailed assessment of the project with the flat statement, "Any findings by the review are suspect and should not be trusted."

Maricopa's elected recorder, Stephen Richer, a lifelong avid Republican, issued a lengthy, savage "prebuttal" in August. Richer's office, along with the county's board of supervisors, oversees the county's elections. He reviewed his conservative Republican credentials, which included campaign work in 2020 alongside Trump's own supporters.

"I'm incredibly amused thinking about what my college, graduate school, or law school friends would say if they heard I was being accused of not being 'pro-market or conservative enough,'" he wrote. He had shunned the spotlight, declining every request for an interview until months after Joe Biden was sworn in.

"But I am human," he wrote. "If you prick me, I bleed. And if you consistently defame me and the people in my office, I eventually fight back. . . . Nobody stole Maricopa County's election. Elections in Maricopa County aren't rigged."

Richer detailed the elaborate precautions the county had taken to avoid fraud. He pointed out that any significant fraud would have produced obvious distortions in normal county voting patterns and that, in fact, the patterns of the 2020 election "almost exactly match" those in 2016. Contrasting the Fann-inspired audit with those already conducted, he noted the obvious bias of Cyber Ninjas.

"Finally—and the absurdity of this is mind boggling—the Ninjas appeared in a conspiracy-theory film about the election and allowed the film to be shot at the audit, while performing the audit," he wrote. Richer noted that previous work by the film's director, Roger Richards, "includes a movie allegedly exposing the workings of 'the deep state,' as well as [a] movie alleging extraterrestrial involvement in the September 11 terrorist attacks and that the Nazis had a settlement on the moon and Mars." The Arizona film starred Patrick Byrne, Trump's ally who founded the

Overstock site and who doled out more than $3 million for the private recount. Meanwhile, Trump and his committees contributed nothing, suggesting he knew it was a charade.

Not that Richer is against audits. He proposed at the end of his prebuttal that images of all of the county's hundreds of thousands of scanned ballots be posted on the internet.

"This way anyone in the world who wants to run his own count or own audit, or do his own data, could do so," he proposed. "This will take out some of the mystery of the process and invite a crowdsourced review. No more questions about if the machines accurately read the ballots."

Instead, Arizona has chosen, in the words of *New York Times* editorial board member Michelle Cottle, "clown-car chaos."

Despite its clear intent, the partisan "audit" failed to produce the desired result. It ended in September in fitting confusion. While the recount showed once more that Trump had lost Maricopa County, and by a slightly larger margin than officially reported, it nevertheless concluded that the election results were flawed. Or possibly flawed. It found the results were "very close to the margin of error." The report was spiced with a recitation of the usual suspicious circumstances, doubts, and conspiracy theories, none of it had been able to prove. For the elected officials who had certified the results, it was clear vindication. If a group created and funded by Trumpists, with the stated intent of finding Biden's victory fraudulent, had failed so plainly, who could continue to believe it was so? Trump, for one. The former president claimed that the "close to the margin of error" comment vindicated him, and showed that he had, in fact won—even though the report itself reached no such conclusion. In short, it was a decision that had something for everyone, and swayed no one.

Clint Hickman was the biggest Trump supporter on the county board. He worked hard for him. Just about everyone in his neighborhood, the folks who rallied around him and his family when The Steal protesters descended on their block, voted for Trump. He is now disappointed in the man.

"I don't like how he has punched down on local officials," Hickman said. "He or his people continue to punch down on people way underneath them to get what they want and I don't think it's appropriate for a former president to be too concerned with people in way, way lower levels just trying to do their job. I didn't think it was appropriate with Secretary of State Raffensperger. I don't think it's appropriate here. Punch somebody at the federal level, but there's no reason to punch down on people at the state and local level."

He was bewildered by Fann's Cyber Ninjas "audit."

"It's extremely strange to have an audit conducted by people who are not auditors," he said. With all his years in the family egg business, he was familiar enough with audits, but he'd never seen anything like this. He was "anxiously awaiting" the results. Anxious, perhaps, more than eager, because more than anything he wanted to put the whole issue of the 2020 election behind him, and behind the country.

So he was gratified by the Cyber Ninja's findings. He had gotten an early copy of them and was so astonished that a project so clearly partisan, so designed to discredit Maricopa County's election, had confirmed Biden's victory "by even more votes!" that he feared it was fake, that he was being set up. He credits the "honest Americans" hired by the company to do the work, to actually inspect each ballot, who, despite whatever pressure they were under, "remembered that they were handling something precious, the votes of real Americans," not just props in a stage-managed production.

"I don't feel like my final chapter can be written until all this bullshit is over," he said, noting new efforts to "goad the attorney general into investigating. We need to stay focused now on what happens going forward. This isn't over."

For her part, Fann insisted all along that she had undertaken the audit not to overturn the results but to restore trust in the state's election process, to which Richer replied, "Harm does come from witch hunts, even if you're not a witch."

Bill Gates believes that Fann deserves all the scorn that has come her way. She was the one person who could have stopped it.

"You can say if she hadn't done it, she would have been removed as president—well, she did do it," he said. "It's all on her. . . . People need to understand Karen and what happened and how we got here. 'Moderate' is a dirty word but many of us would have described her as a moderate or reasonable Republican with a background in local government— someone who looks for solutions, that's how people would have described her before all this."

Not anymore. He also points a finger at Kelli Ward, the state's Republican chair, who he feels led Fann astray.

"One of the main reasons for all this hullabaloo," Gates explained, "was that Kelli Ward lost the state for Trump. As Republican chair, do you wanna sit there and have everyone Monday morning quarterback you and say how you lost the state for Trump? Or is it a lot more fun to go out and say, 'Actually Trump did win: It was stolen from him, and I'm going to go out after the people who stole it from him.'"

It would be laughable if it weren't so dangerous. Gates says he hears people joke about "audit-tourism," lawmakers from other states trekking to Phoenix to gape at Cyber Ninjas at work, "kicking the tires on the audit and then going back to their home state—Georgia, Pennsylvania, New Hampshire, etc.—and arguing they should have the same sort of proceeding." Gates worries about the domino concept, that if Trumpists can overturn the votes in Arizona, it will trigger similar actions in one state after another. As we have seen, this is already being advocated in Pennsylvania.

"So this is dangerous, and I keep saying, *I'm going to wake up from a dream; this nightmare is over*, but it's not." Already, he says, candidates are positioning themselves for the 2022 elections, and the first question being asked potential Republican candidates is, "What's your position on the audit?" The right answer, for those who want the party's nod, is that you are in favor of it.

"Which is crazy," said Gates.

Lynie Stone, who saw the sign of the devil in voting spreadsheets, believes that the Capitol riot on January 6 was staged.

"*Something* was staged," she said. "The videos that I watched, they didn't make sense if something was organic, that was happening naturally. It was all like people moving in funny ways."

Erick Kaardal, the lawyer for the Amistad Project who filed the sweeping lawsuit contesting the election on her behalf and others, may be punished for it. US District Court judge James Boasberg formally referred him to the district's grievance committee, decrying, in particular, the Blunderbuss Strategy.

"Plaintiffs spend scores of pages cataloguing every conceivable discrepancy or irregularity in the 2020 vote in the five relevant states, already debunked or not, most of which they nonetheless describe as a species of fraud," the judge wrote. "The only reason the Court can see for the Complaint to spend 70+ pages on irrelevant allegations of fraud, not one instance of which persuaded any court in any state to question the election's outcome, is political grandstanding."

If the grievance committee concurs, Kaardal could face penalties from reprimand to disbarment. He has appealed.

Stone continues to pray and meditate on truth, love, and light. "My experience is that it's slowly, hopefully, slowly being revealed. . . . For me, it's, 'Please, God, let the truth be shown.' It could be anything, 'Please, consciousness.' To me, it's whatever you believe in, that's great; and hopefully, it's love and light only. Truth, love, and light."

NEVADA

During the battles in Nevada, with his offices and workers under siege, with his integrity questioned every day, Clark County elections director Joe Gloria lost his love for the work. His wife watched him get dressed in the early morning darkness in December—he was routinely going to work before five during those days—and she could see his attitude wasn't the same.

"I don't know how much more of this I can take," he told her.

"You know, Joe, you've been a public servant for a long time," she said. "You've done your duty. You don't owe anybody anything."

Gloria says that for him, those days were like the movie *Groundhog Day*, where the hero is forced to live the same day over and over again until he gets it right. In Gloria's case, there seemed to be no way to get it right since the very root of the complaints against him is his expertise. If you presuppose fraud, then he is, as the man in Clark County most responsible, the least credible.

Speaking of his wife, he said, "She sees me there, and she knows it affects my health, too. So she knows that I don't sleep at night, that I wake up in the middle of the night, oftentimes thinking about something that I need to get done or concerns that I have. . . . There's no going back to sleep. I usually end up going and sitting down and seeing if I can write down what it is that I'm thinking about. If I can't get sleepy doing that, then I take a shower and just go to work. . . . She sees all of that and she saw how this past election affected me day, by day, by day, and it was just an endless run."

He's done. He may go into consulting, but as far as election administration goes, "unless something crazy happens, I think that was my last one."

His wife made the call, as he remembers it.

"It was December, when it's usually over, and it wasn't over."

Jesse Binnall still thinks Trump won in Nevada. He is proud of the work he and his team did there—part of which was making Joe Gloria's life miserable—even though none of their claims held up in court. Much as Trump blamed local election officials for his loss at the polls, Binnall blames the judges. He doesn't believe his cases got a fair hearing.

"I felt that this is one of the most important fights I'd be in in my entire life," he said. "And I had to give it everything I had. Because that's what I had to control. I couldn't control what a judge can do. I couldn't control what the other side can do. Me and my team could control what we can do and we put together the best damn case we could . . . and I'm really really proud of it. . . . The most incredible thing is we appealed to the supreme court in Nevada where it's being heard by judges who have already commented on the issues publicly and refused to recuse themselves. Even after we requested it."

Binnall watched the storming of the Capitol on TV and later expressed sympathy for the rioters. He said he feels there was as much anger on the left after the election as there was on the right and rationalizes the January 6 eruption by circling back to the cases he failed to win in Nevada.

"I remember thinking to myself at the moment this is why it's so important to have election transparency," he said. "This is why it's so critical that elections not be done in the dark and the shadows."

He'll need that stubborn tenacity to deal with the backlash against attorneys, like him, who rallied around Trump in defeat. Some of the companies and officials accused of rigging the vote have come after them, and as with the judge who referred Kaardal for discipline, courts have not looked kindly on the Trump blizzard of litigation. Binnall is now defending Trump from the lawsuits filed by the Capitol Police and Congressman Eric Swalwell, and he is defending Sidney Powell from the defamation suit brought against her by Dominion Voting.

He was not one of the lawyers who joined Powell's failed November lawsuit in Michigan, seeking to decertify the election there. Much as Binnall had done in Nevada, Powell had employed the full-on Blunderbuss Strategy, alleging "multifaceted schemes and artifices" to defraud the vote, citing doctored Dominion machines, widespread "double voting," rejection of Republican observers, and the familiar list of charges. So he escaped being sanctioned by federal judge Linda Parker, who in August characterized Powell's filing as "a historic and profound abuse of the judicial process." Parker suggested that Powell and the other attorneys listed as cocounsels—Lin Wood in Atlanta was one—deserved to be disbarred. She slammed the Blunderbuss Strategy as "the haze of confusion, commotion, and chaos counsel intentionally attempted to create. . . . [O]ne thing is perfectly clear: Plaintiffs' attorneys have scorned their oath, flouted the rules, and attempted to undermine the integrity of the judiciary along the way," Parker wrote. "It is one thing to take on the charge of vindicating rights associated with an allegedly fraudulent election. It is another to take on the charge of deceiving a federal court and the American people into believing that rights were infringed, without regard to whether any laws or rights were in fact violated. This is what happened here. Individuals may have a right (within certain bounds) to disseminate allegations of fraud unsupported by law or fact in the public sphere. But attorneys cannot exploit their privilege and access to the judicial process to do the same. And when an attorney has done so, sanctions are in order."

She formally requested that the bar associations in states where the lawyers are licensed investigate disbarment, calling their lawsuit "frivolous." She also ordered Powell and the others to attend classes on the legal and ethical requirements for filing legal claims.

Rudy Giuliani, who led Trump's legal front, was suspended from practicing law in New York State. A panel of appellate judges wrote, "There is uncontroverted evidence that [Giuliani] communicated demonstrably false and misleading statements to courts, lawmakers and the public at large" in his whirlwind, multistate effort to overturn the 2020 election.

None of this has inhibited Binnall, the lifelong contrarian, from continuing to advocate their case.

"We were right on the facts, we were right on the law," he said. "I'll say it a million times."

He probably will.

GEORGIA

Stubborn plays both ways. Even after all the abuse, the threats, the scorn heaped on Gabriel Sterling following his speech calling for civility from the president, he has never considered leaving government work. "You couldn't drag me away right now," he said.

Some of that is down to personality. Sterling has a "streak of obsti-nacy. If you tell me I'm not going to be able to do it, then it's going to make me want to do it more."

In a larger sense, though, it's about the importance of the American public servant: the faceless, gray-suited figure tabulating and triplicat-ing, certifying and verifying. That anonymous toil inspires passion in Sterling, who raises his voice almost to a shout:

"The whole point of government is you're not supposed to know it's there," he said. "The road is supposed to get paved, the election's supposed to come off, you're not supposed to have to think about it. And all these people on the left and the right that organize their lives around, *and live and die by*, who is president, who isn't president, those are the unhealthy people that *cause problems in the long term of a demo-cratic republic.*"

Meanwhile, Sterling's boss, Secretary of State Brad Raffensperger, faces serious consequences for his steadfast refusal to lie. Georgia's politi-cos expect he will lose his next bid for reelection, in 2022, to primary challenger Jody Hice, a US representative and Trumpist. After Trump lost the 2020 election, Hice lustily promoted The Steal and attacked Raffensperger as he told the truth. On January 6, as protesters gathered before the Capitol assault, Hice said in a now-deleted Instagram post, "This is our 1776 moment."

"Right now, running for reelection, I know I'm in the election of my life," Raffensperger said. "It's going to be tough because I'm really fight-ing a disinformation, misinformation machine that's not been honest and truthful to the American people."

Raffensperger's stand was a lonesome one in a sense. It left him with few friends on either side of the political divide in Georgia. So he looked for inspiration from a distance, watching fellow sojourner Michigan state senator Ed McBroom. "I've not met with him, not talked to him. But the reason I believe that he speaks the truth is for one really big reason. It's a crazy reason perhaps. He's a dairy farmer. That man probably gets up at four every morning," Raffensperger said. "Maybe you don't trust an engineer that's your secretary of state. Maybe you don't trust the politician that has some office. But you can trust a dairy farmer."

Trump's call to Raffensperger—the one where he instructed the secretary of state to "find" enough votes—may result in the only criminal charges against Trump rooted in The Steal. Fulton County's district attorney, Fani Willis, is investigating Trump's efforts to influence the election and has requested that Raffensperger's office preserve all documents related to Trump's call. Willis's letter to Raffensperger outlined a serious set of potential charges against the former president, including "potential violations of Georgia election law prohibiting the solicitation of election fraud, the making of false statements to state and local government bodies, conspiracy, racketeering, violation of oath of office, and any involvement in violence or threats related to the election's administration."

In Raffensperger's view, Trump damaged his own political hopes more than anyone else could, with his false talk of fraud and downplaying mail-in ballots. "We do know now looking at the data that 28,200 people skipped the presidential race," he said. "Everything down ballot, but they actually skipped the presidential race."

That meant more than twenty-eight thousand people filled out their ballots but didn't mark a choice for any presidential candidate. "So I'm sure that people will dig into the data and look at, of those twenty-eight thousand people, did they vote in the Democrat primary, Republican primary, and then do some projections of what that would have looked like."

The implication is that Trump—who lost Georgia by about twelve thousand votes out of five million—might have won, if he hadn't turned off his own potential supporters.

Raffensperger, meanwhile, hopes the Republican Party can survive Trump and find a new leader. "What do we need to do? How do we build that unifying message and build a coalition of fifty plus one?" he said. "I think our best model will be someone of the order of Ronald Reagan."

Is Raffensperger laying the foundation to run for higher office? "No, I'm looking for who that person is. When I find that person"—here he grinned—"I'll say, hey, I found a dairy farmer."

MICHIGAN

Ed McBroom has about three hundred cows and about half need milking. He has a wife, a sister-in-law, and thirteen children who need him. He chuckled at the notion of running for any political office that takes him farther from the farm than Lansing.

"No, no," he said.

Besides, right now his own party is displeased with him. This past summer, when he finished his investigation into The Steal, he wrote a *sulfurous* thirty-five-page report that disassembled every conspiracy theory he could find. Dead voters, unsolicited ballots, vote-flipping computers, wagons and vans full of illicit ballots. In his opening letter he wrote, "Our present times are full of reasons for citizens to distrust their government, politicians, and leaders. The last year has seen so much amplification of this distrust. Perhaps it has never been more rampant and, certainly, modern communication helps to fan the flames of lies and distrust into an unquenchable conflagration."

McBroom wrote the report around the edges of his daily life, getting up before the sun rose over his red barns, or writing late into the night at his office in Lansing. The entire composition is a rebuke to conspiracy theorists, but McBroom reserved his fieriest words for the people who attempted to overturn an American election using the small and slight lever of Antrim County.

"Events in Antrim County sparked a significant amount of concern about the technology used to count ballots," he wrote. "This concern led to much speculation, assumptions, misinformation, and in some cases, outright lies meant to create doubt and confusion. The many hours of testimony before the Committee showed these claims are unjustified and unfair to the people of Antrim County and the state of Michigan. It has also been unfair to people across America."

Then, in bold script, he issued a roaring call for legal action:

> The Committee recommends the attorney general consider investigating those who have been utilizing misleading and false information about Antrim County to raise money or publicity for their own ends. The Committee finds those promoting Antrim County as the prime evidence of a nationwide conspiracy to steal the election place all other statements and actions they make in a position of zero credibility.

At the end of his report, McBroom slammed his point home by including page after page of the tally tapes recorded by voting machines across Antrim County. His colleagues and constituents could see the proof for themselves.

Aaron Van Langevelde, who stood up to pressure from fellow Republicans when his board voted to certify the election in Michigan, lost his spot on the board. When his term ended in January, the state GOP replaced him with a Republican activist. Van Langevelde has remained quiet about his decision and its consequences. But in March, he did accept an award for "professional courage" from Cardozo School of Law in New York. The speech he gave there provides some insight on his thinking. "We were asked to take power we didn't have," he said. "What would have been the cost if we had done so? Constitutional chaos and the loss of our integrity. Our institutions and the rule of law were being tested. And as tensions worsened, it was clear that my family and I were in danger. . . . I did everything I could to make it to that meeting, even though I knew it would cost me my position on the Board. Despite all the chaos, I did everything I could to advocate for the truth and defend the rule of law."

In the months since Antrim County clerk Sheryl Guy stepped forward to admit she had erred in counting votes, her detractors have harassed her.

Most painfully for her, as a Christian, this took the form of a pro-Trump "prayer vigil" outside her office that ended with protesters asking which door Guy used to leave for the day. Police escorted her to her car that evening. When her current term ends in 2024, she said, she will leave public life to spend time boating on Torch Lake with her granddaughter. That sounds pleasant, she said, but she expects to live the rest of her life in the shadow of one mistake. Even after more than four decades of public service, people will talk. "If you work somewhere this long and then you retire, that's kind of like, 'Remember 2020?'"

The deeds of these Michiganders—Van Langevelde, Guy, McBroom—do not move Bill Bailey, who filed the original Antrim suit. "Ed McBroom is a slimy person," he said. "I don't like the guy. I didn't like him before this stuff; I like him a lot less now."

Bailey's election suit is the only one remaining. The last vestige of The Steal. In May, Circuit Court judge Kevin Elsenheimer dismissed the case.

Bailey sees himself as following a long line of his ancestors, dating back to a John Bailey who fought in the Revolutionary War, a great-great-great-uncle who fought in the Civil War, a relative at Iwo Jima, and so forth.

He speaks of his suit in grand terms. Trumpian terms. Freedom and tyranny, life and death, a battle waged against Marxists and infiltrators. "We've appealed to the Court of Appeals," he said. "If they don't side our way, then we go to the Michigan Supreme Court."

His tone darkened. "I mean, I will follow this to the last drop of blood I have."

WISCONSIN

Bill Feehan, the state's third district Republican Party chairman and elector and one of those who ignored the popular will to cast his official state vote for Trump, has made his peace with the outcome.

In May, he was at a GOP "listening session" in Almond when a man stood up to announce that he wasn't going to vote anymore because of the fraud in the last election. Feehan admitted doubts remain. He said, "It's really hard to know how many fraudulent votes were cast in Wisconsin," but "there comes a point when the election is over, and that point has come and gone. Joe Biden is the president of the United States."

For even this half-hearted retreat, Feehan has been dubbed by some in his party a RINO.

Rohn Bishop, the burly red-bearded Republican chairman of Fond du Lac, took down the Trump sign in his front yard on the Thursday after the election. When some of his neighbors complained, he told them simply, "We lost."

He saw the Capitol riot in part as vindication.

He said, "As awful as it was, there was a part of me that wanted to say, 'See? I told you so.' You could see this coming up. . . . It's a stain on [Trump's] record he won't be able to erase. When you spend eight weeks lying to your base, what do you expect is going to happen?"

A woman called him in June to ask if he still had Trump signs. "Are you following what's going on in Arizona?" she asked. She told him that Trump would be president again later in the year—many of his supporters were holding out for August, when the private audit of the state's vote was expected to wrap up. But, the woman added, she didn't want a sign with Pence's name on it. Bishop told her he didn't have any that didn't read "Trump-Pence."

"You can take a marker and cover the Pence name if you want," he told her.

He was proud, and said so publicly, when his congressman, the man he had just helped reelect, Glenn Grothman, voted to confirm Biden as president.

In February, months after the state elections commission struggled over whether to certify the election results over the protests of Republican electors, Bishop was reelected to his party chairmanship. His neighbors came out in a blizzard to support him. After all the abuse he had taken for telling the truth, Bishop was touched.

"Despite the snowstorm, we had pushing forty people," he said proudly. "The sheriff was there, the district attorney was there, the county clerk was there, and these were locally elected Republicans that wanted to make sure I was reelected because they agreed with me, they appreciated the stance I took."

Bishop had wavered about seeking the job again. He feared that Trump loyalists would challenge him. But the vote was unanimous. He would remain the most authentic Republican in America, at least as things are seen in Wisconsin. When he stood to accept and to offer thanks, one of his friends thought he might be about to cry.

He didn't, and proud as he was, he didn't plan to keep the position for long. He decided to run for mayor of Waupun. He had T-shirts that read, "Rohn for Waupun."

His affection for the town gushed forth in one breath: "It's a part-time mayor and it's a nonpartisan position, but I like Waupun, and we have a lot of history in Waupun, and I was raised here, and I love the town, and the history of the town, and the people who live here and I'm a good advocate for Waupun, and the best part about being the mayor is basically you're the cheerleader for the city, and I'm kind of like, 'Well, who better than me?' And plus, we have a cute little slogan, 'Rohn for Waupun.'"

In Wisconsin, "Rohn" (Raahn) is pronounced the same as the "Waah" in Waupun. He says, "It helps people finally learn how to pronounce Waupun correctly."

Acknowledgments

The attempt to overthrow the 2020 presidential election, and the effort to save it, involved many people working across a great range.

This book, likewise, reflects the work of many hands.

We would like to thank publisher Morgan Entrekin, who conceived and guided the book throughout its creation. And assistant editor Sara Vitale, who kept the whole project organized.

Researchers Alice Lloyd, Jordan Howell, Grace Bartlett, Joanna Arcieri, and Allen Entrekin tracked down material with skill and perseverance.

And thanks to Bo Teague for her endless patience.

Cast of Characters

Bill Bailey: Antrim County, MI, real estate agent and Republican activist.

William Barr: US attorney general under Trump.

Rick Barron: Fulton County, GA, election director.

Valerie Biancaniello: Republican activist and Trump campaign head in Delaware County, PA.

Joe Biden: 46th president of the United States.

Jesse Binnall: Trump lawyer who headed legal efforts in Nevada.

Rohn Bishop: Republican party chair, Fond du Lac, WI.

John Capuzzi: Judge, Delaware County, PA, Court of Common Pleas.

Tucker Carlson: Fox News personality and Trump supporter.

Chris Carr: Georgia attorney general.

Geoff Duncan: Republican lieutenant governor of Georgia.

Jenna Ellis: Trump lawyer.

Karen Fann: Republican state senate leader in Arizona.

Bill Feehan: Wisconsin Third District Republican Party chairman.

Heather Flick: Lawyer for Trump's Nevada legal effort.

Ruby Freeman: Election worker in Atlanta, GA.

Jordan Fuchs: Georgia deputy secretary of state.

Bill Gates: Board of supervisors member, Maricopa County, AZ.

Ryan Germany: General counsel for the Georgia secretary of state.

Rudy Giuliani: Former New York City mayor, chief lawyer for Trump's election challenge.

Joe Gloria: Clark County, NV, registrar of voters.

Sheryl Guy: Antrim County, MI, county clerk.

Clint Hickman: Former chairman of the Maricopa County, AZ, Board of Supervisors.

Leah Hoopes: Republican committeewoman and poll watcher in Delaware County, PA.

Richard Hopkins: Erie, PA, postal worker.

Scott Jarrett: Codirector of elections, Maricopa County, AZ.

Jesse Kamzol: Former researcher for the Republican National Committee.

Dean Knudson: Hudson, WI, veterinarian. He has served as Hudson mayor, state assemblyman, and head of the state's elections commission.

Chris Krebs: Head of US Cybersecurity and Infrastructure Security Agency.

Howard Lazarus: Delaware County, PA, executive director.

Tom Liddy: County attorney for Maricopa County, AZ.

Kelly Loeffler: Former US senator from Georgia, who lost campaign for reelection in 2021.

Bill Martin: Delaware County, PA, solicitor.

Doug Mastriano: Republican state senator in Pennsylvania.

John McBlain: Attorney for the Delaware County, PA, Republican Committee, former county council chairman.

Ed McBroom: Republican state senator in Michigan.

Mitch McConnell: Republican US senator from Kentucky and the Senate majority leader, now minority leader.

Amanda Milius: Media director for Trump's legal effort in Nevada.

James O'Keefe: Right-wing activist and provocateur, founder of Project Veritas.

Mike Pence: Trump's vice president.

David Perdue: Former US senator from Georgia, who lost bid for reelection in 2021.

John Porter: Chief of staff for Georgia's Republican lieutenant governor Geoff Duncan.

Sidney Powell: Attorney for Trump and conspiracy theorist.

Brad Raffensperger: Republican secretary of state for Georgia.

Christine Reuther: Democratic councilwoman in Delaware County, PA, responsible for preparing for the county's 2020 election.

Bruce Robinson: Georgia Republican political consultant.

Mike Roman: Trump's director of election day operations, former director of Special Projects and Research.

Jeff Rosen: Acting US attorney general after William Barr's resignation.

Norm Shinkle: Republican member of the Michigan State Board of Canvassers.

Lawrence Sloan: Election worker in Atlanta, GA.

Greg Stenstrom: Republican poll watcher in Delaware County, PA.

Gabriel Sterling: Republican chief operating officer for Georgia secretary of state.

Lynie Stone: An animal chiropractor in Arizona who feared her vote for Trump wasn't counted.

Marko Trickovic: Trump activist in Maricopa County, AZ.

Donald Trump: 45th president of the United States.

Rey Valenzuela: Codirector of elections, Maricopa County, AZ.

Aaron Van Langevelde: Republican member of the Michigan State Board of Canvassers.

Kelli Ward: Chair, Arizona Republican Party.

Rob Weisenbach: Postmaster, Erie County, PA.

Lin Wood: Atlanta lawyer and conspiracy theorist.

Appendix A

List of House Members Who Objected to Certifying the Electoral College Results

Name (Party, District)	Arizona	Pennsylvania	Quote(s)
Robert Aderholt (R-AL-4)	Yes	Yes	
Rick Allen (R-GA-12)	Yes	Yes	"Objecting to certify the electors in certain states today will not undermine our beleaguered institutions, as some critics charge, but rather reinforce and defend them."—January 6, 2021[1]
Jodey Arrington (R-TX-19)	Yes	Yes	
Brian Babin (R-TX-36)	Yes	Yes	
Jim Baird (R-IN-4)	Yes	Yes	
Jim Banks (R-IN-3)	Yes	Yes	"Many of us believe that COVID has exposed a number of problems in the election systems in states, especially states who unconstitutionally changed their voting laws and election rules on the eve of the election."—January 4, 2021[2]
Cliff Bentz (R-OR-2)	No	Yes	
Jack Bergman (R-MI-1)	Yes	Yes	
Stephanie Bice (R-OK-5)	Yes	Yes	

(continued)

Name (Party, District)	Arizona	Pennsylvania	Quote(s)
Andy Biggs (R-AZ-5)	Yes	Yes	
Dan Bishop (R-NC-9)	Yes	Yes	
Lauren Boebert (R-CO-3)	Yes	Yes	
Mike Bost (R-IL-12)	Yes	Yes	
Mo Brooks (R-AL-5)	Yes	Yes	"I and 55 other members of the United States House of Representatives object to the electoral vote for the State of Nevada in order to protect the lawful votes of Nevada and all other American citizens."—January 6, 2021 (from House floor)[3]
Ted Budd (R-NC-13)	Yes	Yes	
Tim Burchett (R-TN-2)	Yes	Yes	
Michael Burgess (R-TX-26)	Yes	Yes	
Ken Calvert (R-CA-42)	Yes	Yes	
Kat Cammack (R-FL-3)	Yes	Yes	
Jerry Carl (R-AL-1)	Yes	Yes	
Buddy Carter (R-GA-1)	Yes	Yes	"When the Capitol was stormed, when the House chamber was stormed by a few who got out of control and who should be held accountable . . . But it's important to note why we were there, and it's important to note, these are two separate incidents . . . I'm not questioning the results of the election, I'm questioning the process."—January 7, 2021[4]
John Carter (R-TX-31)	Yes	Yes	

Name (Party, District)	Arizona	Pennsylvania	Quote(s)
Madison Cawthorn (R-NC-11)	Yes	Yes	"When other officials who are not vested with constitutional authority usurp their role and grind the Constitution under their heel, I must object."—January 6, 2021 (from House floor)
Steve Chabot (R-OH-1)	No	Yes	
Ben Cline (R-VA-6)	Yes	Yes	
Michael Cloud (R-TX-27)	Yes	Yes	
Andrew Clyde (R-GA-9)	Yes	Yes	
Tom Cole (R-OK-4)	Yes	Yes	
Rick Crawford (R-AR-1)	Yes	Yes	"It's not the electors that I question, it's the method by which those electors were chosen. It's not necessarily about this election, as much as it is about the next election."—January 4, 2021[5]
Warren Davidson (R-OH-8)	Yes	Yes	
Scott DesJarlais (R-TN-4)	Yes	Yes	
Mario Diaz-Balart (R-FL-25)	Yes	Yes	
Byron Donalds (R-FL-19)	Yes	Yes	
Jeff Duncan (R-SC-3)	Yes	Yes	"Our mission is simple: Count every legal vote, throw out every illegal vote, and investigate every irregularity and allegation. All Americans should be on board with this mission."—December 30, 2021[6]
Neal Dunn (R-FL-2)	Yes	Yes	
Ron Estes (R-KS-4)	Yes	Yes	
Pat Fallon (R-TX-4)	Yes	Yes	

(continued)

Name (Party, District)	Arizona	Pennsylvania	Quote(s)
Michelle Fischbach (R-MN-7)	Yes	Yes	
Scott Fitzgerald (R-WI-5)	Yes	Yes	
Chuck Fleischmann (R-TN-3)	Yes	Yes	
Virginia Foxx (R-NC-5)	No	Yes	
Scott Franklin (R-FL-15)	Yes	Yes	
Russ Fulcher (R-ID-1)	Yes	Yes	
Matt Gaetz (R-FL-1)	Yes	Yes	"I don't know if the reports are true, but the *Washington Times* has just reported some pretty compelling evidence from a facial recognition company showing that some of the people who breached the Capitol today were not Trump supporters. They were masquerading as Trump supporters, and in fact were members of the violent terrorist group, Antifa.... This fraud was systemic, it was repeated. It was the same system and I dare say it was effective. We saw circumstances where when Democrat operatives couldn't get the outcomes they wanted in state legislatures, when they couldn't get the job done there, they went and pressured, and litigated, and usurped the Constitution with extra constitutional action of some officials in some states. They fraudulently laundered ballots, votes, voter registration forms, and then they limited review."—January 6, 2021 (from House floor)
Mike Garcia (R-CA-25)	Yes	Yes	
Bob Gibbs (R-OH-7)	Yes	Yes	

Name (Party, District)	Arizona	Pennsylvania	Quote(s)
Carlos Gimenez (R-FL-26)	Yes	Yes	
Louie Gohmert (R-TX-1)	Yes	Yes	"I object to the electoral votes of the State of Wisconsin because 71 House members, all of who condemn violence as we witnessed today, are firmly committed to the resolution of disagreements in civil, lawful, peaceful institutions with full and fair debate, free of violence. . . . Democrat leaders in Milwaukee illegally and unconstitutionally created more than 200 illegal polling places; tens of thousands of votes were changed by workers despite election workers objections. Plus so many other illegalities to fraudulently create a twenty thousand vote lead." —January 6, 2021 (from House floor)
Bob Good (R-VA-5)	Yes	Yes	
Lance Gooden (R-TX-5)	Yes	Yes	
Paul Gosar (R-AZ-4)	Yes	Yes	
Garret Graves (R-LA-6)	No	Yes	
Sam Graves (R-MO-6)	Yes	Yes	
Mark Green (R-TN-7)	Yes	Yes	
Marjorie Taylor Greene (R-GA-14)	Yes	Yes	"I, along with 70 of my Republican colleagues object to the counting of the electoral votes for the State of Michigan on the grounds that the error rate precedes (sic) the FEC rate allowed at 0.0008 percent and that the people who signed affidavits at risk of perjury, their voices have not been heard in a court of law."—January 6, 2021[7]

(continued)

Name (Party, District)	Arizona	Pennsylvania	Quote(s)
			"We aren't going to let this election be stolen by Joe Biden and the Democrats. President Trump won by a landslide."—December 21, 2020[8]
Morgan Griffith (R-VA-9)	Yes	Yes	
Michael Guest (R-MS-3)	Yes	Yes	
Jim Hagedorn (R-MN-1)	Yes	Yes	
Andy Harris (R-MD-1)	Yes	Yes	
Diana Harshbarger (R-TN-1)	Yes	Yes	
Vicky Hartzler (R-MO-4)	Yes	Yes	
Kevin Hern (R-OK-1)	Yes	Yes	
Yvette Herrell (R-NM-2)	Yes	Yes	
Jody Hice (R-GA-10)	Yes	Yes	
Clay Higgins (R-LA-3)	Yes	Yes	
Richard Hudson (R-NC-8)	Yes	Yes	
Darrell Issa (R-CA-50)	Yes	Yes	
Ronny Jackson (R-TX-13)	Yes	Yes	
Chris Jacobs (R-NY-27)	Yes	Yes	"There's been a lot of questions about election integrity, but I was going in terms of my constitutional role."—January 7, 2021[9]

Name (Party, District)	Arizona	Pennsylvania	Quote(s)
Bill Johnson (R-OH-6)	Yes	Yes	
Mike Johnson (R-LA-4)	Yes	Yes	
Jim Jordan (R-OH-4)	Yes	Yes	
John Joyce (R-PA-13)	Yes	Yes	
Fred Keller (R-PA-12)	No	Yes	
Mike Kelly (R-PA-16)	Yes	Yes	"Notwithstanding these events, I still objected to Pennsylvania's slate of electors. The tragic attack on the U.S. Capitol does not change the fact that Act 77's no excuse mail-in ballot system violates the Pennsylvania Constitution and Governor Wolf and Secretary Boockvar disregarded the law in multiple ways leading up to the election."—January 7, 2021[10]
Trent Kelly (R-MS-1)	Yes	Yes	
David Kustoff (R-TN-8)	No	Yes	
Doug LaMalfa (R-CA-1)	Yes	Yes	
Doug Lamborn (R-CO-5)	Yes	Yes	
Jacob LaTurner (R-KS-2)	Yes	Not Voting	
Debbie Lesko (R-AZ-8)	Yes	Yes	
Billy Long (R-MO-7)	Yes	Yes	
Barry Loudermilk (R-GA-11)	Yes	Yes	

(continued)

Name (Party, District)	Arizona	Pennsylvania	Quote(s)
Frank Lucas (R-OK-3)	Yes	Yes	
Blaine Luetkemeyer (R-MO-3)	Yes	Yes	
Nicole Malliotakis (R-NY-11)	Yes	Yes	
Tracey Mann (R-KS-1)	Yes	Yes	
Brian Mast (R-FL-18)	Yes	Yes	
Kevin McCarthy (R-CA-23)	Yes	Yes	
Lisa McClain (R-MI-10)	Yes	Yes	"The American people need to have confidence in our democratic elections and the Rule of Law. If the ECA, as followed by myself and my colleagues, conflicts with our Constitution, then that needs to be addressed in the appropriate manner. What we saw is the rule of law and due process at work—just as our Founding Fathers intended."—January 6, 2021[11]
Daniel Meuser (R-PA-9)	No	Yes	
Carol Miller (R-WV-3)	Yes	Yes	
Mary Miller (R-IL-15)	Yes	Yes	
Alex Mooney (R-WV-2)	No	Yes	
Barry Moore (R-AL-2)	Yes	Yes	
Markwayne Mullin (R-OK-2)	Yes	Yes	
Gregory Murphy (R-NC-3)	No	Yes	

Name (Party, District)	Arizona	Pennsylvania	Quote(s)
Troy Nehls (R-TX-22)	Yes	Yes	
Ralph Norman (R-SC-5)	Yes	Yes	
Devin Nunes (R-CA-22)	Yes	Yes	
Jay Obernolte (R-CA-8)	Yes	Yes	
Burgess Owens (R-UT-4)	No	Yes	
Steven Palazzo (R-MS-4)	Yes	Yes	
Gary Palmer (R-AL-6)	Yes	Yes	
Greg Pence (R-IN-6)	No	Yes	
Scott Perry (R-PA-10)	Yes	Yes	"Sadly, but resolutely I object to the electoral votes of my beloved Commonwealth of Pennsylvania on the grounds of multiple constitutional infractions, that they were not, under all of the known circumstances regularly given."—January 6, 2021 (from House floor)
August Pfluger (R-TX-11)	Yes	Yes	
Bill Posey (R-FL-8)	Yes	Yes	
Guy Reschenthaler (R-PA-14)	Yes	Yes	
Tom Rice (R-SC-7)	Yes	Yes	
Hal Rogers (R-KY-5)	Yes	Yes	

(continued)

Name (Party, District)	Arizona	Pennsylvania	Quote(s)
Mike Rogers (R-AL-3)	Yes	Yes	"These allegations of election fraud must be thoroughly investigated before Congress can act. The results of a handful of states critical to both campaigns are in serious doubt. Our elections should be free, fair and transparent. The 2020 election was not. Therefore, I will object to the results of the Electoral College."—January 4, 2021[12]
John Rose (R-TN-6)	Yes	Yes	
Matt Rosendale (R-MT-AL)	Yes	Yes	
David Rouzer (R-NC-7)	Yes	Yes	
John Rutherford (R-FL-4)	Yes	Yes	"To be clear, my objection and those of my colleagues did not have enough support to change the outcome of the election; yet it was a vote rooted in what I believe is my oath to uphold our Constitution And hold states accountable. Objecting to electoral votes is a regular part of Congress's role in certifying electors and ensuring the integrity of our elections."—January 15, 2021[13]
Steve Scalise (R-LA-1)	Yes	Yes	
David Schweikert (R-AZ-6)	No	Yes	
Pete Sessions (R-TX-17)	Yes	Yes	
Adrian Smith (R-NE-3)	Yes	Yes	
Jason Smith (R-MO-8)	Yes	Yes	
Lloyd Smucker (R-PA-11)	No	Yes	"My objection is not about voter fraud, it is grounded on unconstitutional measures taken by bureaucrats and partisan justices on the Commonwealth of Pennsylvania that have unlawfully changed how this election was carried out."—January 6, 2021 (from House floor)

Name (Party, District)	Arizona	Pennsylvania	Quote(s)
Elise Stefanik (R-NY-21)	No	Yes	
Greg Steube (R-FL-17)	Yes	Yes	
Chris Stewart (R-UT-2)	No	Yes	
Glenn Thompson (R-PA-15)	No	Yes	
Tom Tiffany (R-WI-7)	Yes	Yes	
William Timmons (R-SC-4)	Yes	Yes	
Jefferson Van Drew (R-NJ-2)	Yes	Yes	"It's not so much that I want to overturn the election. It is the fact that some really, really—if everybody would clear their head and look at this—that some really wrong things did happen."—January 6, 2021[14]
Beth Van Duyne (R-TX-24)	No	Yes	
Tim Walberg (R-MI-7)	Yes	Yes	
Jackie Walorski (R-IN-2)	Yes	Yes	
Randy Weber (R-TX-14)	Yes	Yes	
Daniel Webster (R-FL-11)	Yes	Yes	
Roger Williams (R-TX-25)	Yes	Yes	
Joe Wilson (R-SC-2)	Yes	Yes	

(continued)

Name (Party, District)	Arizona	Pennsylvania	Quote(s)
Rob Wittman (R-VA-1)	No	Yes	
Ron Wright (R-TX-6)	Yes	Yes	
Lee Zeldin (R-NY-1)	Yes	Yes	"I have a duty to speak out about confirmed, evidence-filled issues with the administration of the 2020 presidential election in certain battle ground states."—January 6, 2021[15]

1. Rick W. Allen, "Objecting to . . . Defend Them," Twitter, January 6, 2021. Accessed October 12, 2021. https://twitter.com/RepRickAllen/status/1346843860530552835?s=20.
2. Dirk Rowley, "Jim Banks Explains His Plan to Protest Some Electoral Votes," wane.com, January 4, 2021, https://www.wane.com/news/local-news/jim-banks-explains-his-plan-to-protest-some-electoral-votes/.
3. https://www.govinfo.gov/content/pkg/CREC-2021-01-06/html/CREC-2021-01-06-pt1-PgH76-4.htm.
4. Buddy Carter, "When the Capitol . . . the process," Twitter, January 7, 2021. Accessed October 12, 2021. https://twitter.com/repbuddycarter/status/1347258973548924930?lang=en.
5. Shelby Rose, "Arkansas Rep. Rick Crawford Supports Objection to Electoral College Vote," January 4, 2021, https://katv.com/news/local/rep-rick-crawford-supports-objection-to-the-electoral-college.
6. https://jeffduncan.house.gov/media/press-releases/duncan-plans-object-electoral-college-certification.
7. The Recount, "Rep. Marjorie Taylor Greene (R-GA) Unsuccessfully Objects to Michigan's Electoral Votes," Twitter, January 7, 2021. Accessed October 12, 2021. https://twitter.com/therecount/status/1347047594460119040?lang=en.
8. Scott Dworkin, "Here's Video . . . by a Landslide" Twitter, January 28, 2021. Accessed October 12, 2021. https://twitter.com/funder/status/1354919728888881158?lang=en.
9. Hannah Buehler, "Chris Jacobs Talks about Election Certification Objection," ABC News Buffalo, January 7, 2021, https://www.wkbw.com/news/local-news/chris-jacobs-talks-about-election-certification-objection.
10. Mike Kelly, "Kelly Statement on Breach of U.S. Capitol and Objection to Pennsylvania's Electors," January 7, 2021. https://kelly.house.gov/press-release/kelly-statement-breach-us-capitol-and-objection-pennsylvanias-electors.
11. Lisa McClain, "Congresswoman McClain on Certifying the 2020 Election," January 6, 2021. https://mcclain.house.gov/media/press-releases/congresswoman-mcclain-certifying-2020-election.
12. Mike Rogers, "Rogers to Oppose Upcoming Electoral College Results for 2020 Election," January 4, 2021. https://mikerogers.house.gov/news/documentsingle.aspx?DocumentID=1807.
13. John Rutherford, "Rutherford Details Objections to State Electors," January 15, 2021. https://rutherford.house.gov/media/press-releases/rutherford-details-objections-state-electors.
14. Mike Catalini, "Van Drew Only New Jersey Rep to Oppose Biden Certification," Associated Press, January 7, 2021. https://apnews.com/article/election-2020-joe-biden-donald-trump-new-jersey-elections-6a9c7283e973f248bf66158fb760d753.
15. "Jan. 6 Statement in Congress by Lee Zeldin," East Hampton Star, January 7, 2021, https://www.easthamptonstar.com/202117/jan-6-statement-congress-lee-zeldin.

Appendix B

List of Senators Who Objected to Certifying the Electoral College Results

Name, State	Quote
Ted Cruz (TX)	"But for those who respect the voters, simply telling the voters, go jump in a lake, the fact that you have deep concerns is of no moment to us. That jeopardizes, I believe, the legitimacy of this, and subsequent elections." January 6, 2021
Josh Hawley (MO)	"The state of Pennsylvania, quite apart from allegations of any fraud. You have a state constitution that has been interpreted for over a century to say that there is no mail-in balloting permitted except for in very narrow circumstances that's also provided for in the law. And yet, last year Pennsylvania elected officials passed a whole new law that allows universal mail-in balloting, and did it irregardless [sic] of what the Pennsylvania constitution says." January 6, 2021
Cindy Hyde-Smith (MS)	"The people I represent do not believe the presidential election was constitutional and cannot accept the Electoral College decision; therefore, I cannot in good conscience support certification." January 6, 2021[1]
Cynthia Lummis (WY)[2]	"Let me be clear: My objecting to the certification of the votes in Pennsylvania was never intended to change the outcome of the election. Congress cannot and shall not dictate the results of a presidential election to our states." January 7, 2021[3]
John Kennedy (LA)[4]	"I joined several Senate colleagues in calling for a bipartisan commission to inspect election issues raised across the country. Our proposal was not successful, but our goal to ensure full confidence and transparency in our elections—for all Americans—is a noble one, and I'll keep pursuing it." January 7, 2021[5]

(continued)

Name, State	Quote
Roger Marshall (KS)	"I rise today to restore integrity to our republic." January 6, 2021
Rick Scott (FL)[6]	"We simply cannot tolerate partisan political attempts to change the rules and tip the scales in our elections." January 6, 2021[7]
Tommy Tuberville (AL)	"I have serious concerns that the state of Arizona did not act in accordance with their own duly enacted laws when conducting this election." January 7, 2021[8]

1. Adam Ganucheau, "Sen. Cindy Hyde-Smith Supports Losing Effort to Overturn Biden Presidential Victory," *Mississippi Today*, January 6, 2021, https://mississippitoday.org/2021/01/06/sen-cindy-hyde-smith-supports-losing-effort-to-overturn-biden-presidential-victory/.

2. Objected to Pennsylvania, Certified Arizona.

3. "Cynthia Lummis: Here's Why I Objected To Pennsylvania's Electors," *Cowboy State Daily*, January 9, 2021, https://cowboystatedaily.com/2021/01/09/cynthia-lummis-heres-why-i-objected-to-pennsylvanias-electors/.

4. Objected to Arizona, Certified Pennsylvania.

5. John Kennedy, "Kennedy Again Condemns Mob Violence at Joint Session of Congress," January 7, 2021. https://www.kennedy.senate.gov/public/2021/1/kennedy-again-condemns-mob-violence-at-joint-session-of-congress.

6. Objected to Pennsylvania, Certified Arizona.

7. Rick Scott, "Sen. Rick Scott Fights to Defend Free and Fair Elections," January 6, 2021, https://www.rickscott.senate.gov/2021/1/sen-rick-scott-fights-defend-free-and-fair-elections.

8. Tommy Tuberville, "TUBERVILLE PRESS RELEASE: TUBERVILLE STATEMENT ON ELECTORAL VOTE CERTIFICATION," January 7, 2021, https://www.tuberville.senate.gov/newsroom/press-releases/tuberville-statement-on-electoral-vote-certification/.

Appendix C

Guide to the Lawsuits Filed to Challenge the Election Results

The following sources provide further details, court documents, and analysis of post-2020 election challenges filed in US states and territories:

- Democracy Docket—www.democracydocket.com
- Stanford-MIT Healthy Elections Project—https://healthyelections-case-tracker.stanford.edu/
- Brennan Center for Justice Voting Rights Litigation Tracker 2020—https://www.brennancenter.org/our-work/court-cases/voting-rights-litigation-tracker-2020

State	Date Filed	Description	Lawsuit Outcome
		Arizona	
AZ	November 4	*Aguilera v. Fontes*[1] This lawsuit claimed that Sharpies damaged ballots and votes were not properly counted. The lawsuit was voluntarily dismissed on November 7.	Voluntarily Dismissed
AZ	November 7	*Donald J. Trump for President, Inc. v. Hobbs*[2] The Trump campaign filed a lawsuit claiming votes in Maricopa County were mishandled and wrongly rejected. Like *Aguilera v. Fontes* (filed on November 4; voluntarily dismissed on November 7), it alleged that ballots completed with a Sharpie were not counted by the ballot processing machine. The Trump campaign then dropped the suit because the small number of ballots would not have overturned Biden's lead.[3] The lawsuit was dismissed on November 13.	Dismissed

(continued)

State	Date Filed	Description	Lawsuit Outcome
AZ	November 12	*Arizona Republican Party v. Fontes*[4]	Dismissed
		A suit by the Arizona Republican Party against Maricopa County. It sought to expand the state's election audit by calling for a hand count of "precincts" not "voting centers." Superior Court of Arizona judge John H. Hannah dismissed the case on November 18.	
AZ	November 12	*Aguilera v. Fontes*[5]	Dismissed
		Filed by two Republican voters who claimed their votes were not counted. The superior court dismissed the case with prejudice on November 29.	
AZ	November 24	*Ward v. Jackson*[6]	Denied
		This lawsuit, filed by the Arizona Republican Party chair Kelli Ward, sought to block the certification of the 2020 presidential election. It was rejected by the supreme court of Arizona. The US Supreme Court denied the petition on February 22, 2021.	
AZ	December 2	*Bowyer v. Ducey*[7]	Dismissed; Denied
		Republican electors sought to decertify the 2020 presidential election results. US District Court judge Diane Humetawa dismissed the election challenge on December 9. In her ruling, Humetawa wrote, "Allegations that find favor in the public sphere of gossip and innuendo cannot be a substitute for earnest pleadings and procedure in federal court. They most certainly cannot be the basis for upending Arizona's 2020 General Election."[8] The US Supreme Court denied a subsequent writ of mandamus.	
AZ	December 4	*Stevenson v. Ducey*[9]	Voluntarily Dismissed
		Republican voters, members of the Arizona Election Integrity Association, sought to vacate the certification of the 2020 presidential election. Their claims included a charge that state officials allowed for "double voting."	

State	Date Filed	Description	Lawsuit Outcome
AZ	December 7	*Burk v. Ducey*[10] Pinal County judge Kevin D. White dismissed a lawsuit filed by Staci Burk, an individual voter. Burk filed the challenge late and she was not a registered voter during the 2020 general election. Therefore, she was not eligible to file the election contest. The Arizona Supreme Court upheld the dismissal on January 5. An appeal was made to the US Supreme Court on March 3, 2021, no decision has been reached. [11]	Dismissed
		Georgia	
GA	November 4	*In re: Enforcement of Election Laws*[12] A lawsuit filed by the Georgia GOP and the Trump campaign in Chatham County. The petition alleged that election officials improperly tabulated late absentee ballots. On November 5, Superior Court judge James Bass ruled that "there is no evidence that the Chatham County Board of Elections or the Chatham County Board of Registrars has failed to comply with the law."	Dismissed
GA	November 11	*Brooks v. Mahoney*[13] A lawsuit filed by Georgia voters that sought to stop the certification of the election results in Democratic-leaning counties. The petition claimed that elections officials included "illegal Presidential Elector results." The plaintiffs filed for voluntarily dismissal on November 16.	Voluntarily Dismissed
GA	November 13	*Wood v. Raffensperger*[14] This lawsuit, filed by pro-Trump lawyer L. Lin Wood, challenged the use of absentee ballots in the general election results. On November 19, federal judge Steven Grimberg, a Trump appointee, rejected the lawsuit, responding, "He has not presented any evidence demonstrating how he will suffer any particularized harm. . . . The fact that his preferred candidate did not prevail in the General Election . . . does not create a legally cognizable harm, much less an irreparable one."	Dismissed with Prejudice

(continued)

State	Date Filed	Description	Lawsuit Outcome
		Wood appealed to the 11th US Circuit Court of Appeals, which affirmed the district court's decision. The US Supreme Court denied Wood's petition on February 22, 2021, and the case was dismissed with prejudice on February 24.	
GA	November 25	*Wood v. Raffensperger*[15]	Dismissed
		Filed by the right-wing group Georgia Voters Alliance on behalf of an "aggrieved elector." This election contest sought to "nullify the presidential election results in Georgia and block the state from certifying the results so that the Georgia General Assembly could appoint electors." Biden electors successfully intervened, and the superior court of Fulton County granted their motion to dismiss on December 8.	
GA	November 25	*Pearson v. Kemp*[16]	Dismissed
		This lawsuit alleged that Dominion Voting equipment "rigged" the presidential election and it attempted to decertify Georgia's election results.	
		On November 30, a federal judge barred election officials from "altering, destroying, or erasing, or allowing the alteration, destruction, or erasure of, any software or data on any Dominion voting machine" pending the lawsuit.[17]	
		After this ruling, the plaintiffs (represented by a legal team that included Sidney Powell) embarked on a lengthy court process that included several appeals. Ultimately, Powell withdrew the lawsuit from the 11th Circuit and US Supreme Court on January 19, 2021.	

State	Date Filed	Description	Lawsuit Outcome
GA	November 30	*Boland v. Raffensperger*[18] A lawsuit filed by Paul Andrew Boland, an individual voter. It alleged that ballots were cast by out-of-state voters. Judge Emily K. Richardson of the superior court of Fulton County dismissed the case on December 8, writing, "The allegations in the complaint rest on speculation rather than duly pled facts." Following an emergency appeal to the Georgia Supreme Court (which was dismissed), the voter voluntarily dismissed the lawsuit on January 7, 2021.	Voluntarily Dismissed
GA	December 4	*Trump v. Raffensperger*[19] An election contest filed by Trump, the Trump campaign, and a Trump elector. It alleged "significant systemic misconduct, fraud, and other irregularities" occurred and "many thousands of illegal votes" were included in the vote tabulations. At one point, the petitioners claimed a lower court judge was not qualified to preside over the case—the Georgia Supreme Court dismissed this appeal. The petitioners voluntarily dismissed the case on January 7, 2021.	Voluntarily Dismissed
GA	December 31	*Trump v. Kemp*[20] Like the previous lawsuits filed by Donald Trump, this emergency injunction attempted to decertify the 2020 election results based on claims of "illegal voting." It also claimed that "unqualified individuals," including convicted felons, underage individuals, out-of-state voters, and deceased individuals, were permitted to vote. It was voluntarily dismissed on January 7, 2021.	Voluntarily Dismissed

(continued)

State	Date Filed	Description	Lawsuit Outcome
		Michigan	
MI	November 4	*Donald J. Trump for President, Inc. v. Benson*[21]	Denied
		The Trump campaign filed a lawsuit against Michigan secretary of state Jocelyn Benson to stop the absentee vote count. The Michigan Court of Claims denied the plaintiffs' motion for declaratory judgment. The Michigan Court of Appeals and Michigan Supreme Court then denied further appeals, closing the case on January 6, 2021.	
MI	November 4	*Stoddard v. City Election Commission*[22]	Dismissed
		Filed by an individual voter and the Election Integrity Fund, a conservative nonprofit. It attempted to block absentee ballots in Detroit. Circuit Court judge Timothy Kenny dismissed the case on November 6, calling the allegations "mere speculation." He argued a delay in counting the vote "without any evidentiary basis for doing so" would harm public interest and it "engenders a lack of confidence in the City of Detroit to conduct full and fair elections."	
MI	November 9	*Costantino v. Detroit*[23]	Dismissed
		A lawsuit filed by GOP poll challengers in Detroit, the majority of which allege fraud. The plaintiffs' requested that the board of election conduct an audit of the election, stop the certification of the vote, and order a new election. All requests were denied by the trial court and both the Michigan Court of Appeals and Supreme Court. Wayne County Circuit Court judge Timothy M. Kenny dismissed the case on January 8, 2021.	

State	Date Filed	Description	Lawsuit Outcome
MI	November 11	*Donald J. Trump for President, Inc. v. Benson*[24] This lawsuit, filed by individual voters and the Trump campaign, claimed Wayne County officials did not follow election code. It claimed that credentialed poll challengers were denied "meaningful opportunity" to review ballots during the tabulation process. The lawsuit was voluntarily dismissed on November 19, 2020.	Voluntarily Dismissed
MI	November 11	*Bally v. Whitmer*[25] An attempt by individual voters to exclude election results from Wayne, Washtenaw, and Ingraham Counties. Among the complaints, the plaintiffs argued that poll watchers were excluded from the canvassing process and cited *Costantino v. Detroit* and *Trump v. Benson* in the court filings.	Voluntarily Dismissed
MI	November 25	*King v. Whitmer*[26] Individual voters sought to decertify Michigan's election results. The complaint alleged "hundreds of thousands of illegal, ineligible, duplicate or purely fictitious ballots" were cast through the "systemic adaptation of old-fashioned 'ballot-stuffing.'" The district court denied the request for injunctive relief, and the US Supreme Court denied the petition.	Denied
MI	November 25	*Johnson v. Benson*[27] Filed by the Thomas More Society, this lawsuit asked the Michigan Supreme Court to "segregate" ballots and delay the certification of the election results. The lawsuit alleged that "respondent state officials failed to allow meaningful poll observation, instructed election workers to count invalid ballots, and permitted grant funding from Mark Zuckerberg."[28] The Michigan Supreme Court denied the petition.	Denied

(continued)

State	Date Filed	Description	Lawsuit Outcome
		Nevada	
NV	November 5	*Stokke v. Cegavske*[29] This lawsuit, filed by individuals and two congressional campaigns, challenged the use of mail ballot processing machines in Clark County. It claimed that the county's ballot processing machines used software that did not verify signatures on absentee ballots. After the district court denied the plaintiffs' motion for injunctive relief, the plaintiffs voluntarily dismissed the case.	Voluntarily Dismissed
NV	November 17	*Law v. Whitmer*[30] Individual Trump electors alleged voter fraud. It alleged that ballot processing machines either mismatched or did not verify signatures. It asked that Biden's election be annulled "and no candidate for elector for the office of President of the United States of America be certified from the state of Nevada." On December 4, the state court dismissed the lawsuit saying, "Contestants did not prove under any standard of proof that any illegal votes were cast and counted, or legal votes were not counted at all, for any other improper or illegal reason."[31] The Nevada Supreme Court upheld the decision and dismissed the lawsuit on December 8.	Dismissed
		Pennsylvania	
PA	October 28	*Woodruff v. Philadelphia County Board of Elections*[32] A lawsuit filed by a conservative group, Public Interest Legal Foundation, that sought to void mail-in ballots in Philadelphia. The court denied the petition on November 2, the day prior to Election Day, but it is indicative of the legal challenges that would follow.	Denied

State	Date Filed	Description	Lawsuit Outcome
PA	November 4	*Donald J. Trump for President, Inc. v. Philadelphia County Board of Elections*[33] This lawsuit claimed poll watchers for the Trump campaign were not given equal access to observe the ballot counting in Philadelphia. After Trump's attorneys admitted their observers had indeed been given access, Judge Diamond—a George W. Bush appointee—asked, "I'm sorry, then what's your problem?"[34] The US District Court judge Paul Diamond denied the case without prejudice after the Trump campaign reached an agreement with Pennsylvania election officials.[35]	
PA	November 5	*In re: Canvass of Absentee and Mail-in Ballots of November 3, 2020, General Election*[36] In Montgomery County, the Trump campaign, Republican National Committee, and Republicans filed a similar lawsuit to stop the board of elections from counting absentee ballots, claiming inaccuracies. Judge Richard Haaz ruled against Trump on November 13, writing, "Voters should not be disenfranchised by reasonably relying upon voting instructions provided by election officials."	Denied without Prejudice
PA	November 9	*Donald J. Trump for President, Inc. v. Boockvar*[37] Filed by the Trump campaign on November 10, this lawsuit challenged election results in key Democratic counties. Among the charges it argued include that election officials "did not undertake any meaningful effort to prevent the casting of illegal or unreliable absentee or mail-in ballots. Pennsylvania attorney general Jos Shapiro called the suit "meritless."[38] The lawsuit underwent a lengthy sequence of appeals.	Denied

(continued)

State	Date Filed	Description	Lawsuit Outcome
		Federal judge Matthew Brann dismissed the suit on November 21. Brann wrote, "In the United States of America, this cannot justify the disenfranchisement of a single voter, let alone all the voters of its sixth most populated state."	
		He added, "One might expect that when seeking such a startling outcome, a plaintiff would come formidably armed with compelling legal arguments and factual proof of rampant corruption. . . . That has not happened."[39]	
		On November 27, the 3rd US Circuit Court of Appeals denied a preliminary injunction pending appeal. Judge Stephanos Bibas, a Trump appointee, wrote, "Free, fair elections are the lifeblood of our democracy. Charges of unfairness are serious. But calling an election unfair does not make it so. Charges require specific allegations and then proof. We have neither here."	
PA	November 9	*Donald J. Trump for President, Inc. v. Bucks County Board of Elections*[40]	Denied
		An attempt by the Trump campaign, Republican National Convention, and other Republicans to not count a number of "defective" absentee ballots in Bucks County.	
PA	November 10	*In re: Canvass of Absentee and Mail-in Ballots of November 3, 2020, General Election*[41]	Dismissed
		On November 13, the Court of Common Pleas rejected five separate Trump petitions claiming that voters in Philadelphia County had improperly filled out their mail-in ballots or envelopes. Judge James Crumlish ruled that 8,329 ballots should be processed and counted.[42]	

State	Date Filed	Description	Lawsuit Outcome
		The Pennsylvania Supreme Court upheld the order on November 23, writing that although some "failures" such as a missing date on the outer envelope of a ballot are a "technical violation of the Election Code, do not warrant the wholesale disenfranchisement of thousands of Pennsylvania voters."	
PA	November 21	*Kelly v. Pennsylvania*[43]	
		Republican candidates, including US representative Mike Kelly, and individual voters sought to block the certification of the presidential election results. "Specifically, the suit asked the court to exclude vote-by-mail ballots from the certified results or alternatively direct the general assembly to choose its own electors."	
		On November 25, the Pennsylvania Appeals Court ordered to stop the certification process. But on the 28th, the Pennsylvania Supreme Court overturned the decision following an emergency appeal from Governor Tom Wolf, which stated there was no "conceivable justification" to stop the certification.[44]	
		Ultimately, the lawsuit was denied.	
PA	December 4	*Metcalfe v Wolfe*[45]	Dismissed. The US Supreme Court denied the petition
		An attempt by two GOP state representatives and two Republican voters to decertify the election results.	
PA	December 20	Rudy Giuliani filed a petition with the US Supreme Court to overturn three decisions by the Pennsylvania Supreme Court and by extension the election there. One law expert called the suit "frivolous."	Voluntarily Dismissed

(continued)

State	Date Filed	Description	Lawsuit Outcome
		Wisconsin	
WI	November 12	*Langenhorst v. Pecore*[46]	Voluntarily Dismissed
		Individual voters alleged illegal votes were cast in Menomonie, Dane, and Milwaukee Counties, citing fraud that may occur with mail-in ballots. The plaintiffs asked the court to not include the presidential election votes from these counties and to stop the certification of election.	
		On November 16th, the plaintiffs voluntarily dismissed the case after the Democratic National Committee intervened.	
WI	November 18	*Trump v. Biden*[47]	Voluntarily Dismissed
		Filed by the Trump campaign, this lawsuit called for a recount in Dane and Milwaukee Counties. It attempted to invalidate 221,000 ballots.	
		On December 14, Justice Brian Hagedorn wrote, "Our laws allow the challenge flag to be thrown regarding various aspects of election administration. The challenges raised by the Campaign in this case, however, come long after the last play or even the last game; the Campaign is challenging the rulebook adopted before the season began."[48]	
WI	November 23	*Wisconsin Voters Alliance v. Wisconsin Elections Commission*[49]	Denied
		An attempt by the Wisconsin Voters Alliance, a conservative nonprofit group, and several Wisconsin voters to nullify and block the certification of the presidential election results. It claimed that "a systemic effort . . . using millions of dollars in private money sourced to Mark Zuckerberg" led to tens of thousands illegal absentee ballots being cast.	
		The Wisconsin Supreme Court denied the petition on December 4.	

State	Date Filed	Description	Lawsuit Outcome
WI	December 1	*Trump v. Evers*[50] The Trump campaign's attempt to challenge the legality of absentee ballots in Wisconsin. The Wisconsin Supreme Court denied the petition on December 3.	Denied
WI	December 1	*Feehan v. Wisconsin Elections Commission*[51] A lawsuit filed by a Trump elector and a Republican congressional candidate. It alleged manipulation and fraud due to the Wisconsin State Board of Canvassers's use of Dominion Voting Systems. It called for the decertification of the elections results. The lawsuit also referenced "the voting process at the TCF Center," a polling location that did not exist in Wisconsin. On December 9, federal judge Pamela Pepper dismissed the suit, writing, "Federal judges do not appoint the president in this country. One wonders why the plaintiffs came to federal court and asked a federal judge to do so." The US Supreme Court denied the petition on March 1, 2021. It was the final lawsuit from attorney Sidney Powell to be tossed.[52]	Denied
WI	December 2	*Trump v. Wisconsin Elections Commission*[53] In this lawsuit, the Trump campaign petitioned the district court to "declare the election a failure, with the results discarded, and the door thus opened for the Wisconsin Legislature to appoint Presidential Electors in some fashion other than by following the certified voting results."[54]	Dismissed

(continued)

State	Date Filed	Description	Lawsuit Outcome
		Both the Democratic National Committee and the NAACP intervened. On December 12, the district court dismissed the case with prejudice, with Judge Brett Ludwig writing that a "sitting president who did not prevail in his bid for reelection has asked for federal court help in setting aside the popular vote based on disputed issues of election administration." The US Supreme Court denied Trump's petition on March 8, 2021.	
TX	December 7	*Texas v. Pennsylvania*[55]	Dismissed
		Filed by Texas attorney general Ken Paxton with seventeen states in support, this attempted to invalidate elections results in Georgia, Michigan, Pennsylvania, and Wisconsin. The District of Columbia and twenty-two states and territories filed opposition to Texas's petition.	
		The US Supreme Court denied the request for "lack of standing" on December 11.	

1. "*Aguilera v. Fontes*," Democracy Docket, August 13, 2021, https://www.democracydocket.com/cases/arizona-public-interest-ballot-cure.
2. "*Donald J. Trump for President, Inc. v. Hobbs*," Democracy Docket, August 13, 2021, https://www.democracydocket.com/cases/arizona-trump-sharpie-lawsuit.
3. Sara Randazzo, "Trump Drops Legal Challenge in Arizona," *Wall Street Journal*, https://www.wsj.com/livecoverage/latest-updates-biden-trump-election-2020/card/jU8pMZdnj6SyRqNBnYgl.
4. "*Arizona Republican Party v. Fontes*," Democracy Docket, August 13, 2021, https://www.democracydocket.com/cases/arizona-election-audit-challenge; "*Arizona Republican Party v. Fontes*," Healthy Elections Project, May 13, 2021, https://healthyelections-case-tracker.stanford.edu/detail?id=376.
5. "*Aguilera v. Fontes II*," Democracy Docket, November 11, 2020, https://www.democracydocket.com/cases/arizona-vote-recasting-challenge/.
6. "*Ward v. Jackson*," Democracy Docket, August 13, 2021, https://www.democracydocket.com/cases/arizona-election-contest/.
7. "*Bowyer v. Ducey*," Democracy Docket, August 13, 2021, https://www.democracydocket.com/cases/arizona-decertification-challenge; "*Bowyer v. Ducey*," Healthy Elections Project, December 13, 2020, https://healthyelections-case-tracker.stanford.edu/detail?id=409.
8. Maria Polletta, "Last Election Challenge Pending in Arizona Courts Thrown Out by Federal Judge in Blistering Ruling," *Arizona Republic*, December 9, 2020, https://www.azcentral.com/story/news/politics/elections/2020/12/09/federal-judge-throws-out-last-election-challenge-pending-arizona/6506927002.

9. *"Stevenson v. Ducey,"* Democracy Docket, August 13, 2021, https://www.democracydocket
.com/cases/arizona-election-contest-2; *"Stevenson v. Ducey,"* Healthy Elections Project,
December 12, 2020, https://healthyelections-case-tracker.stanford.edu/detail?id=416.

10. *"Burk v. Ducey,"* Democracy Docket, August 13, 2021, https://www.democracydocket
.com/cases/arizona-pinal-county-decertification-challenge; *"Burk v. Ducey,"* Healthy
Elections Project, May 12, 2021, https://healthyelections-case-tracker.stanford.edu
/detail?id=422.

11. https://www.democracydocket.com/wp-content/uploads/2020/12/cert-petition.pdf.

12. *"In re: Enforcement of Election Laws,"* Democracy Docket, August 13, 2021, https://www
.democracydocket.com/cases/georgia-absentee-ballot-counting-chatham-county; WTOC
Staff, "Chatham Co. Judge Dismisses Lawsuit Filed by Ga. GOP, Trump Campaign over
Absentee Ballots," WTOC, November 5, 2020, https://www.wtoc.com/2020/11/04/ga
-republican-party-president-trumps-campaign-files-lawsuit-against-chatham-co-board
-elections-over-absentee-ballots/.

13. *"Brooks v. Mahoney,"* Democracy Docket, August 13, 2021, https://www.democracydocket
.com/cases/ga-democratic-counties-election-challenge; *"Brooks v. Mahoney,"* Healthy
Elections Project, May 13, 2021, https://healthyelections-case-tracker.stanford.edu/detail
?id=373.

14. *"Wood v. Raffensperger,"* Democracy Docket, August 13, 2021, https://www
.democracydocket.com/cases/georgia-presidential-electors-challenge; *"Lin Wood v.
Raffensperger,"* Healthy Elections Project, May 13, 2021, https://healthyelections-case
-tracker.stanford.edu/detail?id=377.

15. *"Wood v. Raffensperger,"* Democracy Docket, August 13, 2021, https://www
.democracydocket.com/cases/georgia-election-law-contest; *"Wood v. Raffensperger,"*
Healthy Elections Project, December 7, 2020, https://healthyelections-case-tracker
.stanford.edu/detail?id=417.

16. *"Pearson v. Kemp,"* Democracy Docket, August 13, 2021, https://www.democracydocket
.com/cases/georgia-certification-challenge; *"Pearson v. Kemp,"* Healthy Elections Tracker,
December 9, 2020, https://healthyelections-case-tracker.stanford.edu/detail?id=401.

17. Zack Burdyck, "Judge Directs State Officials Not to Reset Georgia Voting Machines,"
The Hill, November 29, 2020, https://www.documentcloud.org/documents/20417947
-pearonvkempfiledorder112920.

18. *"Boland v. Raffensperger,"* Democracy Docket, August 13, 2021, https://www
.democracydocket.com/cases/georgia-decertification-challenge/; *"Boland v. Raffensperger,"* Healthy Elections Project, December 15, 2020, https://healthyelections-case
-tracker.stanford.edu/detail?id=403.

19. *"Trump v. Raffensperger,"* Democracy Docket, August 13, 2021, https://www
.democracydocket.com/cases/georgia-trump-election-contest/; *"Trump v. Raffensperger,"*
Healthy Elections Project, January 1, 2021, https://healthyelections-case-tracker.stanford
.edu/detail?id=414.

20. *"Trump v. Kemp,"* Democracy Docket, August 12, 2021, https://www.democracydocket
.com/cases/georgia-trump-decertification-challenge; *"Trump v. Kemp,"* Healthy Elections Project, January 6, 2021, https://healthyelections-case-tracker.stanford.edu
/detail?id=446.

21. *"Donald J. Trump for President Inc. v. Benson,"* Democracy Docket, August 16, 2021,
https://www.democracydocket.com/cases/michigan-absentee-counting-intervention;
"Donald J. Trump for President v. Benson," Healthy Elections Project, May 12, 2021, https://
healthyelections-case-tracker.stanford.edu/detail?id=338.

22. *"Stoddard v. City Election Commission,"* Democracy Docket, August 16, 2021, https://
www.democracydocket.com/cases/michigan-election-integrity-oversight-process;
"Stoddard v. City Election Commission," Healthy Elections Project, May 13, 2021, https://
healthyelections-case-tracker.stanford.edu/detail?id=353.

23. *"Costantino v. Detroit,"* Democracy Docket, August 16, 2021, https://www
.democracydocket.com/cases/michigan-detroit-election-challenge; *"Costantino v.
Detroit,"* Healthy Elections Project, May 13, 2021, https://healthyelections-case-tracker
.stanford.edu/detail?id=367.

24. *"Donald J. Trump for President, Inc. v. Benson,"* Democracy Docket, August 16, 2021,
https://www.democracydocket.com/cases/michigan-wayne-county-results-challenge.

25. *"Bally v. Whitmer,"* Healthy Elections Project, May 13, 2021, https://healthyelections-case
-tracker.stanford.edu/detail?id=374.

26. *"King v. Whitmer,"* Democracy Docket, August 16, 2021, https://www.democracydocket
.com/cases/michigan-certification-challenge/; *"King v. Whitmer,"* Healthy Elections Project, January 12, 2021, https://healthyelections-case-tracker.stanford.edu/detail?id=410.

27. *"Johnson v. Benson,"* Democracy Docket, August 16, 2021, https://www.democracydocket
.com/cases/michigan-thomas-more-society-election-challenge/.

28. *"Johnson v. Benson III,"* Healthy Elections Project, December 12, 2020, https://
healthyelections-case-tracker.stanford.edu/detail?id=411.

29. *"Stokke v. Cegavske,"* Democracy Docket, August 16, 2021, https://www.democracydocket
.com/cases/clark-county-vote-count-halt; *"Stokke v. Cegavske,"* Healthy Elections Project,
May 13, 2021, https://healthyelections-case-tracker.stanford.edu/detail?id=352.

30. *"Law v. Whitmer,"* Democracy Docket, August 16, 2021, https://www.democracydocket
.com/cases/nevada-election-law-contest/; *"Law v. Whitmer,"* Healthy Elections Project,
May 13, 2021, https://healthyelections-case-tracker.stanford.edu/detail?id=387.

31. Riley Snyder, "Judge Rejects Trump Campaign Lawsuit Seeking to Block State's Presidential Election Results, Says No Evidence Election Was Affected by Fraud," *Nevada Independent*, December 4, 2020, https://thenevadaindependent.com/article/judge-rejects-trump
-campaign-lawsuit-seeking-to-block-states-presidential-election-results.

32. *"Woodruff v. Philadelphia County Board of Elections,"* Democracy Docket, August 17, 2021,
https://www.democracydocket.com/cases/philadelphia-mail-ballot-intervention/.

33. *"Donald J. Trump for President, Inc. v. Philadelphia County Board of Elections,"* Healthy
Elections Project, May 15, 2021, https://healthyelections-case-tracker.stanford.edu/detail
?id=350.

34. "As Trump's Lead Weakened in Pennsylvania, His Allies Tried to Discredit the Count,"
Washington Post, November 6, 2020, https://www.washingtonpost.com/investigations
/philadelphia-republican-observers-vote-count/2020/11/06/982385ac-2055-11eb-ba21
-f2f001f0554b_story.html.

35. *"Donald J. Trump for President, Inc. v. Philadelphia County Board of Elections,"*
Democracy Docket, November 4, 2021, https://www.democracydocket.com/cases/
philadelphia-county-boe-count/.

36. *"In re: Canvass of Absentee and Mail-In Ballots of November 3, 2020, General Election,"* Democracy Docket, August 17, 2021, https://www.democracydocket.com/cases
/montgomery-county-board-of-elections-vote-count/.

37. *"Donald J. Trump for President, Inc. v. Boockvar,"* Democracy Docket, August 17, 2021,
https://www.democracydocket.com/cases/pennsylvania-democratic-counties-challenge.

38. "Nine Legal Experts Say Trump's Lawsuit Challenging Election Results in Pennsylvania Is
Dead on Arrival," *USA Today*, November 10, 2020, https://www.usatoday.com/story/news
/politics/elections/2020/11/09/legal-experts-say-trumps-election-lawsuit-pennsylvania
-baseless/6228914002/.

39. Josh Gerstein, Kyle Cheney, and Zach Montellaro, "'This Is Simply Not How the Constitution Works': Federal Judge Eviscerates Trump Lawsuit over Pennsylvania," Politico,
November 21, 2020, https://www.politico.com/states/new-york/albany/story/2020/11
/21/this-is-simply-not-how-the-constitution-works-federal-judge-eviscerates-trump
-lawsuit-over-pennsylvania-results-1337595.

40. "*Donald J. Trump for President, Inc. v. Bucks County Board of Elections*," Healthy Elections Project, May 13, 2021, https://healthyelections-case-tracker.stanford.edu/detail?id=369.

41. "*In re: Canvass of Absentee and Mail In Ballots of November 3, 2020, General Election*," Democracy Docket, August 17, 2020, https://www.democracydocket.com/cases/philadelphia-county-boe-appeal/.

42. Matthew Santoni, "Pa. Judges Deny Trump's Bid to Throw Out 8900 Ballots," Law 360, November 13, 2020, https://www.law360.com/articles/1328932/pa-judges-deny-trump-s-bid-to-throw-out-8-900-ballots.

43. "*Kelly v. Pennsylvania*," Democracy Docket, August 17, 2021, https://www.democracydocket.com/cases/pennsylvania-vbm-certification-challenge; "*Kelly v. Pennsylvania*," Healthy Elections Project, May 13, 2021, https://healthyelections-case-tracker.stanford.edu/detail?id=392.

44. Alison Durkee, "Pennsylvania Court Temporarily Blocks State from Certifying Votes in Response to GOP Challenge," *Forbes*, November 25, 2020, https://www.forbes.com/sites/alisondurkee/2020/11/25/pennsylvania-court-temporarily-blocks-state-from-certifying-votes-in-response-to-gop-challenge/?sh=88d674259074.

45. "*Metcalfe v. Wolfe*," Democracy Docket, August 17, 2021, https://www.democracydocket.com/cases/pennsylvania-decertification-challenge/.

46. "*Langenhorst v. Pecore*," Democracy Docket, August 17, 2021, https://www.democracydocket.com/cases/wisconsin-democratic-counties-election-challenge; "*Langenhorst v. Pecore*," Healthy Elections Project, May 13, 2020, https://healthyelections-case-tracker.stanford.edu/detail?id=375.

47. "*Trump v. Biden*," Democracy Docket, August 17, 2021, https://www.democracydocket.com/cases/wisconsin-2020-election-recount/;

48. Scott Bauer, "Wisconsin Supreme Court Tosses Trump Election Lawsuit," Associated Press, December 14, 2020, https://apnews.com/article/wisonsin-supreme-court-trump-lawsuit-e6b3aa222b4141c0844d541c4b041964.

49. "*Wisconsin Voters Alliance v. Wisconsin Elections Commission*," Democracy Docket, August 17, 2021, https://www.democracydocket.com/cases/wisconsin-certification-challenge/; "*Wisconsin Voters Alliance v. Wisconsin Election Commissions*," Healthy Elections Project, May 13, 2021, https://healthyelections-case-tracker.stanford.edu/detail?id=393.

50. "*Trump v. Evers*," Democracy Docket, August 17, 2021, https://www.democracydocket.com/cases/wisconsin-absentee-count-challenge/; "*Trump v. Evers*," Healthy Elections Project, December 5, 2020, https://healthyelections-case-tracker.stanford.edu/detail?id=412.

51. "*Feehan v. Wisconsin Elections Commission*," Democracy Docket, August 17, 2021, https://www.democracydocket.com/cases/wisconsin-decertification-challenge/.

52. Alison Durkee, "Sidney Powell's Remaining 'Kraken' Cases Thrown Out by Supreme Court," *Forbes*, March 1, 2021, https://www.forbes.com/sites/alisondurkee/2021/03/01/sidney-powell-remaining-kracken-cases-thrown-out-by-supreme-court.

53. "*Trump v. Wisconsin Elections Commission*," Democracy Docket, August 17, 2021, https://www.democracydocket.com/cases/wisconsin-federal-election-challenge/; "*Trump v. Wisconsin Elections Commission*," Healthy Elections Project, January 12, 2021, https://healthyelections-case-tracker.stanford.edu/detail?id=406.

54. "*Donald J. Trump v. The Wisconsin Elections Commission, et al.*," Democracy Docket, December 12, 2020, https://www.democracydocket.com/wp-content/uploads/2020/12/2020-12-12-Decision-And-Order-dckt-134_0-1.pdf.

55. "*Texas v. Pennsylvania*," Democracy Docket, August 17, 2021, https://www.democracydocket.com/cases/texas-scotus-decertification-challenge; "*Texas v. Pennsylvania*," SCOTUS Blog, December 11, 2020, https://www.scotusblog.com/case-files/cases/texas-v-pennsylvania.

Notes

Most of the material in this book comes from interviews with the principal characters, supplemented by research into news reports, court documents, books, and academic papers. More material was obtained by researching the social media of key characters who were posting comments and videos contemporaneously, including Donald Trump on his now-suspended Twitter account. While we have made every effort to provide current links to the social media posts and videos cited in the text, some of these platforms are fluid. Any changes that occurred after publication will not be reflected in these notes.

Chapter 1

1 *he could feel it in his bones*   Michael C. Bender, *Frankly, We Did Win This Election* (New York: Twelve, 2021), 328.

1 *the system was "totally rigged"*   NBC News, "Donald Trump Goes All In On Unsupported 'Large Scale Voter Fraud' Election Claims," October 17, 2016, video, 3:07. https://www.youtube.com/watch?v=20PSky9hU4I

1 *it became simply "The Swamp"*   Trump has a thing about swamps. I spent a weekend with him at Mar-a-Lago in November 1996 on assignment from *Playboy* magazine. This was six months after ValuJet Flight 592 took off from Miami and crashed into the Everglades, killing all 110 people on board. It was still very much on his mind. He told me, "And you're going down in the Everglades, in the swamp, so if the crash doesn't kill you—I got these Seminole Indian guys, friends of mine, great guys, you should meet these guys, the plane went down just a few miles from their reservation. They tell me they've got the world's fucking hungriest gators in this swamp—so if you're lucky enough to be alive after you hit, the fucking gators are coming after you. And if the gators miss you, the

moccas—that's what they call water moccasins; you guys ain't from New York, we got our own machas up there—will get you. And these fucking things are vicious. They bite you and in two minutes you're completely paralyzed and in three minutes you're dead. Can you fucking imagine this?" *Playboy*, May 1997, "The Art of the Donald."—Mark Bowden

1   *the "lying" mainstream press*   During Trump's political rise in 2016, I attended several of his rallies and each shared common themes: boasts about crowd size, chants about building a wall on the southern border, and, consistently, attacks on the press.

We sat in a pen, usually, surrounded by fencing. "I have to put up with some of the most dishonest people in the world: the media," Trump told his supporters during a typical speech in Pensacola. "They never show crowds like that—look at that, it goes all the way back. They never show crowds. They don't show crowds."

Before the rallies, we had signed papers acknowledging rules set out by the campaign, on pain of losing coverage credentials. Most of them didn't apply to me—technical details about camera focal throw, cable length—but one rule specified that television cameras must remain focused on the speaker at the podium. So Trump's call for cameras to turn and reveal his big, beautiful crowds was an empty dare; he knew the cameras couldn't move.

The crowds, though, believed him. Jeers and boos came in waves, from every direction. I tried to explain to people about the cameras, the contract, the general aims of the press; of course, none of it mattered. Talking to individuals is futile in the face of an orator like Trump, who had mastered speaking to the crowd as a collective creature. He could direct its gaze, its sneer, its movement wherever he wanted.

These rallies were miniature models for the protests of January 6. For eight weeks in advance, Trump spoke to the collective creature, in whispers and shouts, about theft and deceit and fraud. And the crowds believed him.—Matthew Teague

1   *with him the American dream*   Noah Bierman, "Trump Shifts Meaning of 'Drain the Swamp' from Ethics to Anything He Objects To," *Los Angeles Times*, February 9. 2018, https://www.latimes.com/politics/la-na-pol-swamp-20180209-story .html

2   *only in rare instances—local election results*   "A Sampling of Recent Election Fraud Cases from Across the United States," The Heritage Foundation. https:// www.heritage.org/voterfraud

3   *"will be prosecutions at the highest level"*   Amy Gardner, "Without Evidence, Trump and Sessions Warn of Voter Fraud in Tuesday's Elections," *Washington*

Post, November 5, 2018. https://www.washingtonpost.com/politics/without
-evidence-trump-and-sessions-warn-of-voter-fraud-in-tuesdays-elections/2018
/11/05/e9564788-e115-11e8-8f5f-a55347f48762_story.html

3   *"missing or forged, ballots massively infected"*   Joseph Ax, "Trump's Baseless
Voter Fraud Allegations Could Hurt U.S. Faith in Elections," *Reuters*, November 14, 2018. https://www.reuters.com/article/us-usa-election-trump-claims
/trumps-baseless-voter-fraud-allegations-could-hurt-u-s-faith-in-elections
-idUSKCN1NJ30L

3   *"signing ballots all over the place"*   This is untrue. A study by the American Statistical Association found no evidence that mail voting is more susceptible to fraud
than in-person voting. Jonathan Auerbach and Steve Pierson, "Does Voting by
Mail Increase Fraud?," *Statistics and Public Policy* 8, no. 1 (2021): 18–41.

3   *"in my opinion, is massive fraud"*   *The Hill*, "Trump: 'The Only Way We Can Lose
in My Opinion Is Massive Fraud,'" October 26, 2020, video, 5:03. https://www
.youtube.com/watch?v=Rt6nCZRKChE

3   *Georgia*   This section is based primarily on interviews with Rick Barron, State
Farm Arena staff, Georgia state election officials, an examination of the rooms
in question at the arena, and security-camera footage from Election Day: "Stop
Voter Fraud—Ensure Secure Georgia Elections." Secure the Vote GA. https://
securevotega.com/fact-check/

4   *the machinery of freedom to a stop*   Johnny Kauffman, "Inside the Battle for
Fulton County's Votes," WABE, February 3, 2021. https://www.wabe.org/inside
-the-most-beleaguered-election-office-in-the-nation/

5   *Pennsylvania*   This section is based primarily on interviews with Leah Hoopes
and on testimony given by state voters at the November 25, 2020, state legislative
hearing about the election in Gettysburg: C-Span, "Pennsylvania Republican
Hearing on 2020 Election," November 25, 2020. https://www.c-span.org/video
/?478422-1/president-trump-tells-pennsylvania-gop-lawmakers-election-rigged
-overturned

5   *the PA State Watchdogs*   Facebook, https://www.facebook.com/leahmhoopes,
October 26, 2020.

6   *She maintained two accounts*   https://www.facebook.com/leahmhoopes;
https://www.facebook.com/search/top?q=leah%20hoopes%20pennsylvania

8   *whom she called a "stuttering prick"*   https://www.facebook.com/leahmhoopes,
October 22, 2020, in reference to Biden's struggle, as a boy, with stuttering.

9   *the consequences of a Democratic win*   https://www.facebook.com/leahmhoopes,
September 25, 2020.

9   to *"expose and bring to light election fraud"*   https://www.facebook.com
/leahmhoopes, October 26, 2020.

10 *as a "data forensic scientist"* Mark Bowden interview with Leah Hoopes, June 2, 2021.

10 *her county neighbors, "lying hacks"* https://www.facebook.com/leahmhoopes, October 25, 2020.

11 *"voting and at the counting boards"* https://www.facebook.com/watch/?v =2640587549523836

11 *issue a statement defending them* "Advisory: Secretary Pablos Provides Additional Guidance to Voters, Election Officials Regarding Hart eSlate Electronic Voting Systems in 78 Texas Counties," Texas Secretary of State, October 27, 2018. https://www.sos.texas.gov/about/newsreleases/2018/102718 .shtml

12 *being set up by their superiors to fail* Mark Bowden interview with Leah Hoopes, June 2, 2021: "So, it's like, you ever watch, like, the old movies or whatever, or you watch, like, a Nazi operation? So, you have your little monkeys working and nobody knows what anybody else is doing. After you do your job, you don't know what happens next, or you put people in a position who think that what they're doing is the right thing, but in reality, it's not."

13 la grand traverse, *they called it* "How Did Michigan Cities Get Their Names?" Pure Michigan. https://www.michigan.org/article/trip-idea/how-did-michigan -cities-get-their-names

13 *About twenty-three thousand people live in Antrim* "U.S. Census Bureau Quick-Facts: Antrim County, Michigan," U.S. Census Bureau. https://www.census. gov/quickfacts/antrimcountymichigan

13 *the "cherry capital of the world"* Chris Duerksen and Cara Snyder, *Nature-Friendly Communities: Habitat Protection and Land Use Planning* (Island Press, 2013): 395. https://books.google.com/books?id=MpXK01AUIj4C&pg =PA395

14 *and a particular local favorite, Ulsters* "Northern Michigan Sweet and Tart Cherries: Varieties," King Orchards. https://www.kingorchards.com/our-fruits /cherries/

14 *finally flowing into the Grand Traverse* "Chain of Lakes," Elk Rapids Area Chamber of Commerce. https://www.elkrapidschamber.org/chain-of-lakes/

14 *Native Americans fished by torchlight* Trevor Nace, "Michigan's Torch Lake Looks Exactly Like the Caribbean Sea," *Forbes*, June 11, 2018. https://www .forbes.com/sites/trevornace/2018/06/11/michigans-torch-lake-looks-exactly -like-the-caribbean-sea/?sh=c19d5857013f

14 *you never know what might go wrong* Details in the following section come largely from interviews with Sheryl Guy.

15 *Central Lake village, and so forth*   "Townships in Michigan," Michigan Townships Association. https://www.michigantownships.org/mi_twps.asp

15 *"Old Man Thunder" (braised beef)*   Short's Brewing Company. https://www.shortsbrewing.com

16 *in a county as reliably Republican as Antrim*   J. Alex Halderman, "Analysis of the Antrim County, Michigan November 2020 Election Incident," Michigan Department of State, March 26, 2021. https://www.michigan.gov/documents/sos/Antrim_720623_7.pdf

16 *"with us while we get to the bottom of this"*   Antrim County, "November 4, 2020—For Immediate Release—Antrim County Unofficial Election Results," Facebook, November 4, 2020. https://www.facebook.com/AntrimCountyMI/posts/november-4-2020for-immediate-releaseantrim-county-unofficial-election-resultsant/186111776300742/

17 *Arizona*   This section is based on interviews with Lynie Stone.

20 *then shaved down to moustaches and voted again*   "Foot Powder Wins in a Landslide, and Other Unsavory Election Trivia," NPR, November 1, 2014. https://www.npr.org/2014/11/01/360629459/foot-power-wins-in-a-landslide-and-other-unsavory-election-trivia

20 *including a straw hat*   The Editors of Encyclopaedia Britannica, "The Mysterious Death of Edgar Allan Poe," *Britannica*. https://www.britannica.com/story/the-mysterious-death-of-edgar-allan-poe

20 *"To Dr. J. E. Snodgrass"*   Natasha Geiling, "The (Still) Mysterious Death of Edgar Allan Poe," *Smithsonian Magazine*, October 7, 2014. https://www.smithsonianmag.com/history/still-mysterious-death-edgar-allan-poe-180952936/

21 *with millions of illegal votes—a farce*   Philip Bump, "There Have Been Just Four Documented Cases of Voter Fraud in the 2016 Election," *Washington Post*, December 1, 2016. https://www.washingtonpost.com/news/the-fix/wp/2016/12/01/0-000002-percent-of-all-the-ballots-cast-in-the-2016-election-were-fraudulent/

21 *stealing an American ballot box*   "Crooked Voting By Immigrants." Retrieved from Getty Images. https://www.gettyimages.com/detail/news-photo/cartoon-charging-irish-and-german-immigrants-with-stealing-news-photo/96817567

22 *it didn't decide the race in Illinois*   Edmund F. Kallina, "Was the 1960 Presidential Election Stolen? The Case of Illinois," *Presidential Studies Quarterly*, 15, no. 1 (1985): 113–118. https://www.jstor.org/stable/27550168

22 *"the agony of a constitutional crisis"*   Scott Bomboy, "The Drama Behind President Kennedy's 1960 Election Win," *Constitution Daily*, November 7, 2017. https://constitutioncenter.org/blog/the-drama-behind-president-kennedys-1960-election-win

22 *toward George W. Bush over John Kerry* Christopher Hitchens, "Ohio's Odd Numbers," *Vanity Fair*, March 2005: 214–217. https://archive.vanityfair.com /article/2005/3/ohios-odd-numbers

22 *"There is no evidence of vote theft or errors on a large scale"* "Opinion: About Those Election Results," *New York Times*, November 14, 2004. https://www.nytimes .com/2004/11/14/opinion/about-those-election-results.html

22 *the claims as "conspiracy theories"* Manuel Roig-Franzia and Dan Keating, "Latest Conspiracy Theory—Kerry Won—Hits the Ether," *Washington Post*, November 11, 2004. https://www.washingtonpost.com/wp-dyn/articles /A41106-2004Nov10.html?nav=rss_technology/techpolicy/epolitics

22 Preserving Democracy: What Went Wrong in Ohio John Conyers, *What Went Wrong in Ohio: The Conyers Report on the 2004 Presidential Election* (Chicago: Academy Chicago Publishers, 2005).

22 *it didn't add up to fraud* Mark Hertsgaard, "Recounting Ohio," *Mother Jones*, November 2005. https://www.motherjones.com/media/2005/11/recounting -ohio/

22 *the other side of the political aisle* Robert F. Kennedy Jr., "Was the 2004 Election Stolen?" *Rolling Stone*, June 15, 2006, 46–48, 50, 52, 54, 56, 110–114.

23 *"deliberate omission of key bits of data"* Farhad Manjoo, "Was the 2004 Election Stolen? No" *Salon*, June 3, 2006. https://www.salon.com/2006/06/03 /kennedy_39/

23 *according to Dunlap, "glaringly empty"* Marina Villeneuve, "Report: Trump Commission Did Not Find Widespread Voter Fraud," Associated Press, August 3, 2018. https://apnews.com/article/north-america-donald-trump-us-news-ap -top-news-elections-f5f6a73b2af546ee97816bb35e82c18d

23 *interview with journalist David Daley* David Daley, "Kobach and Trump's Spectacular Voter-Fraud Failure," *Rolling Stone*, April 27, 2020. https://www.rollingstone .com/politics/politics-features/kris-kobach-donald-trump-voter-fraud-myths-vote -suppression-990300/. The article is an excerpt from David Daley's book *Unrigged: How Americans Are Battling Back to Save Democracy* (New York: Live-right, 2020).

23 *but decided against it* "Abrams Says She Can't Win Georgia Governor Race," *Valdosta Daily Times*, November 16, 2018. https://www.valdostadailytimes.com /news/local_news/abrams-says-she-cant-win-georgia-governor-race/article _33bfa5fc-23a5-5c09-a530-27c445619650.html

24 *Pennsylvania* This section is based on interviews with Greg Stenstrom, Leah Hoopes, Bill Miller, Christine Reuther, Howard Lazarus, John McBlain, and Gerry Lawrence.

25 *By a sneaky infusion of bogus Biden ballots* Mark Bowden interview with Greg Stenstrom, June 9, 2021: "Now, what I think happened—and I'm just saying what

I think happened—was they had ballots already prefilled out in the building on some other floor. And the ballots that were introduced into the BlueCrest sorter, which is where the data is ingested, I believe those were fake ballots."

26 *forty-one solar-powered ballot drop boxes*   Delaware County Bureau of Elections, "Our Secured Ballot Drop Boxes: A Quick Overview." https://www.delcopa. gov/vote/ballotdropbox.html

27 *Center for Tech and Civic Life*   Adrienne Marofsky, "Delaware County Awarded $2.2 Million Grant for Safe Elections," Delaware County Government Center. August 19, 2020. https://delcopa.gov/publicrelations/releases/2020/safeelec tionsgrant.html

32 *Georgia*   Details in this section come largely from interviews with Lawrence Sloan and Rick Barron.

32 *It surrounded him. He piloted it*   Matthew Teague interview with Lawrence Sloan, July 18, 2021: "It's a big desk. I was like, 'Yo, this looks like a shuttlecraft from *Star Trek: The Next Generation!*' It's the same color, the same lines, it's gigantic—it's the size of a very large desk; you feel more like you're sitting in it than you pull up to it."

34 *Wisconsin*   This section is based on interviews with Rohn Bishop, Dean Knudson, and Joe Handrick.

36 *"they loved him"*   Michael Miller, a political science professor at Barnard College, was teaching a class at Columbia in the fall of 2019. He had met Rohn earlier while researching a book about local party organizations. Interviewed in July 2021.

37 *"I think mail-in voting is going to rig the election, I really do"*   Fox Business, "President Trump's First Interview Since Coronavirus Diagnosis," October 8, 2020, video, 55:20. https://video.foxbusiness.com/v/6198767208001#sp=show-clips

37 *"the most CORRUPT ELECTION in our Nation's History!"*   https://www .thetrumparchive.com/?results=1, July 21, 2020.

37 *invited Bishop on to explain himself*   WISN 12 News, "GOP Chairman Speaks Up for Voting by Mail," July 26, 2020, video, 4:45. https://www.youtube.com /watch?v=HHeEKaST2Hg

39 *difference in voting by mail or in person*   River Channel, "Western Wisconsin Journal: Dean Knudson Wisconsin Elections Cmsn.," October 27, 2020, video, 40:55. https://www.youtube.com/watch?v=n6_hzYMz5c4

41 *Arizona*   This section is based primarily on interviews with Clint Hickman and Rey Valenzuela.

41 *Marko Trickovic, a self-professed patriot*   https://www.facebook.com/marko .trickovic.3

42 *This may or may not have been scripted*   https://www.facebook.com/marko .trickovic.3, November 3, 2020. The video now comes with a fact-check warning from Facebook, noting that its allegation about Sharpies is false.

42 *Sharpies had fouled the election* "AZ Lawsuit: Maricopa County's Sharpies Denied Voting Rights," Public Interest Legal Foundation, November 4, 2020. https://publicinterestlegal.org/press/az-lawsuit-maricopa-countys-sharpies -denied-voting-rights/

43 *Mark Brnovich announced an immediate investigation* Michael T. Catlett, "Re: Use of Sharpie Brand Markers at Maricopa County Voting Centers," Office of the Arizona Attorney General. November 4, 2020. https://www.azag.gov/sites /default/files/2020-11/LT%20Jarrett%20re%20Use%20of%20Sharpie%20 Markers_Redacted.pdf

43 *Sharpie-marked ballots perfectly* https://twitter.com/GeneralBrnovich/status /1324526305677750272

43 *The lawsuit was withdrawn by the plaintiffs* Bree Burkitt and Jen Fifield, "Sharpie Lawsuit Officially Dropped by Plaintiffs Hours after Biden Win Announced," *Arizona Republic*, November 7, 2020. https://www.azcentral.com/story/news /politics/elections/2020/11/07/sharpie-lawsuit-officially-dropped-plaintiffs -hours-after-biden-win-announced/6209529002/

43 *the Maricopa County Recorder's Office* https://www.facebook.com/marko .trickovic.3/videos/4133394300010902, November 4, 2020.

Chapter 2

47 *They had four TVs going* Bender, *Frankly, We Did Win This Election*, 343–344.

48 *"Call Rupert! Call James and Lachlan!"* Carol Leonnig and Phillip Rucker, *I Alone Can Fix It: Donald J. Trump's Catastrophic Final Year* (New York: Penguin, 2021), 344. Rupert is Rupert Murdoch, owner of Fox; James and Lachlan are his sons.

48 *"This is a major fraud"* Jane Mayer, "The Big Money Behind the Big Lie," *New Yorker*, August 2, 2021. https://www.newyorker.com/magazine/2021/08/09 /the-big-money-behind-the-big-lie

49 *Pennsylvania* This section is based on interviews with Leah Hoopes, Greg Stenstrom, Bill Martin, John McBlain, and Rob Weisenbach.

52 *sitting in her car outside The Wharf* https://www.facebook.com/leahmhoopes /videos/10158045560057983, November 4, 2020.

53 *a video on her Facebook page* https://www.facebook.com/leahmhoopes/videos /10158045595857983, November 4, 2020.

55 *from the chairman of the elections board* "Erie County, Board of Elections Praises Branches for a Successful Election Process," Erie County. November 4, 2020. https://eriecountypa.gov/erie-county-board-of-elections-praises-branches-for -a-successful-election-process/

55 *he stayed home and rested*   "First Amended Complaint - Weisenbach v. Project Veritas," Protect Democracy. https://protectdemocracy.org/resource-library /document/first-amended-complaint-weisenbach-v-project-veritas/

55 *"from November 4th and 5th"*   Project Veritas, "Pennsylvania USPS Whistleblower Exposes Anti-Trump Postmaster's Illegal Order to Back-Date Ballots," Nov 5, 2020, video, 2:18. https://www.youtube.com/watch?v=AR_XpJ287Iw

56 *a group of self-styled "guerrilla journalists"*   "Work for Us," Project Veritas. https:// www.projectveritas.com/jobs/

56 *making wildly false accusations, and deceptive editing*   Matthew Feeney, "Misleading Project Veritas Accusations of Google 'Bias' Could Prompt Bad Law," The Cato Institute, June 15, 2019. https://www.cato.org/blog/misleading-veritas-accusation -google-bias-could-result-bad-law; Brennan Weiss, "The 33-Year-Old Who Tried to Trick the *Washington Post* with a Fake Sexual Harassment Story Has a Long History of Sting Operations Backfiring," *Business Insider*, November 27, 2017. https:// www.businessinsider.com/james-okeefe-project-veritas-sting-fails-2017-11; Casey Newton and Russell Brandom, "Project Veritas' YouTube Sting Was Deeply Misleading—and Successful," *The Verge*, June 27, 2019. https://www.theverge.com /interface/2019/6/27/18760463/project-veritas-youtube-sting-james-okeefe

56 *the country for prostitution*   Tony Perry, "Conservative Activist Pays $100,000 to Former ACORN Worker," *Los Angeles Times*, March 7, 2013. https://www .latimes.com/local/la-xpm-2013-mar-07-la-me-0308-acorn-20130308-story .html

56 *Judge Roy Moore, a Trump supporter*   "*Washington Post* Uncovers Fake Roy Moore Story 'Sting'," BBC, November 28, 2017. https://www.bbc.com/news /world-us-canada-42150322

56 *"the lies and deceipt* [sic] *of the liberal MSM"*   Alec Jenkins, "The *Washington Post* Says a Woman Tried to Give Them a Fake Roy Moore Story," *Time*, November 27, 2017. https://time.com/5038629/jaime-phillips-roy-moore-washington -post-project-vertias-james-okeefe/

56 *Project Veritas as a "flak mill"*   Brian Michael Goss, "Veritable Flak Mill: A Case Study of Project Veritas and a Call for Truth," *Journalism Studies* 19, no. 4 (2018): 548–563. https://doi.org/10.1080%2F1461670X.2017.1375388

56 *"flak mill" and "disinformation outfit"*   Yochai Benkler, Robert Faris, and Hal Roberts, *Network Propaganda: Manipulation, Disinformation, and Radicalization in American Politics* (New York: Oxford University Press, 2018): 351–380. https:// oxford.universitypressscholarship.com/view/10.1093/oso/9780190923624.001 .0001/oso-9780190923624-chapter-13

56 *in part, by the Trump Foundation*   https://pdf.guidestar.org/PDF_Images/2015 /133/404/2015-133404773-0d216463-F.pdf

58 *At home, Weisenbach pulled his red Jeep into the driveway* Account from an interview with Weisenbach attorney, David Houck, and lawsuit text: "First Amended Complaint: Weisenbach v. Project Veritas," Protect Democracy. https://www.docu mentcloud.org/documents/21041667-first-amended-complaint-final-w-exhibits.

59 *the allegations of fraud in Erie* Kerry Picket, "Lindsey Graham Calls for DOJ Investigation After USPS Whistleblower Affidavit Alleges Ballot Fraud," *Washington Examiner*, November 7, 2020. https://www.washingtonexaminer.com /news/lindsey-graham-calls-for-doj-investigation-after-usps-whistleblower -affidavit-alleges-ballot-fraud

59 *certification of Pennsylvania's election* "Pennsylvania Democratic Counties Challenge," Democracy Docket. https://www.democracydocket.com/cases /pennsylvania-democratic-counties-challenge

59 *Project Veritas then pumped on social media* David Covucci and Zachary Petrizzo, "Why Do So Many of Project Veritas' Right-Wing 'Whistleblowers' Land GoFundMe Paydays?," Daily Dot, November 11, 2020. https://www .dailydot.com/debug/project-veritas-gofundme/

59 *immediately and showed no signs of slowing* Matthew Rink, "Erie Postmaster Files Lawsuit Against Mail Carrier, Project Veritas Over Ballot Fraud Claims," *Erie Times-News*, April 26, 2021. https://www.goerie.com/story/news/politics /elections/2021/04/26/erie-ballot-fraud-case-postmaster-sues-hopkins-okeefe -project-veritas/7376713002/

60 *a central site for counting absentee ballots* Tim Alberta, "The Inside Story of Michigan's Fake Voter Fraud Scandal," *Politico*, November 24, 2020. https:// www.politico.com/news/magazine/2020/11/24/michigan-election-trump-voter -fraud-democracy-440475

60 *the Republican Party posted to its Facebook page* https://www.facebook.com /LivingstonGOP/posts/2789597161254573

60 *each party was allowed 134 challengers* Breana Noble and Craig Mauger, "Shouting, Confrontation at Detroit Vote Count Center: Poll Challenger Barred by Police," *The Detroit News*, November 4, 2020. https://www.detroitnews.com /story/news/politics/2020/11/04/poll-challengers-converge-detroit-amid -close-election-results/6161484002/

61 *the Wayne County 11th Republican Committee posted* https://www.facebook .com/191580460894439/posts/3723145394404577

61 *Trump's director of election day operations* In the White House, Roman was "Director, Special Projects and Research," a job title *Politico* described as "a vague title that reveals almost nothing." He is a Republican political operative who maintains a blog that he describes as dedicated to "fraud, cheating, dirty tricks, absurdity and other election news."

61 *of fake ballots smuggled in*   Ali Swenson, "Wagon Filmed at Detroit Vote Center Held Camera Gear, Not Ballots," AP News, November 5, 2020. https://apnews.com /article/fact-check-detroit-wagon-had-camera-gear-afs:Content:9707800234

61 *a hand-pulled wagon and later by industrial van*   Clara Hendrickson, "Video Does Not Provide Evidence of Election Fraud in Detroit," *Detroit Free Press*, February 5, 2021. https://www.freep.com/story/news/local/michigan/detroit/2021/02/05 /gateway-pundit-video-doesnt-show-election-fraud-detroit/4411975001/

62 *"denied access to observe any counting in Detroit"*   Clara Hendrickson, "More than 100 Republican Challengers Monitored Absentee Ballot Count in Detroit," *Detroit Free Press*, November 6, 2020. https://www.freep.com/story/news/local /michigan/detroit/2020/11/06/republican-challengers-barred-detroit-tcf /6190533002/

62 *"the state may undercut Trump's number of votes"*   Steven Nelson, "Michigan Republicans Claim Software Issue Undercounted Trump Votes," *New York Post*, November 6, 2020. https://nypost.com/2020/11/06/michigan-gop-claims -software-issue-undercounted-trump-votes/

62 *to the county commissioners*   Matthew Teague interview with Sheryl Guy, August 11, 2021: "I mean, I'm the boss, I'm elected. It's my job to take the heat. I would never throw my staff, who I fight for with this board, to improve working conditions, wages, and benefits—I would never throw one of my staff under the bus. I ran for it; I own it. Period."

63 *a terrible episode in Guy's public life*   "Report on the November 2020 Election in Michigan," Michigan Senate Oversight Committee, June 23, 2021. https:// committees.senate.michigan.gov/testimony/2021-2022/Senate%20Commit tee%20on%20Oversight%20Report%20on%20the%20November%202020%20 Election%20in%20Michigan,%20adopted.pdf

63 *a vote for the local marijuana shop*   File 2020009238CZ in *William Bailey v. Antrim County*.

63 *Nevada*   The section is based on interviews with Joe Gloria.

63 *on Wednesday afternoon, November 4*   8 News NOW Las Vegas, "Clark County Registrar Joe Gloria Provides a Brief Update from the Election Center," November 4, 2020, video, 12:18. https://www.youtube.com/watch?v=Pu5bm47s4Co

66 *Georgia*   This section is based largely on interviews with John Porter.

67 *and testimony, delivered via video calls*   Brad Schrade, "Georgia Judge Dismisses Trump Campaign Case in Chatham Ballot Dispute," *Atlanta-Journal Constitution*, November 5, 2020. https://www.ajc.com/news/georgia-judge-dismisses-trump-campaign -case-in-chatham-ballot-dispute/YKBA6IYQKBB4JCSQEIJBQQT6QI/

67 *their electric bill—the machine didn't slice cleanly*   This section is largely based on interviews with Lawrence Sloan and Rick Barron.

68 *Someone had recorded it, added narration, and posted it*   https://twitter.com
/fleccas/status/1324239926641262593

69 *"and explain what is happening in this video"*   https://twitter.com/DavidShafer
/status/1324482209919717376

69 *"Nothing to see here"*   https://twitter.com/erictrump/status/132433795
1866802178?lang=en

69 *Donald Trump Jr. retweeted it, adding, "WTF?"*   https://twitter.com
/donaldjtrumpjr/status/1324351563473833987?lang=en

69 *"we will have a margin of a few thousand"*   C-Span, "Georgia Secretary of State
Update on 2020 Election Results," November 6, 2020. https://www.c-span.org
/video/?477860-1/georgia-secretary-state-recount

70 *he learned to look out for himself*   The following account is based on interviews
with Gabriel Sterling.

71 *"Secretary of State Brad Raffensperger to resign"*   Greg Bluestein and Mark
Niesse, "Citing No Evidence, Georgia's U.S. Senators Demand Elections Head
Resign," *Atlanta-Journal Constitution.* November 9, 2020. https://www.ajc.com
/politics/georgias-senators-seek-secretary-of-states-resignation-over-election
/A3JUFWTWORDH7LTL2XSZ7ODWPA/

71 *She had taken some shots*   The following section is based largely on interviews
with Jordan Fuchs.

71 *"Something ain't right in GA"*   Jessica McBride, "Georgia's Deputy Secretary of
State Prominent Voter Fraud Critic's 'Little Man Ego'," Heavy.com, March 16,
2021. https://heavy.com/news/jordan-jordy-fuchs/

72 *an internal memo to that effect*   Alan Feuer, "Trump Campaign Knew Lawyers'
Voting Machine Claims Were Baseless, Memo Shows," *New York Times*, September 21, 2021. https://www.nytimes.com/2021/09/21/us/politics/trump
-dominion-voting.html

72 *"to perform spells, curses, potions, hexes and vexes just like Harry"*   Father Jose
Maniyangat Eucharistic Healing Ministry, "The Effects of Harry Potter." http://
www.frmaniyangathealingministry.com/UserFiles/NewsPdf/9f7c07339fb74
d14a12e05128bb07704.pdf

73 *Pennsylvania*   This section is based on interviews with Greg Stenstrom, Leah
Hoopes, John McBlain, Dr. Jonathan Briskin, and Valerie Biancaniello.

75 *the estimate would swell to seventy thousand*   Six months later, he was using the
larger number. Mark Bowden interview with Greg Stenstrom, June 9, 2021:
"What I saw in the rear canvassing area—the rear room that we'd been barred
from and in the locked ballot room—were seventy thousand unopened mail-in
ballots."

75 *ending on Sunday evening, the 8th* The Wayback Machine allows a search of what was being reported throughout the days in question: www.web.archive .org; "Pennsylvania Presidential Election Results," *New York Times.* https:// www.nytimes.com/interactive/2020/11/03/us/elections/results-pennsylva nia-president.html. "Delaware County Results," CNN via Wayback Machine. https://docs.google.com/spreadsheets/d/1Z37F2zMKsvsbAQ85OrgG92S25 -AJyDFtuPyUSASS9ds/edit#gid=1666471655

76 *Democrats were filling in false ballots* McKenzie Sadeghi, "Fact Check: Viral Video Shows Pennsylvania Poll Workers Fixing Damaged Ballots," *USA Today,* November 6, 2020. https://www.usatoday.com/story/news/factcheck/2020/11/06/fact-check -video-shows-pennsylvania-poll-workers-fixing-damaged-ballots/6185589002/

80 *with his background in fraud and security* Mark Bowden interview with Greg Stenstrom, June 9, 2021: "But my expertise is in fraud and security. I've been working in security. And my background is, like, I encrypted the Federal Depository Insurance Corporation—FDIC—the Federal Reserve, the Bank of New York, Naval Space Warfare. I helped introduce firewalls into the country, intrusion detection, a lot of technology into the country from Israel and from other programs. So I've been involved in a number of fraud investigations and been very successful at it. Put quite a few people in jail and got a lot of money back for the government for the citizens."

80 *in a position of power was corrupt. All being paid* Mark Bowden interview with Greg Stenstrom, June 9, 2021: "The Republican Party and the Democrat Party in these counties act as a uniparty. They make deals with each other. Okay? Basically, my guy gets here. My woman gets here. Basically, everything is prearranged. They decide what they are going to fight and who is going to get what contract. Then what they do is, the way they suck money out of the system is by controlling the Delaware County council, which appoints the board of elections, which approves money, pensions, and payments from Geo. Geo [The Geo Group Inc.] is a private company. I am trying to remember which one. Delcora [a regional water authority] is the water company; Geo is the prison. I cannot remember which is which. Geo and Delcora, okay?"

John McBlain, the Republican Party lawyer who argued initially on Stenstrom's behalf and then washed his hands of him, told me, "Really? I'm still waiting for my first check."

81 *Wisconsin* This section is based on interviews with Rohn Bishop.

83 *"There's enough states outstanding"* "Biden Wins Wisconsin-Local Reaction," 98.7 FM The Great 98 WMDC-FM, November 5, 2020. http://www.great98. net/2020/11/04/11-5-20-biden-wins-wisconsin-local-reaction/

83 *Trump at this moment.* "Biden Wins Wisconsin-Local Reaction," 98.7 FM The Great 98 WMDC-FM, November 5, 2020. http://www.great98.net/2020/11/04 /11-5-20-biden-wins-wisconsin-local-reaction/

84 *take orders from Biden as commander in chief* https://www.facebook.com/jeff .respalje/posts/389115962376206.

85 *Arizona* This section is based on interviews with Clint Hickman and Rey Valenzuela.

87 *in his fifteen minutes of Sharpie-gate fame* https://www.facebook.com/marko .trickovic.3/videos/4133394300010902, November 4, 2020.

87 *disparaging term for the left-wing group Antifa* https://www.urbandictionary .com/define.php?term=pantifa

89 *"The Patriot Party of Arizona"* Patriot Party of Arizona, "Patriotism Does NOT Reside in Political Parties," March 10, 2021, video, 1:34. https://www.youtube .com/watch?v=SBmdkMmiJCw

90 *crowned with a flowing fur cap with horns* Chansley, who also went by the name Jake Angeli, left a threatening note on the desk of Mike Pence—"It's only a matter of time, justice is coming." Justice instead came for him. He would plead guilty in September 2021 to obstructing Congress and face up to four years in federal prison. He renounced his support for Trump and blamed him for inciting him and others to storm the Capitol building. Alan Feuer, "Capitol Rioter Known as QAnon Shaman Pleads Guilty," *New York Times*, September 3, 2021. https://www.nytimes.com/2021/09/03/us/politics/qanon-shaman-capitol-guilty.html

90 *Georgia* This section is based on interviews with Lawrence Sloan and Adonay Deglel.

92 *"U.S. Supreme Court should decide!"* https://www.thetrumparchive.com/, November 6, 2020.

93 *in the event of discovered irregularities* Elise Viebeck, Robert Barnes and Emma Brown, "Justice Alito Temporarily Grants Pennsylvania GOP Request to Enforce Segregation of Ballots that Arrive after Election Day," *Washington Post*, November 6, 2020. https://www.washingtonpost.com/politics/pennsylvania-ballots -gop/2020/11/06/064fdf94-2056-11eb-90dd-abd0f7086a91_story.html

93 *For a fee of something like $20,000 per day* Maggie Haberman, "Giuliani Concedes that an Associate Did Ask for $20,000 a Day to Help Trump Post-Election," *New York Times*, January 21, 2020. https://www.nytimes.com/2021 /01/22/us/giuliani-concedes-that-an-associate-did-ask-for-20000-a-day-to -help-trump-post-election.html?searchResultPosition=2

93 *"FRAUD like you've never seen"* Shane Goldmacher, "Trump Camp Uses Online Gimmick to Fuel Donations Into December," *New York Times*, October 30,

2020. https://www.nytimes.com/2020/10/31/us/politics/trump-fundraising -donations.html

93 *a purported chilling rise of pedophilia*   Will Sommer, "Rudy Giuliani's Twitter Feed Is a Boomer Conspiracy-Theory Sh*tshow," *Daily Beast,* October 17, 2019. https://www.thedailybeast.com/rudy-giulianis-twitter-feed-is-a-boo mer-conspiracy-theory-shtshow

94 *a legitimate tactic in the political realm*   Devlin Barrett, "Giuliani Told Agents It Was Okay to 'Throw a Fake' During Political Campaign," *Washington Post,* August 11, 2021. https://www.washingtonpost.com/national-security/giuliani-fbi -surprise-fake/2021/08/11/754e9b4c-fabc-11eb-9c0e-97e29906a970_story.html

94 *"Lawyers Press Conference at Four Seasons, Philadelphia, 11 a.m."*   https://www .thetrumparchive.com/, November 7, 2020, 9:45:37 a.m.

94 *"at Four Seasons Total Landscaping—11:30am!"*   https://www.thetrumparchive .com/, November 7, 2020, 9:45:37 a.m.

94 *Four Seasons Hotel in Center City*   This faux pas has turned the landscaping company into a Philadelphia landmark and tourist attraction. The company's clever owners have capitalized on it—"Make America Rake Again!"—by marketing T-shirts, caps, beer, coffee mugs, posters, and other merchandise. The press conference has inspired, in a nod to the city's annual ten-mile Broad Street Run, the Fraud Street Run, beginning at the landscaping company's parking lot and ending at the "lesser known" Four Seasons Hotel.

94 *of lawsuits all over the country*   AP Archive, "Four Seasons Total Landscaping Press Conference - Long Version," November 17, 2020, video, 40:17. https:// www.youtube.com/watch?v=7QTRO9MG6z8

95 *"SENT TO PEOPLE WHO NEVER ASKED FOR THEM!"*   https://www.the trumparchive.com/, November 7, 2020, 4:53:34 p.m.

96 *to switch ballots from Trump to Biden*   nyronic, "Sidney Powell, Tom Fitton, Lou Dobbs Discuss," November 7, 2020, video, 8:36. https://www.youtube .com/watch?v=9GNX8XTWsG4 https://videobanned.nl/aiovg_videos /sidney-powell-tom-fitton-lou-dobbs-discuss-hammer-scorecard/

96 *"tens of thousands of votes in Pennsylvania"*   https://archive.org/details/FOX NEWSW_20201107_170000_Fox_News_Democracy_2020_Election_Coverage

97 *only sees the United States*   C-Span, "Joe Biden and Kamala Harris Victory Speeches," November 7, 2020. https://www.c-span.org/video/?477916-1 /president-elect-joe-biden-vice-president-elect-kamala-harris-address-nation

Chapter 3

98 *winning by 3 percent, 3,276 votes to 3,127*   "Election Results," Delaware County, Pennsylvania. https://delcopa.gov/vote/results.html

98 *In a flurry of postings on November 7* https://www.facebook.com/leahmhoopes, November 7, 2020.

99 *"for being blissfully ignorant" (64 likes, 8 shares)* https://www.facebook.com /leahmhoopes, November 8, 2020.

99 *had always been central in Trump's creed* "Donald Trump: The Genius of Self-Promotion," ABC News, January 6, 2006. https://abcnews.go.com/Primetime /story?id=132337&page=1

100 *still more hopeful headlines resulted* Matt Zapotosky and Devlin Barrett, "Barr Clears Justice Dept. to Investigate Alleged Voting Irregularities as Trump Makes Unfounded Fraud Claims," *Washington Post*, November 9, 2020. https://www .washingtonpost.com/national-security/trump-voting-fraud-william-barr-justice -department/2020/11/09/d57dbe98-22e6-11eb-8672-c281c7a2c96e_story.html

100 *"it's hard to trust anything you hear right now"* Fox News, "Tucker: We heard you. It's hard to trust anything. Here's what we know," November 9, 2020, video, 23:20. https://www.youtube.com/watch?v=R5ki6S-WsKU

100 *which reached an audience of more than four million* Joe Concha, "Trump Dings CNN, 'Morning Joe' Ratings as Tucker Carlson Sets Record," *The Hill*, July 1, 2020. https://thehill.com/homenews/media/505386-trump-dings-cnn -morning-joe-ratings-as-tucker-carlson-sets-record

102 *She received 174 likes, and 29 shares* https://www.facebook.com/leahmhoopes, November 7, 2020.

102 *"without merit and speculative accusations"* Darryl Coote, "Trump Files Lawsuit Against Pennsylvania's 'Two-Tier' Voting System," UPI, November 9, 2020. https://www.upi.com/Top_News/US/2020/11/09/Trump-files-lawsuit-against -Pennsylvanias-two-tier-voting-system/8071604979529/; "Pennsylvania Democratic Counties Challenge," Democracy Docket. https://www.democracydocket .com/cases/pennsylvania-democratic-counties-challenge/

102 *"Theatrics, not really lawsuits"* Joe Biden, "Post-Election Legal Briefing LIVE with Bob Bauer, Dana Remus & Kate Bedingfield," November 10, 2020, video, 24:45. https://www.youtube.com/watch?v=-2Jv_vH8Epk

102 *"[but] it doesn't go far in court"* MSNBC, "After Trump Lost Election, See How He's Losing in Court—The Beat with Ari Melber," November 12, 2020, video, 6:44. https://www.youtube.com/watch?v=Ciy81z0eoPM

104 *the very people who would notice red flags first. None had* Nick Corsaniti, Reid J. Epstein, and Jim Rutenberg, "The Times Called Officials in Every State: No Evidence of Voter Fraud," *New York Times*, November 10, 2020. https://www .nytimes.com/2020/11/10/us/politics/voting-fraud.html

104 *"a shit ton!" (45 likes, 1 share)* https://www.facebook.com/leahmhoopes, November 10, 2020, accessed September 23, 2021.

105 *His efforts to overturn the election consumed him* Michael Wolff, *Landslide: The Final Days of the Trump Presidency* (New York: Henry Holt, 2021), 138–139.

105 *replaced several other senior Pentagon officials* Lara Seligman and Daniel Lippman, "'Devastating': Top Pentagon Leadership Gutted as Fears Rise over National Security," *Politico*, November 10, 2020. https://www.politico.com /news/2020/11/10/pentagon-top-policy-official-resigns-435693

105 *"These are dictator moves"* Charlotte Klein, "National Security Experts Alarmed at Trump's 'Dictator Moves' at the Pentagon," *Vanity Fair*, November 11, 2020. https://www.vanityfair.com/news/2020/11/trump-fires-mark-esper -pentagon

105 *for many, a real possibility* *The Late Show with Stephen Colbert*, "Trump Has Yet to Show Real Evidence of Fraud, but Getting Him Out of Office May Be a Bumpy Ride," November 11, 2020, video, 12:02. https://www.youtube.com/watch?v =7mJwuKhfvqY

106 *"REPORT: DOMINION DELETED 2.7 MILLION TRUMP VOTES NATION- WIDE"* https://www.thetrumparchive.com/, November 12, 2020, 11:34 a.m.

106 *"changed votes, or was in any way compromised"* Alana Wise, "Trump Fires Elec- tion Security Director Who Corrected Voter Fraud Disinformation," NPR, November 17, 2020. https://www.npr.org/2020/11/17/936003057/cisa-director -chris-krebs-fired-after-trying-to-correct-voter-fraud-disinformati

106 *"except for what the Democrats did. Rigged Election!"* https://www .thetrumparchive.com/, November 13, 2020, 10:59:29 a.m.

106 *Hoopes posted on November 12 (101 likes, 1 share)* https://www.facebook.com /leahmhoopes, November 12, 2020, accessed September 24, 2021.

106 *"Four more years!" and "Stop The Steal!"* https://www.facebook.com /leahmhoopes/videos/10158067304887983, November 14, 2020.

107 *"I'm still shaky, so that's why I'm like, 'Oh!'"* Project Veritas, "Raw Audio: USPS Whistleblower Richard Hopkins FULL COERCIVE INTERROGATION by Federal Agents," November 11, 2020, video, 2:02:49.

110 *It quickly shot to more than $236,000, which Hopkins withdrew* "Backdated Ballot Whistleblower Coerced by Feds," Give Send Go. https://givesendgo.com/bebrave

110 *Of those, only two came through the Erie post office* Matthew Rink, "Only 2 Ballots That Arrived Late and Had Nov. 3 Postmark Came from Erie Postal Facility," *Erie Times-News*, November 10, 2020. https://www.goerie.com/story/news/politics /elections/2020/11/10/only-2-late-ballots-postmarked-nov-3-came-erie-postal -facility/6230622002/

111 *Georgia* Much of this section is based on interviews with John Porter, Brad Raffensperger, and Rick Barron.

111 *"didn't win doesn't rise to the level of harm"* FOX 5 Atlanta Digital Team, "Federal Judge Dismisses Trump Campaign Lawsuit Seeking to Halt Georgia Election Certification," FOX 5 Atlanta, November 19, 2020. https://www.fox5atlanta .com/news/judge-dismisses-trump-campaign-lawsuit-seeking-to-halt-georgia -election-certification

111 *"in which millions of people have voted"* Josh Gerstein, "Federal Judge Rejects Trump Ally's Bid to Block Election Certification in Georgia," *Politico*, November 19, 2020. https://www.politico.com/news/2020/11/19/federal-judge-rejects-trump-allys-bid -block-election-certification-georgia-438563

112 *"I will execute that duty and follow Georgia law"* https://twitter.com/GaSecofState /status/1325917055611265024

112 *"all legally-cast ballots—and only legally-cast ballots"* SBJ Staff Report, "Nov. 7— Gov. Kemp, Lt. Gov. Duncan, Speaker Ralston Issue Joint Statement on Georgia Election," *Savannah Business Journal*, November 7, 2020. https://www .savannahbusinessjournal.com/news/elections/nov-7—gov-kemp-lt-gov -duncan-speaker-ralston-issue-joint-statement-on/article_8a7927ea-2109-11eb -99ac-fb0522ff34a4.html

112 *"We've not seen any sort of credible examples"* Chandelis Duster, "Georgia GOP Lieutenant Governor Says 'No Credible Examples' of Voter Fraud," CNN, November 9, 2020. https://www.cnn.com/2020/11/09/politics/geoff-duncan -georgia-election-fraud-cnntv/index.html

113 *If you could imagine it, it might be true!* Matthew Teague interview with Rick Barron, July 18, 2021: "We had all sorts of things going on. We had people that would try to come and bring lunch to our warehouse, and they would come in with pizzas and they would say, 'Oh, we're bringing lunch to all you guys.' But their intent was to get back into our lunchroom because they thought that there was secret Dominion hacking training going on in our lunchroom. . . . And they thought we had snipers on the roof, that was one of the other things that all of them thought. But they would have people camped out outside our warehouse, and they would take pictures of all of my guys going in and out, take all their license plates. So, there was just a lot of really weird things that happened this election."

113 *"a fake 'water main break', to recover!"* https://www.thetrumparchive.com/ ?searchbox=%22"Why+did+the+Swing+States+stop+counting+in+the+mi ddle+of+the+night%3F%22

114 *"just been told to go home because of a pipe burst?"* https://www.facebook.com /102785054906864/posts/ruby-freeman-of-larubys-unique-treasures-identified -surrounding-suitcase-ballot-/154547516397284/

114 *"excellent man named Joe Biden while counting the ballots"* Kim LaCapria, "'Ruby-Freeman_Georgia' Instagram Post," *Truth or Fiction*, December 7, 2020. https://www.truthorfiction.com/rubyfreeman_georgia-instagram-post/

116 *they certified the election unanimously* Colin Dwyer, "Michigan's Wayne County Certifies Election Results after Brief GOP Refusal," NPR, November 18, 2020. https://www.npr.org/sections/live-updates-2020-election-results/2020/11/18/936120411/michigans-wayne-county-certifies-election-results-after-brief-gop-refusal

117 *"Huge win for @realDonaldTrump"* https://twitter.com/jennaellisesq/status/1328844700883808260?lang=en

117 *at least one $500 bottle of Dom Pérignon champagne* David Boucher and Clara Hendrickson, "Trump Tweets Undermine Michigan Leaders; Images Show Chatfield Drinking at Trump Hotel," *Detroit Free Press*, November 21, 2020. https://www.freep.com/story/news/politics/elections/2020/11/21/michigan-gop-trump-meeting-shirkey-chatfield/6374174002/

117 *A call from Washington, DC. Strange* This account is based on interviews with Monica Palmer.

118 *rescind certification of the vote* Paul Egan, "GOP Members of Wayne County Board of Canvassers Say They Want to Rescind Votes to Certify," *Detroit Free Press*, November 19, 2020. https://www.freep.com/story/news/politics/elections/2020/11/19/wayne-county-board-of-canvassers-monica-palmer-william-hartmann/3775242001

118 *the otherwise white, windowless expanse* C-Span, "Michigan Board of State Canvassers Certifies Election Results," November 23, 2020. https://www.c-span.org/video/?478327-1/michigan-board-state-canvassers-certifies-election-results

120 *"I don't care who you are, that affects you"* Account based on an interview with Norm Shinkle.

120 *Arizona* This section is based on interviews with Clint Hickman and Bill Gates and video of the November 20, 2020, meeting: "Special Meeting Summary-Friday, November 20, 2020, 3:30 PM." Maricopa County Board of Supervisors. https://maricopa.hylandcloud.com/198AgendaOnline/Meetings/ViewMeeting?id=3669&doctype=3

121 *"This was a RIGGED ELECTION!"* https://www.thetrumparchive.com/, November 15, 2020, 7:47:54 a.m.

123 *They had alleged a plot, popularized by Sidney Powell* Powell, colorful in style and speech, had characterized the multifarious plot to defraud the election as a "Kraken," an octopus-like monster from Scandinavian folklore. It was arguably apt, since both monster and plot were purely fictional.

123　*and error that they were laughable*　Liddy statement before Maricopa County Board of Supervisors on November 20, 2020: https://maricopa.hylandcloud .com/198AgendaOnline/Meetings/ViewMeeting?id=3669&doctype=3.

124　*"the basis for upending Arizona's 2020 election"*　Bowyer v. Ducey, No. CV-20 -02321-PHX-DJH (D. Ariz. Dec. 9, 2020). https://s3.documentcloud.org /documents/20422013/bowyer-v-ducey-dismissal-order.pdf

125　*"Why can't we wait a few days? What's the harm?"*　According to Gates.

125　*all of them masked and well-spaced according to the COVID guidelines*　"Special Meeting Summary-Friday, November 20, 2020, 3:30 PM," Maricopa County Board of Supervisors. https://maricopa.hylandcloud.com/198AgendaOnline /Meetings/ViewMeeting?id=3669&doctype=3

128　*"a community of knowledge"*　Elizabeth Kolbert, "Why Facts Don't Change Our Minds," *New Yorker,* February 19, 2017. https://www.newyorker.com/maga zine/2017/02/27/why-facts-dont-change-our-minds?utm_campaign=falcon &utm_source=twitter&mbid=social_twitter&utm_medium=social&utm _social-type=owned&utm_brand=tny

134　*"including challenging the ballots or ballot signatures"*　Zach Montellaro and Josh Gerstein, "Pennsylvania Supreme Court Rejects Complaints about Philadelphia Election Observations," *Politico,* November 17, 2020. https://www.politico.com /news/2020/11/17/pennsylvania-supreme-court-philadelphia-ballots-437082

135　*"could have easily established such parameters; however, it did not"*　https:// www.pacourts.us/assets/opinions/Supreme/out/J-116-2020mo%20-%20 104608159120049033.pdf?cb=1

135　*further representation of the president*　Rachel Abrams, David Enrich, and Jessica Silver-Greenberg, "Once Loyal to Trump, Law Firms Pull Back from His Election Fight," *New York Times,* November 13, 2020. https://www.nytimes.com/2020 /11/13/business/porter-wright-trump-pennsylvania.html

135　*"lose my fucking law license because of these idiots"*　Wolff, *Landslide,* 115.

136　*"this result can possibly be justified?"*　Jon Swaine and Aaron Schaffer, "Here's What Happened When Rudolph Giuliani Made His First Appearance in Federal Court in Nearly Three Decades," *Washington Post,* November 18, 2020. https://www .washingtonpost.com/politics/giuliani-pennsylvania-court-appearance/2020 /11/18/ad7288dc-2941-11eb-92b7-6ef17b3fe3b4_story.html

136　*and the remedy it proposed, "unhinged"*　Jeremy Roebuck, "'Not How the Constitution Works': Federal Judge Tosses Trump Suit Seeking to Disrupt Pa. Election Results," *Philadelphia Inquirer,* November 21, 2020. https://www .inquirer.com/news/pennsylvania-election-lawsuit-trump-dismissed-matthew -brann-certification-vote-results-20201121.html

136 *"a national embarrassment"* Paul Kane and Felicia Sonmez, "Chris Christie Calls the Conduct of Trump's Legal Team a 'National Embarrassment,'" *Washington Post*, November 22, 2020. https://www.washingtonpost.com/politics /republicans-christie-trump-concede/2020/11/22/05c280e6-2cda-11eb-bae0 -50bb17126614_story.html

136 *"Time to put it out there"* Leonnig and Rucker, *I Alone Can Fix It*, 397.

137 *she posted (228 likes, 207 shares)* https://www.facebook.com/leahmhoopes, November 17, 2020.

137 *accompanied by Sidney Powell* etzimanuel, "Full Rudy Giuliani News Conference November 19 2020," November 19, 2020, video, 1:32:58. https://www.youtube .com/watch?v=XEttZKjl7vY

138 *"Past 2 days have been incredible"* https://www.facebook.com/leahmhoopes, November 19, 2020.

138 *"I am asking is for the truth and transparency?"* https://www.facebook.com /leahmhoopes, November 23, 2020.

138 *"Looks like I am a diplomat after all"* https://www.facebook.com/leahmhoopes, November 19, 2020.

138 *"Faith has led me here and no turning back!"* https://www.facebook.com /leahmhoopes, November 24, 2020.

139 *The event was televised live nationally on a number of platforms* C-Span, "Pennsylvania Republican Hearing on 2020 Election," November 25, 2020. https:// www.c-span.org/video/?478422-1/president-trump-tells-pennsylvania-gop -lawmakers-election-rigged-overturned

145 *"All you Americans. This isn't over"* https://www.facebook.com/leahmhoopes, November 25, 2020.

145 *"Poll Watcher from PA Speaks Out"* https://www.dropbox.com/s/abdcw ke1qmqebdn/Leah%20Hoopes.mp4?dl=0&fbclid=IwAR18KCksAHJDI4_8w MPXd2rpzNPGxnXh0KndrffUczuvxbNlYUcvaQ59wnc

145 *her on his broadcast* The War Room https://www.facebook.com/leahmhoopes /videos/10158095478282983

145 *appearing on Fox TV's* Lou Dobbs Tonight https://www.facebook.com/watch /?v=391737748777995

145 *and on* Hannity Charles Creitz, "Pennsylvania Whistleblower Speaks Out After Claiming 'Forensically Destructive' Vote Canvassing Procedure," Fox News, December 2, 2020. https://www.foxnews.com/politics/pennsylvania -whistleblower-speaks-out-hannity

145 *Georgia* This section is based on interviews with Brad Raffensperger and Rick Barron.

Chapter 4

148 *Georgia* This section is largely based on interviews with Jordan Fuchs and Gabriel Sterling.

149 *"because—it—has—all—gone—too—far. All of it!"* GPB, "Gabriel Sterling of Sec of State's Office Blasts Those Threatening Election Workers," December 1, 2020, video, 4:41. https://www.youtube.com/watch?v=jLi-Yo6IucQ

151 *where his TV hangs above the fireplace* This account is based on an interview with Brian Robinson.

151 *the crowd jeered them* https://www.rev.com/transcript-editor/shared/o UyKDZ-s5fyFqYYahefOHtmgRPqF3-MNe17aLZUT4B7inOSq6eyxiJzYaUg5 a13aKra4eXa9d3HaXnGApulIh1SkN7s?loadFrom=PastedDeeplink&ts=50 53.82

153 *so thick that he eventually stopped listening* Account based on interviews with Rick Barron.

154 *election workers cover up the windows in Detroit* This account is based on an interview with Ed McBroom.

154 *"No, absolutely not. You're not doing that."* NTD, "Live: Michigan Senate Committee Holds Hearing on Election Issues (Dec. 1)," December 1, 2020, video, 7:01:20: https://www.youtube.com/watch?v=eZXkAv7yKgw

154 *"folks with firsthand knowledge"* https://twitter.com/jonathanoosting/status /1333511603845816324?s=21

155 *"machines and complete other menial tasks"* Jerry Lambe, "Dominion Attorneys Send Brutal Letter to Trump Campaign's 'So-Called Star Witness' Mellissa Carone," *Law and Crime*, December 24, 2020. https://lawandcrime.com/high -profile/dominion-attorneys-send-brutal-letter-to-trump-campaigns-so-called -star-witness-mellissa-carone/

155 *to the degree that Giuliani reached to touch her arm and shushed her* Teo Armus, "Trump Campaign's Star Witness in Michigan Was Deemed 'Not Credible.' Then, Her Loud Testimony Went Viral," *Washington Post*, December 3, 2020. https://www.washingtonpost.com/nation/2020/12/03/melissa-carone -michigan-trump-giuliani-election/

155 *Trump tweeted, misspelling her name* https://www.thetrumparchive.com /?searchbox=%22Melissa+is+great%22

155 *but Sheryl Guy answered her phone anyway* This section is largely based on interviews with Sheryl Guy and Bill Bailey.

156 *meant that the proposal passed* File 2020009238CZ in *William Bailey v. Antrim County*.

157 *Two hours later, Rudy Giuliani tweeted* https://twitter.com/rudygiuliani/status /1335014224532221952?lang=en

157 *"You want to show that this isn't you"*   Account based on interviews with Sheryl Guy.

157 *"to conduct that forensic examination"*   Paul Egan, "Trump Attorney: 'Our Team' Examining Antrim Voting Experiment after Judge Issued Order," *Detroit Free Press*, December 6, 2020. https://www.freep.com/story/news/politics/elections /2020/12/06/trump-legal-team-examining-antrim-county-voting-equipment /3847931001/

158 *"to create systemic fraud and influence election results"*   "Antrim Michigan Forensics Report," December 13, 2020. https://www.depernolaw.com/uploads/2/7/0/2 /27029178/antrim_michigan_forensics_report_[121320]_v2_[redacted].pdf

158 *"Election changing result!"*   https://www.thetrumparchive.com/?searchbox =%22%5C%22WOW.+This+report+shows+massive+fraud.+Election+chang ing+result%21%5C%22%22

158 *soon to be acting attorney general*   "Selected Documents-President Trump Pressure Campaign on Department of Justice," Committee on Oversight and Reform, U.S. House of Representatives, June 2021. https://oversight.house .gov/sites/democrats.oversight.house.gov/files/documents/COR-SelectedDOJ Documents-2021-6-15-FINAL.pdf

159 *site of the proposed marijuana shop*   Mardi Link, "Up in Smoke: Antrim Voter Fraud Plaintiff Couldn't Have Voted on Pot Ordinance," *Record-Eagle,* December 9, 2020. https://www.record-eagle.com/news/local_news/up-in-smoke-antrim -voter-fraud-plaintiff-couldnt-have-voted-on-pot-ordinance/article_ac902254 -3999-11eb-8cc4-176185db0b11.html

160 *because Friske's defied the pandemic mask mandate*   Neil MacFarquhar, "Sweet Cherries, Bitter Politics: Two Farm Stands and the Nation's Divides," *New York Times,* June 6, 2021. https://www.nytimes.com/2021/06/06/us/michigan -masks-covid-farm-stands.html

160 *for allegedly plotting to kidnap the governor*   Graham Macklin, "The Conspiracy to Kidnap Governor Gretchen Whitmer," CTC Sentinel, 14, no. 6 (July/August 2021): 1–15. https://ctc.usma.edu/the-conspiracy-to-kidnap-governor-gretchen -whitmer/

160 *Wisconsin*   This section is based on an interview with Dean Knudson and on the webcast of his testimony: NTD, "LIVE: Wisconsin State Legislature Election Hearing (Dec. 11)," December 11, 2020, video, 7:41:05. https://www.youtube .com/watch?v=pkqFTUEvMoU.

161 *to make the case plausible enough to move forward*   Wolff, *Landslide,* 131.

161 *who had been appointed by Trump*   Trump v. Wisconsin Elections Commissions, No. 2:20-cv-01785 (E.D. Wis.). https://www.democracydocket.com/wp-content /uploads/2020/12/2020-12-12-Decision-And-Order-dckt-134_0-1.pdf

166   *Nevada*   This section is based on interviews with Jesse Binnall, Amanda Milius, and Heather Flick.

167   *in sunny resort destinations worldwide*   https://www.facebook.com/jbinnall

167   *"MAGA lawyer," warning . . . "RINOs beware!"*   https://twitter.com/jbinnall ?lang=en

169   *"bridge" Biden's winning 33,596-vote margin*   Riley Snyder, "Trump Campaign Files Lawsuit Asking Judge to Overturn or Annul Nevada's Presidential Election Results," *Nevada Independent*, November 17, 2020. https://thenevadainde pendent.com/article/trump-campaign-files-lawsuit-asking-judge-to-overturn -or-annul-nevadas-presidential-election-results

170   *at a press conference before the courthouse*   Donald J. Trump, "Jesse Binnall: President Trump Won the State of Nevada," November 17, 2020, video, 0:31. https://www.youtube.com/watch?v=ZeWfhRUJ0og

170   *"very compelling for any court that hears this evidence"*   https://twitter.com /newsmax/status/1332358521753640966

170   *the interview on his account*   https://www.thetrumparchive.com/, November 27, 2020, 12:48:53 p.m.

171   *"by him referred to the Court is denied"*   Leonnig and Rucker, *I Alone Can Fix It*, 412.

171   *the three appointed by Trump, declined to hear it*   Emma Platoff, "U.S. Supreme Court Throws out Texas Lawsuit Contesting 2020 Election Results in Four Battle-ground States," *Texas Tribune*, December 11, 2020. https://www.texastribune.org /2020/12/11/texas-lawsuit-supreme-court-election-results/

171   *to contest elections in other states*   Nina Totenberg and Barbara Sprunt, "Supreme Court Shuts Door on Texas Suit Seeking to Overturn Election," NPR, December 11, 2020. https://www.npr.org/2020/12/11/945617913/supreme-court -shuts-door-on-trump-election-prospects

171   *"No Wisdom, No Courage!"*   https://www.thetrumparchive.com/, December 11, 2020, 11:50:47 p.m.

172   *Barr was done pretending*   Jonathan D. Karl, "Inside William Barr's Breakup with Trump," *The Atlantic*, June 27, 2021. https://www.theatlantic.com/politics /archive/2021/06/william-barrs-trump-administration-attorney-general /619298/. Barr told Jonathan D. Karl of *The Atlantic*, "We realized from the beginning that it was just bullshit."

172   *The president was furious*   Wolff, *Landslide*, 138.

172   *"You must hate Trump!"*   Leonnig and Rucker, *I Alone Can Fix It*, 407.

172   *He crushed every point Binnall raised*   Law v. Whitmer, No. 10 OC 00163 1B (Nev. Dist. Ct., Carson City). https://www.democracydocket.com/wp-content

/uploads/2020/11/20-OC-00163-Order-Granting-Motion-to-Dismiss-State
ment-of-Contest-1.pdf

172 *to cast their six votes for Biden*   Caroline Bleakley, "Nevada Electors Cast Votes
for Biden in Presidential Race," *8NewsNow*, December 14, 2020. https://www
.8newsnow.com/news/local-news/live-nevada-electoral-college-to-cast-states
-votes-in-presidential-race/

173 *"the hell out of office"*   "Statement by Donald J. Trump, 45th President of the
United States of America," Donald J. Trump, June 24, 2021. https://www
.donaldjtrump.com/news/statement-by-donald-j-trump-45th-president-of-the
-united-states-of-america-06.24.21

173 *that his own party leaders were the ones perpetrating a fraud*   Michigan Senate
Oversight Committee, "Report on the November 2020 Election in Michigan,"
June 23, 2021. https://committees.senate.michigan.gov/testimony/2021-2022
/Senate%20Committee%20on%20Oversight%20Report%20on%20the%20
November%202020%20Election%20in%20Michigan,%20adopted.pdf

175 *"to the unofficial vote count errors"*   "McBroom Statement on Dominion Voting
System Oversight Committee Testimony," Senator Ed McBroom, December 22,
2020. https://www.senatoredmcbroom.com/mcbroom-statement-on-dominion
-voting-systems-oversight-committee-testimony/

175 *"amount of money to litigate these issues"*   Interview with Ed McBroom.

175 *they fought the election and his impeachment*   Brian Schwartz, "Trump PACs Paid
Lawyers Nearly $8 Million as He Fought Election Results and Impeachment,"
CNBC, August 2, 2021. https://www.cnbc.com/2021/08/02/trump-pacs-paid
-lawyers-nearly-8-million-as-they-fought-election-results-impeachment.html

175 *which makes those payments impossible to track*   Meridith McGraw, "Trump
Raised Millions but Spent None of It on Audits and GOP Candidates," *Politico*,
August 3, 2021. https://www.politico.com/news/2021/08/03/trump-spending
-millions-gop-candidates-502233

175 *after admitting a romance with a Russian spy*   Cade Metz and Julie Creswell,
"Patrick Byrne, Overstock C.E.O., Resigns After Disclosing Romance with
Russian Agent," *New York Times*, August 22, 2019. https://www.nytimes.com
/2019/08/22/business/overstock-ceo-patrick-byrne.html

175 *"other people with odd skills"*   Will Sommer, "Ex-Overstock CEO Says He's
Put Together an 'Army of Various Odd People' to Save Trump," *Daily Beast*,
November 28, 2020. https://www.thedailybeast.com/ex-overstock-ceo-says
-hes-put-together-an-army-of-various-odd-people-to-save-trump

175 *followers sent in more than a quarter billion dollars*   Shane Goldmacher and
Rachel Shorey, "Trump's Sleight of Hand: Shouting Fraud, Pocketing Donors'

Cash for Future," *New York Times*, February 1, 2021. https://www.nytimes.com /2021/02/01/us/politics/trump-cash.html

176 *and possibly funding his own run at reelection*   Meridith McGraw, "Trump Raised Millions but Spent None of It on Audits and GOP Candidates," *Politico*, August 3, 2021. https://www.politico.com/news/2021/08/03/trump-spending-millions -gop-candidates-502233

176 *"I bet it's getting close to $2 million now"*   Interview with Bill Bailey.

176 *He's running for attorney general of Michigan*   https://twitter.com/mdeperno /status/1415536441392783360/photo/1

176 *Arizona*   This section is based on an interview with Bill Gates.

176 *"Much more to come!"*   https://www.thetrumparchive.com/, November 15, 2020, 9:21:48 a.m.

177 *Her company, DG Fenn Construction*   https://www.dgfenn.com/

178 *"President Trump thanking us for pushing to prove any fraud"*   Ryan Randazzo and Yvonne Wingett Sanchez, "In Emails, Senate President Tries to Appease Both Critics and Supporters of Election Audit," *Arizona Republic*, June 4, 2021. https:// www.azcentral.com/story/news/politics/elections/2021/06/04/arizona-audit -senate-releases-karen-fann-emails-recount-effort/7553588002/

178 *her moves with Trump directly and with Giuliani*   Jane C. Timm, "Arizona Republican Who Ordered Election Audit Touted Trump Phone Call, Giuliani Support in Emails," NBC News, June 4, 2021. https://www.nbcnews.com/politics /politics-news/arizona-republican-who-ordered-election-audit-touted-trump -phone-call-n1269718

178 *Wisconsin*   This section is based on an interview with Bill Feehan.

179 *to cast their votes for Trump*   Nick Viviani, "Wisconsin GOP Electors Meet to Cast Their Own Votes Too - Just in Case," WMTV, December 14, 2020. https:// www.nbc15.com/2020/12/14/wisconsin-gop-electors-meet-to-cast-their-own -votes-too-just-in-case/

180 *do about it*   Albert Samaha, Amber Jamieson, and Rosalind Adams, "Two Republican Members of the Electoral College Have a Message: Biden Won," *Buzzfeed*, November 10, 2020, https://www.buzzfeednews.com/article/albert samaha/electoral-college-republicans-biden-won?bftwnews&utm_term=4ldqpgc #4ldqpgc

181 *"enough to change 20,000 votes in the state of Wisconsin"*   Albert Samaha, Amber Jamieson, and Rosalind Adams, "Two Republican Members of the Electoral College Have a Message: Biden Won," *BuzzFeed News*, November 10, 2020. https:// www.buzzfeednews.com/article/albertsamaha/electoral-college-republicans -biden-won?bftwnews&utm_term=4ldqpgc#4ldqpgc

181 *in her embrace of election conspiracy*   Wolff, *Landslide*, 114.

181 *in the White House after Giuliani had challenged her* Wolff, *Landslide*, 113.

181 *"became only observers of the circus"* Wolff, *Landslide*, 114.

182 *The complaint alleged "massive election fraud"* Feehan v. Wisconsin Elections Commission, No. 2:20-cv-1771 (E.D. Wis.). https://www.wpr.org/sites/default /files/20314496542.pdf

183 *"This is gibberish. Nonsense"* Wolff, *Landslide*, 173–176; Leonnig and Rucker, *I Alone Can Fix It*, 425–427; Maggie Haberman and Alan Feuer, "Trump Lawyers Disavow Sidney Powell, Another Member of His Legal Team, over Spurious Fraud Accusations," *New York Times*, November 23, 2020. https://www .nytimes.com/2020/11/23/us/trump-lawyers-disavow-sidney-powell-another -member-of-his-legal-team-over-spurious-fraud-accusations.html.html; Jonathan Swan, "Officials Increasingly Alarmed about Trump's Power Grab," Axios, December 19, 2020. https://www.axios.com/trump-officials-alarmed-overturn -election-results-a844d1d2-acb2-47a9-87ce-ac579458b1ea.html

183 *she would be "practicing law on her own," an unofficial combatant* Maggie Haberman and Alan Feuer, "Trump Team Disavows Lawyer Who Peddled Conspiracy Theories on Voting," *New York Times*, November 22, 2020. https://www.nytimes .com/2020/11/22/us/politics/sidney-powell-trump.html

183 *"So that hasn't happened yet"* MSNBC, "It's Over: Watch MAGA Elector Confronted by Certified Vote On Live TV—The Beat with Ari Melber," December 14, 2020, video, 6:05. https://www.youtube.com/watch?v=S3tm3ID0eDM

184 *"Yes it effected (sic) the outcome"* https://www.facebook.com/bill.feehan/posts /10218234915164307, accessed October 12, 2021.

184 *Georgia* This section is largely based on interviews with John Porter and Joan Kirchner Carr.

184 *"Doing the right thing will never be the wrong thing"* https://twitter.com /BaylerDuncan/status/1336108976354828289 [Dec. 7, 2020, 7:42 PM]

184 *afraid Trump's supporters would come after their son* James Hohmann, "Opinion: Georgia's GOP Lieutenant Governor Conducts the 2020 Autopsy His Party Won't," *Washington Post*, September 8, 2021. https://www.washingtonpost.com /opinions/2021/09/08/geoff-duncan-book-gop-20-2020-autopsy/

184 *he had been murdered in a political cover-up* u/wheresmytendies, "Why Is No One Talking About the Guy That Got Seth Rich'ed in Georgia Today for Exposing Voter Fraud?" r/conspiracy, Reddit, December 4, 2020. https://www.reddit.com/r /conspiracy/comments/k6xkqm/why_is_no_one_talking_about_the_guy_that _got_seth/

185 *"donated to him and are now being thrown under the bus by him"* Brad Raffensperger, "Georgia Secretary of State: My Family Voted for Trump. He Threw Us under the Bus Anyway," *USA Today*, November 25, 2020. https://www.usatoday

.com/story/opinion/voices/2020/11/25/georgia-secretary-of-state-election
-integrity-2020-column/6407586002/

185 *an enemy of the people* Fox News, "Trump: Georgia Sec. of State Raffensperger
is an 'enemy of the people,'" November 26, 2020. https://video.foxnews.com
/v/video-embed.html?video_id=6212559542001

185 *"Enemies of the People"* Ionut Ilascu, "Pro-Trump 'Enemies of the People' Dox-
ing Site Is Still Active," Bleeping Computer, January 16, 2021. https://www
.bleepingcomputer.com/news/security/pro-trump-enemies-of-the-people
-doxing-site-is-still-active/

187 *Arizona* This section is based on interviews with Lynie Stone, Leah Hoopes,
and Clint Hickman.

188 *the country into one big federal lawsuit* Wisconsin Voters Alliance v. Pence,
No. 1:20-cv-03791-JEB (D.D.C.). https://electioncases.osu.edu/wp-content
/uploads/2020/12/WVA-v-Pence-Doc1.pdf

189 *the election night request for access to the "back room"* https://uploads.documents
.cimpress.io/v1/uploads/b41dec4b-4e28-47e7-a835-c9f4ebc086b9~110
/original?tenant=vbu-digital

190 *with cars driving past blowing their horns* Dennis Welch, "Trump Supporters
Target Arizona House Speaker Rusty Bowers, Over Election Results," AZ
Family, December 9, 2020. https://www.azfamily.com/news/politics/election
_headquarters/trump-supporters-target-arizona-house-speaker-rusty-bowers
-over-election-results/article_8368a120-3a80-11eb-8106-8be083047f7a
.html

194 *He called Rosen daily* Ann E. Marimow and Josh Dawsey, "What Rosen Told
U.S. Senators: Trump Applied 'Persistent' Pressure to Get Justice to Discredit
Election," *Washington Post*, August 12, 2021. https://www.washingtonpost
.com/national-security/rosen-senate-judiciary-testimony-trump/2021/08/12
/4b500618-fabd-11eb-8a67-f14cd1d28e47_story.html

195 *Nevada* This section is based on interviews with Jesse Binnall.

195 *the Senate Homeland Security and Governmental Affairs Committee* https://www
.facebook.com/watch/?v=1494879947372886

195 *during which he had been cross-examined* https://www.democracydocket
.com/wp-content/uploads/sites/45/2020/11/20-OC-00163-Order-Granting
-Motion-to-Dismiss-Statement-of-Contest-1.pdf

196 *took a hard look at Kamzol's study and his deposition* Derek T. Muller, "Scru-
tinizing One Voter Fraud Allegation: Did 42,000 People Vote More than
Once in Nevada in 2020?," Excess of Democracy, December 23, 2020. https://
excessofdemocracy.com/blog/2020/12/scrutinizing-one-voter-fraud-allegation
-did-42000-people-vote-more-than-once-in-nevada-in-2020

Chapter 5

198 *the 2020 election and lost every one* Amy Sherman and Miriam Valverde, "Joe Biden Is Right That More Than 60 of Trump's Election Lawsuits Lacked Merit," *Politifact*, January 8, 2021. https://www.politifact.com/factchecks /2021/jan/08/joe-biden/joe-biden-right-more-60-trumps-election-law suits-l/

198 *and simply proclaim Trump the victor* Nick Niedzwiadek and Kyle Cheney, "Trump Pressures Pence to Throw Out Election Results—Even Though He Can't," *Politico*, January 5, 2021. https://www.politico.com/news/2021/01/05 /trump-pressures-pence-election-results-455069

199 *to accomplish the same thing* "Read: Trump Lawyer's Memo on Six-Step Plan for Pence to Overturn the Election," CNN, September 21, 2021. https://www .cnn.com/2021/09/21/politics/read-eastman-memo/index.html

199 *who, recruited by Trump campaign consultants* Michael Scherer, "To Build a Crowd for a Pro-Trump Rally, Nevada GOP Consultant Sought Help from Proud Boys," *Washington Post*, June 2, 2021. https://www.washingtonpost .com/politics/proud-boys-nevada-republican/2021/06/01/60da2a58-be5f -11eb-b26e-53663e6be6ff_story.html

199 *"JANUARY SIXTH, SEE YOU IN DC!"* https://www.thetrumparchive.com/, December 30, 2020, 2:06:51 p.m.

199 *Georgia* This section is largely based on interviews with Brad Raffensperger and Brian Robinson, Cobb County police records, and audio of Trump's call to Raffensperger: Amy Gardner, "'I Just Want to Find 11.780 Votes': In Extraordinary Hour-Long Call, Trump Pressures Georgia Secretary of State to Recalculate the Vote in His Favor," *Washington Post*, January 3, 2021. https:// www.washingtonpost.com/politics/trump-raffensperger-call-transcript-georgia -vote/2021/01/03/2768e0cc-4ddd-11eb-83e3-322644d82356_story.html.

200 *"acknowledge God and he shall direct your path"* Ben Collins, "We Need to Learn How to Talk to (and about) Accidental Conspiracists," Nieman Lab, December 2020. https://www.niemanlab.org/2020/12/we-need-to-learn-how-to-talk-to -and-about-accidental-conspiracists/

201 *"not just ballots"* https://twitter.com/BrendanKeefe/status/1337090 630728753153

201 *Kutti works for Kanye West* Diana Bradley, "R. Kelly's Former Publicist Is Now Working with Kanye West," *PR Week*, December 21, 2018. https://www.prweek .com/article/1521732/r-kellys-former-publicist-working-kanye-west

201 *with Trump during visits to the White House* This account is based on interviews with Trevian Kutti and Cobb County police records.

204 *Arizona* This section is based on interviews with Clint Hickman.

205 *Sunday morning, January 3* Ashton Carter, Dick Cheney, William Cohen, Mark Esper, Robert Gates, Chuck Hagel, James Mattis, Leon Panetta, William Perry, and Donald Rumsfeld, "Opinion: All 10 Living Former Defense Secretaries: Involving the Military in Election Disputes Would Cross into Dangerous Territory," *Washington Post*, January 3, 2021. https://www.washingtonpost.com/opinions/10-former-defense-secretaries-military-peaceful-transfer-of-power/2021/01/03/2a23d52e-4c4d-11eb-a9f4-0e668b9772ba_story.html

208 *139 House members and eight senators objected* Harry Stevens, Daniela Santamarina, Kate Rabinowitz, Kevin Uhrmacher, and John Muyskens, "How Members of Congress Voted on Counting the Electoral College Vote," *Washington Post*, January 7, 2021. https://www.washingtonpost.com/graphics/2021/politics/congress-electoral-college-count-tracker/

208 *deny him a second term* Public Records Branch of the Federal Election Commission, "Official 2020 Presidential General Election Results," January 28, 2021: https://www.fec.gov/resources/cms-content/documents/2020presgeresults.pdf

209 *No one in a position to know can be believed* Mark Bowden: *"You cannot dissuade someone rooted in distrust. Once, in a brief essay, I wrote a dismissive throwaway line about people who still believed that NASA had never landed men on the moon. The comment spurred a combative reaction from those who held this belief. I made the mistake of engaging with some. One asked me why, if there had been moon landings, powerful telescopes on earth had never been able to see landers on the moon's surface? This was a reasonable question, so I looked. There were, in fact, such pictures of the landers, all six of them. But when I pointed this out, supplying links to the photos, my critic said, 'How easy would that be to fake?' Certainly a lot easier than faking video of the landings themselves. He had me."*

210 *became a "spineless RINO"* Dave Goldiner, "Trump Lashes Out at 'Spineless' Former A.G. Bill Barr for Calling Out Election Lies," *New York Daily News*, June 28, 2021. https://www.nydailynews.com/news/politics/us-elections-government/ny-election-2020-trump-barr-mcconnell-20210628-nwbsnay2zzakjnanxtdwhhczdu-story.html

Chapter 6

213 *"the ones whose conduct is contemptible"* Vinny Vella, "Judge Dismisses Claim That Delaware County Violated Rules for Poll Watchers in the Presidential Election," *Philadelphia Inquirer*, January 13, 2021. https://www.inquirer.com/news/poll-watchers-presidential-elecion-delaware-county-20210113.html

213 *The amount would likely be between $50,000 and $75,000* Interview with Delaware County solicitor Bill Martin.

214 *of their certified results. They refused*   Danielle Ohl, "What We Know about the Renewed Push for a 'Forensic Audit' of Pennsylvania's 2020 Election," *Philadelphia Inquirer,* August 26, 2021. https://www.inquirer.com/politics/pennsylvania/spl/pa-forensic-audit-explainer-mastriano-corman-20210826.html

214 *"They were grilling the hell out of me"*   Project Veritas, "USPS Whistleblower Richard Hopkins Gives New Interview Detailing Coercion Tactics Used By Fed Agents," November 11, 2020, video, 7:02. https://www.youtube.com/watch?v=gKhXBU_IgYo&t=2s

214 *"suffered unprecedented and irreparable harm"*   Weisenbach v. Project Veritas and Richard Hopkins, April 26, 2021, https://drive.google.com/file/d/1wGGiG2h TfcqV4uObAJ8Rn-9ytomR9JFr/view

215 *"witnessed in modern day America"*   Weisenbach v. Project Veritas and Richard Hopkins, April 26, 2021, https://drive.google.com/file/d/1wGGiG2hTfcqV4u ObAJ8Rn-9ytomR9JFr/view

215 *"which meritless claims are built"*   Matthew Rink, "Erie Postmaster Files Lawsuit against Mail Carrier, Project Veritas Over Ballot Fraud Claims," *Erie Times-News,* April 26, 2021. https://www.goerie.com/story/news/politics/elections/2021/04/26/erie-ballot-fraud-case-postmaster-sues-hopkins-okeefe-project-veritas/7376713002/

215 *"and people better get wise fast"*   Jeremy Duda and Jim Small, "Arizona Senate Hires a 'Stop the Steal' Advocate to Lead 2020 Election Audit," *AZ Mirror,* March 31, 2021. https://www.azmirror.com/2021/03/31/arizona-senate-hires-a-stop-the-steal-advocate-to-lead-2020-election-audit/

216 *"the review are suspect and should not be trusted"*   Barry C. Bruden and Trey Grayson, "Report on the Cyber Ninjas Review of the 2020 Presidential and U.S. Senatorial Elections in Maricopa County, Arizona," States United Democracy Center, June 22, 2021. https://statesuniteddemocracy.org/wp-content/uploads/2021/06/6.22.21-SUDC-Report-re-Cyber-Ninjas-Review-FINAL.pdf

216 *savage "prebuttal" in August*   Stephen Richer, "Dear Arizona Republicans: Let's Do this Right. Let's Build Confidence. Let's Move Forward," August 19, 2021. https://www.politico.com/f/?id=0000017b-6062-d290-a57b-ee62cfa80000

217 *$3 million for the private recount*   Nicholas Reimann, "These Trump-Backing Groups Are Largely Funding the Arizona Audit," *Forbes,* July 29, 2021. https://www.forbes.com/sites/nicholasreimann/2021/07/29/these-trump-backing-groups-are-largely-funding-the-arizona-audit/?sh=29d1f33c28ae

217 *editorial board member Michelle Cottle, "clown-car chaos"*   Michelle Cottle, "The Trump Clown Car Has a Smashup in Arizona," *New York Times,* August 24, 2021. https://www.nytimes.com/2021/08/24/opinion/arizona-results-trump-republicans.html

217 *"very close to the margin of error"* Jack Healy, Michael Wines, and Nick Corasaniti, "Republican Review of Arizona Vote Fails to Show Stolen Election," *New York Times*, September 24, 2021. https://www.nytimes.com/2021/09/24/us/arizona -election-review-trump-biden.html?searchResultPosition=2

220 *"is political grandstanding"* Josh Gerstein, "Lawyer Who Brought Election Suit Referred for Possible Discipline," *Politico*, February 19, 2021. https://www .politico.com/news/2021/02/19/lawyer-election-suit-discipline-470369

223 *multistate effort to overturn the 2020 election* https://www.nycourts.gov /courts/ad1/calendar/List_Word/2021/06_Jun/24/PDF/Matter%20of%20 Giuliani%20(2021-00506)%20PC.pdf

223 *Georgia* This section is based on interviews with Gabriel Sterling and Brad Raffensperger.

224 *"This is our 1776 moment"* Greg Bluestein, "Hice Launches Challenge to Raffensperger in Race for Secretary of State," *Atlanta Journal-Constitution*, March 22, 2021. https://www.ajc.com/politics/politics-blog/hice-launches -challenge-to-raffensperger-in-race-for-secretary-of-state/IBLOYKCCNF BOTN5FCSEM5PMBAA/

225 *"the election's administration"* https://int.nyt.com/data/documenttools/letters -to-georgia-officials-from-fulton-district-attorney/70d7cbc8ba0ae1dd/full.pdf

226 *Michigan* This section is based on interviews with Ed McBroom, Sheryl Guy, and Bill Bailey.

226 *"lies and distrust into an unquenchable conflagration"* Michigan Senate Over-sight Committee, "Report on the November 2020 Election in Michigan," June 23, 2021. https://committees.senate.michigan.gov/testimony/2021-2022/Sen ate%20Committee%20on%20Oversight%20Report%20on%20the%20Novem ber%202020%20Election%20in%20Michigan,%20adopted.pdf

227 *the state GOP replaced him with a Republican activist* Samuel Dodge, "Gov. Whitmer Replaces GOP Canvasser Who Certified Election with Conservative Activist," MLive, January 19, 2021. https://www.mlive.com/public-interest /2021/01/gov-whitmer-replaces-gop-canvasser-who-certified-election-with -conservative-activist.html

227 *"the truth and defend the rule of law"* Jess Bidgood, "Aaron Van Langevelde's Speech about the 2020 Election: 'We Were Asked to Take Power We Didn't Have," *Boston Globe*, July 5, 2021. https://www.bostonglobe.com/2021/07/05 /nation/aaron-van-langeveldes-speech-about-2020-election-we-were-asked-take -power-we-didnt-have/

Due to the timeliness of the events recounted in this book, it was produced on an expedited schedule and does not contain an index. A full index will be made available on the Grove Atlantic website, groveatlantic.com, and will be included in future printings and the eBook.